Direction of Cities

Also by John Guinther

Moralists & Managers: Public Interest Movements in America

The Malpractitioners

Philadelphia (A 300-Year History)

The Jury in America

Brotherhood of Murder
(with Thomas Martinez)

Breaking the Mob
(with Frank Friel)

John Guinther

Direction of Cities

Foreword by Edmund N. Bacon

VIKING

VIKING
Published by the Penguin Group
Penguin Books USA Inc., 375 Hudson Street,
New York, New York 10014, U.S.A.
Penguin Books Ltd, 27 Wrights Lane,
London W8 5TZ, England
Penguin Books Australia Ltd, Ringwood,
Victoria, Australia
Penguin Books Canada Ltd, 10 Alcorn Avenue,
Toronto, Ontario, Canada M4V 3B2
Penguin Books (N.Z.) Ltd, 182–190 Wairau Road,
Auckland 10, New Zealand

Penguin Books Ltd, Registered Offices:
Harmondsworth, Middlesex, England

First published in 1996 by Viking Penguin, a division of Penguin Books USA Inc.

10 9 8 7 6 5 4 3 2 1

Copyright © John Guinther, 1996
Foreword copyright © Edmund N. Bacon, 1996
All rights reserved

Illustration credits appear on page 293.

LIBRARY OF CONGRESS CATALOGING IN PUBLICATION DATA
Guinther, John.
Direction of cities/John Guinther; with a foreword by Edmund N. Bacon.
p.   cm.
Includes bibliographical references and index.
ISBN 0-670-84198-6
1. Cities and towns—United States.   2. City planning—United States.
3. Urban renewal—United States.   4. Bacon, Edmund N.
I. Title
HT123.G85   1996
307.76'0973—dc20   96-14675

This book is printed on acid-free paper.

Printed in the United States of America
Set in Electra
Designed by Francesca Belanger

Foreword

The threat to the future well-being of our nation posed by the growing dominance of the suburban state of mind in national affairs is comparable to the threat to our past well-being posed by the secession of the Southern states in 1860 and 1861. We are becoming a nation divided.

This single most important fact about our current condition is not a major theme in contemporary literature. We should be grateful to any writer who attempts to project the subject of the plight of cities onto the national scene.

John Guinther has given us an encyclopedic view of the inside workings of cities from the days of Boss Tweed to our own times. Particularly significant is the fact that Guinther is a political writer, not a professional city planner or architect, not an academic urbanologist. We professionals can benefit greatly by seeing how someone else sees us. We have had our fill of how we see each other.

It has been tremendously exciting and valuable to have exchanged experiences and ideas with John Guinther over our many hours of conversation—how the world looks to me after the twenty-one years that I labored on the public scene directing the planning of a great city, and the private but contentious years since, and how he sees things from his broad perspective of historical knowledge and acute observation of the current political scene. We stimulated each other to think more deeply about the significance of what we have done than otherwise we would have.

Out of a study of John Guinther's broad panorama of the political scene, his unorthodox interpretation of many things we are familiar with as well as his exposé of things we are not, we may gain better insights into what we have to do to foresee and forestall the impending disaster that we must avoid at all costs.

To do this will require firm resolve, deep discipline, and an acute and ruthless facing up to the real nature of the demon in our path.

John Guinther has helped us along this way.

Edmund N. Bacon

Contents

Author's Note

The writing of *Direction of Cities* was made possible by the collaboration of Edmund N. Bacon, the city designer and architect. Over a period of more than two years, we met to talk about the nature of cities: how they came to be, whom they are intended to serve, which forces harm them and which help develop their potential.

In the book that follows, I attempt to describe Bacon's philosophy and place it within the context of the history of American cities from the earliest days to the present time. Over all those years, few people have been more influential than has Bacon in defining the purpose of the city, and none have more completely devoted their lives to creating a more humane urban habitat. For the better part of a half century, he has been a leading figure, nationally and internationally, as a planner whose ideas have been adopted in many cities in addition to his native Philadelphia. His landmark book, *Design of Cities*, first published in 1967, continues to serve as a guide for students of architecture and planning, for governmental officials, and for others who want to understand the underlying texture of cities and the forces within them that can be developed for their long-term advancement.

Bacon's insights affected and enriched my own thinking about urban life, and that influence is reflected in the text in more ways than I can count. However, our agreement was that the book's thesis and its structure were mine alone to develop, and that is what was done. Therefore, I alone am responsible for the contents, and also for the views expressed, other than those directly attributed to Bacon, and for the conclusions about the past, present, and future of the American city.

Direction of Cities

Prologue

On a wintry day in March 1990—the day on which the idea for this book came into being—Edmund Bacon and I took a walking tour of Philadelphia. It was the city of his birth and where I had lived since 1954. The mid-1950s had been a good time to be in Philadelphia. It then was, as a writer for *Harper's Magazine* put it, "the Renaissance City of America," with its heroic reform mayor, its widely copied constitution that gave promise of assuring good government in perpetuity, its new buildings and new businesses, its population infusion of thousands of young professionals. Philadelphia appeared to be a joyful harbinger: Come to it and learn what the future of urban America could be.

Penn Center, in the heart of the downtown, was the most visible symbol of the Renaissance. A medley of new office towers and plazas, situated just west of the venerable City Hall, Penn Center was Bacon's creation. It had its inception in an experience he had while living in China in 1933.

Bacon was then twenty-three years old. A graduate of the architecture school of Cornell University, he had just received a small inheritance and decided to spend it on a trip around the world. After bicycling through England, France, and Italy, he headed for Egypt. While visiting the pyramids, he met a missionary who told him of a building boom Shanghai was experiencing; jobs for an architect might be available there. This was good news for Bacon, who found he had $35 left over after he booked passage on a steamer heading for that city. There he obtained a job designing houses. A few months later, he visited Beijing, where he

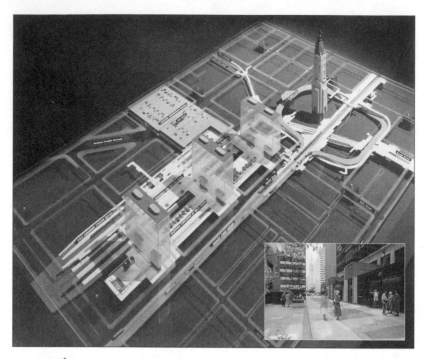

Penn Center as visualized by Bacon (1972). INSET: Penn Center, 1992

learned more about the design of cities than his five years at Cornell had taught him.

"You entered Beijing through a gate," he recalls, "then walked through a city of gateways and archways, of pulsating opening and closing spaces. In the outer city, the roofs were black. And from there, through a gate, you entered into the Manchu City, which was a hollow square around the Forbidden City where the emperor had lived. Suddenly you found yourself in an area where all the roofs were purple — an area of magnificent red doors and gold ornaments. You went over a bridge and then down another bridge, and finally you got to the throne hall, which was not particularly finer or richer than some of the sights you had been passing through before you arrived there. However, your journey in its entirety had now become a modulated, rhythmical, physical experience, with point and counterpoint, recall and anticipation. It was overwhelming, and it scarcely exists in anything we have [in America]."

From Bacon's experience in Beijing "came my basic idea that cities are not a collection of objects. Rather, they are a sequential continuum of sensory experiences."

Penn Center was Bacon's first opportunity to express his Beijing revelation. His idea, which came to him in 1947, called for three office towers, connected by an underground garden open to the sky; the sun, Bacon thought, wouldn't mind going down those additional few feet. The garden began at 18th Street and ended three blocks later at 15th, approaching the ancient, rococo City Hall. "By creating the three-block continuum," Bacon said to me, "I managed to build a sense of forceful direction." (See Diagram 1.) "And because a direction reacts when it hits an object, when it came up against City Hall, which is very solid and granite, it ricocheted back like a billiard ball, first at a northwestern angle to establish the site for what became Kennedy Plaza, and then a few years later hit again to the southwest, establishing the point for the Center Square building." (See Diagrams 2 and 3.) "The thing that was surprising to me was that the arrow wasn't content to just bounce back but finally, like a laser beam, penetrated City Hall and thirty years later came to rest to produce Market East." (See Diagram 4.)

In the mid-1950s, real estate developers took over the Penn Center project. Soon the number of office towers doubled, the buildings themselves architecturally undistinguished. Moreover, instead of Bacon's open underground gardens lined with retail shops, a concrete plaza was laid out on the street level; below it was placed an equally undistinguished concourse abutting the commuter railroad station. Nevertheless, so powerful was the original idea that the mistreatment did not destroy it. The integrity of the direction line had been maintained in the route of the plaza, so that the sense of openness and connections among the buildings was not lost. Penn Center has also acted as progenitor. Westward from it on Market Street, by 1990 a string of office towers had

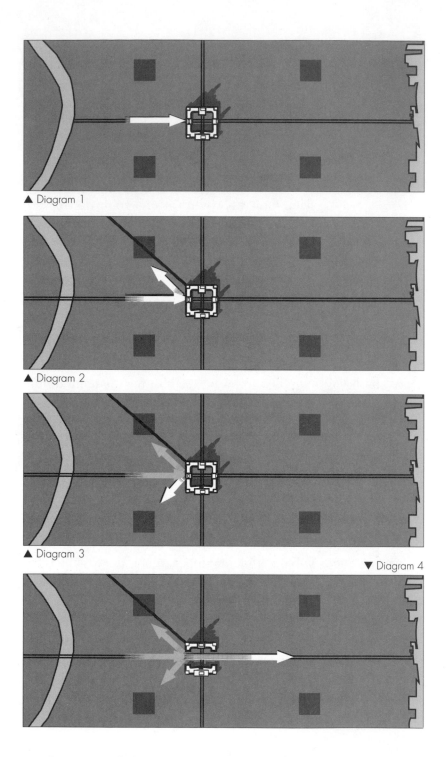

▲ Diagram 1

▲ Diagram 2

▲ Diagram 3

▼ Diagram 4

4   Direction of Cities

replaced the amalgam of railroad yards and warehouses and all but a few of the low-rent retail outlets that had given the area an economically depressed and miscellaneous appearance. While not all the new buildings were aesthetically successful, the total impression was one of expanding vigor.

Bacon and I began our tour by entering the Penn Center underground concourse by a flight of stairs at 17th Street; at the foot of the steps, in a recess where it is not likely to be noticed, is a metallic-winged Alexander Calder sculpture. Originally it was intended for the plaza above, but developers had exiled it to this spot. Heading east under artificial lighting, rather than the natural daylight Bacon had proposed, we passed the train station, a series of fast-food restaurants, shoe repair shops, and other businesses.

Leaving the concourse by winding stairs and walking east past City Hall, we emerged onto Market East. The project had not yet been completed; ground was still being cleared in preparation for a new convention center and a hotel, but the sensory shift from the depressing concourse was, even so, a startling one. The street, from City Hall to the facade of the historic Lit Department Store building five blocks on, had been scrubbed clean. The gaslight era lampposts were garlanded near the top by metal baskets, laden with ivy and flowers. The old Reading Terminal, with nearly a century of grime removed from its renovated facade, revealed an unexpected Victorian-style bounty of cornices, keystones, and arches.

Bacon and I entered One Reading Center, an office building next to the Terminal. Passing through its foyer, with its splendid little garden and fountain, we descended a flight of stairs to be greeted in an extravagant way that nothing in the Penn Center concourse could have prepared us for. The pervading sense was of light and space, produced by a high-vaulted glass roof, fountains, mobiles, escalators leading to balconies adorned with greenery, and an external elevator. Adjoining the courtyard is the Market East commuter rail station, which may be the most striking of its kind anywhere in the world, with its skylight, crosswalks, escalators, and walls done in ceramics of strong and vivid colors.

Extending from the courtyard and station, on the right, are the shopping galleries. They do not entirely escape the overweening sense of artificiality and fragmentation of suburban malls, but the many shafts of natural lighting from above are an unusual saving grace; more important is the maintenance of a sense of direction, aided by the regular orienting glimpses of the streets above.

The sense of welcome initiated by the courtyard below One Reading Center eventually culminates in a subdued blending of grays, blacks, and whites within the restored Lit building, which opens into a multilevel atrium ascending in an understated manner to the high, triangular roof. When Lit's is the end of the journey, the effect is both conclusory and restful, as of a musical diminuendo. But when the traveler enters through Lit's, the effect is equally satisfying, as the quiet overture is overtaken by the brightness and energy ahead, as on crescendo. When Bacon and I left the Lit's enclave and began to work our way back to City Hall, he stopped, just for a moment, and said, more to himself than to me: "This is an odd feeling. You know, all this was once a figment of my imagination."

In *Direction of Cities*, I will return to Bacon's career in describing the development of his ideas and their practical and philosophic applications. Consideration will also be paid to earlier city planners whose work to one degree or another expressed an understanding of the continuum in their attempts to create an amenable urban environment.

The book will argue that the principles that should be applied to planning the physical city have equal vitality when used to guide governmental decisions. Only when that happens can a coherent urban direction be developed and can it become possible to reverse the decline that has been the lot of most cities during the second half of the twentieth century.

In one sense, such an effort means that the planning that led to the successful revitalization of downtowns in places as diverse as Philadelphia, St. Paul, and Milwaukee needs be extended in order to begin the recovery of blighted inner-city neighborhoods. To date, the concept of the central district as a continuum and the city as a total continuum has rarely been acted upon or even recognized in either of its elements, although where it has been the results have been encouraging. In a broader sense, the idea of the continuum means that we as citizens must learn to expect and demand from those who hold public office that they deal with problems of the present in terms of both the present and the future. The continuum to which Bacon refers is one not only of space but of time as well.

1

Seeing the City

The pages of an atlas showing the United States reveal, among other features, the locations of many towns and cities. Should the atlas be a very extensive one, it may also include maps of the largest cities and their metropolitan areas. The depictions, however, will likely show only boundaries and main routes, and would not be of much practical help to strangers who visit these places. Fortunately, detailed street maps will be available to them from the city's tourist information service or from vendors. Special-purpose maps for each city also abound: Those meant for tourists locate sites of cultural or historic interest; maps of public transportation show its routes; the telephone book has local and regional calling-zone maps; the post office offers zip-code maps; utility companies print maps showing underground power lines, water and sewage pipes, gas mains, and the like; police departments map the city into enforcement districts and patrol sectors within each district; the United States Commerce Department draws maps of census tracts; and politicians from time to time will pore over ward and division maps. With enough maps, the city is knowable in a linear fashion even if one never sets foot in it.

These contemporary maps are not the only ones available. In libraries or history books, a map can be found showing the first street plan for the city; still others, of more recent vintage, depict the directions in which it expanded over the years. It is even possible to unearth maps that outline growth plans that never materialized, so that the maps, as a totality, lay out the city that was, that is, and that also never was.

A number of inferences can be drawn about a city's life from its maps. Those of the utility company, by the very complexity of their lines, demonstrate the extraordinary activity and amount of construction required to make basic services available to the citizens every day. The fact that some police districts are larger than others indicates that the smaller ones have the highest population densities or highest crime rates or—most likely—both. Cluster points of the entertainment and cultural centers offer solid evidence of the location of the city's downtown area. The degree of criss-crossing of bus and rail lines provides a fairly reliable notion of the priority the city gives to mass transit.

No people are shown on the maps, but people is their subject. The old maps reveal how those who are now dead made decisions that formulated the city for those who are living. The contemporary maps suggest people at work and play, people in trouble (as in the high-crime districts), people seeking power (as with the political maps), and people hurtling about each day from one place to another within the city and its suburbs (as with the street and bus maps).

Cities also contain maps of neighborhoods. They exist not on paper but in people's minds, and their boundaries and the meaning of them can differ from person to person in the neighborhood. For example, suppose we have two women who live next door to each other: Mary Smith, a recent arrival, and Jane Brown, who has lived in the neighborhood all her life. For Mary Smith, the boundaries of the neighborhood are likely to be pragmatic ones: the drugstore three blocks north of where she lives, a grocery for small purchases two blocks south, a supermarket and dry cleaner four blocks west, while one block east is the park where she takes her baby on sunny days. Her initial idea of the neighborhood, therefore, carries with it no personal meaning. Jane Brown, on the other hand, is not likely to think of her neighborhood as bounded by places where one does things, as it is for Mary Smith. For her, the associations and therefore the boundaries are of community, of the quick and the dead, even of places that no longer exist, a long-gone penny candy emporium or the settlement house where she played as a child.[1]

Even though, or perhaps because, the boundaries of a neighborhood exist only within the minds of its people, they have a firm sense of when they are no longer within it. Their neighborhood, for instance, may be situated only a few blocks from the central shopping section of the city, but the residents, when heading there, will say they are going "in town," exactly as a farmer who lives outside a village uses that phrase. In Brooklyn, a different formulation can be heard. There, instead of "in town," people go to "the city," by which they don't mean any place in their own borough, but Manhattan. The Brooklynites' use of "the city" carries with it an explicit recognition, which is more fuzzily defined by "in town" and "downtown," that within any city can be found a polis or central core of its institutions—governmental, cultural, financial, mercantile—which, in aggregate, affect the rest of the city in a vibrant and rippling way that no neighborhood affects another neighborhood.

The polis, in that sense, is like the capital of a nation, and the neighborhoods that spread from it are like states or districts within the nation. However, if for the moment we eliminate the polis from the equation, then it becomes apparent that each neighborhood itself is like a small nation with its understood rules and customs. Its people may dislike or fear those who live in other nations, and feel at home only in those nations that have customs and demographics closest to their own.

Both these visualizations—that of the city as a single nation with a capital and as a series of neighborhood nations—show us why the city is a place simultaneously possessed of a sense of "us" and of "them." The animosities, whether based on race or on differences in economic status, have always been at their most pungent on a group rather than an individual basis. A man may rail against "their" kind moving into "our" neighborhood; however, when bounded by another kind of map, that of the workplace, he probably will have a good—or at least not an openly antagonistic—

relationship with the very individuals whom he regards as a threat in the neighborhood setting.

But each individual's idea of the city is also in part created by another kind of map that is highly personal and can provoke a sense of fragmentation and isolation. Workers, for instance, regardless of whether they walk or use their cars or public transportation, generally follow the same route each day as they go to and from their jobs. Variations can occur, but they are insignificant and themselves often tend to be repetitious (as with working parents who alternate on a regular basis driving out of the way to pick up a child at a day care center). In this fashion, people who work far from home can travel many miles each week but see very little of the city in which they live.

Not only are these urban corridors narrow, but the more frequently we travel along them the less receptive we are to them visually. We tend, that is, to be more attentive to the new than to the commonplace. This is why we will vividly remember a street seen on a vacation twenty years ago but might be hard pressed to describe the appearance of the houses on a block we have passed a thousand times.

To the extent that familiarity breeds visual contempt, our daily travel corridors not only put blinders on our capacity to grasp the city as a whole but also cause us to "see" ever less of that small portion we regularly travel. Nevertheless, such impressions of the city as the corridors do create (which were established when we were seeing them more freshly) can become important references for us. For example, if our corridor causes us to drive through one downtrodden neighborhood after another, long after we are no longer "seeing" these sectors, the early impressions remain and can cause us to think of the whole city as "ugly," because they have a greater subjective impact upon us than other and more sporadic visual information we are receiving.

For some people, travel corridors are not only narrow but short. Children of poverty-level families are restricted, much of the time, to corridors that are no greater than the distance between home and school. Their parents may not fare a great deal better, and if unemployed probably won't. Such people, old and young alike, are unlikely to have access to automobiles, so that their non-neighborhood corridors will largely be defined by public transit lines, which are narrow in themselves and which in a very large city may be partly underground.

The truncated corridors of an impoverished population can at times take on a military significance. Control of a single block, even a corner of a block, can prompt battles between gangs when one is accused of invading the other's nation. The fight to control a block or a corner of a block represents the psychic fragmentation of a city in its most dire form.

To think of the city in terms of daily corridors is, however, no more adequate an explanation of its nature than is a description of it as a series of individual neighborhoods, police districts, and so on. The maps we have been considering describe only elements of the landscape of the city, and neither individually nor collectively do they define what a city is. Rather, a city—and this, not size, is what distinguishes it from the village and town—is a container inside which are to be found multiple functions. Unlike the village or town, everything about the city is pluralistic. The kaleidoscope of sensory impressions it offers combines unremitting motion with a procession of buildings, monuments, parks, streets, boulevards. Each procession is alike in that the same elements are to be found from city to city, but the order in which the procession occurs and the individual tastes that went into creating it make each city unique. That is why when we are in Boston, we do not think we are in New York, nor do we mistake New York for Los Angeles. It is this specific sequentiality that provides a city's residents with what Bacon has called "a sense of orientation and structure. Because of it people feel, as they move about the city, that they are part of a larger system and not simply atoms among chaotic and disconnected elements."

The multiple interests that congregate in a city give it—far more so than the town or village, which lacks that many players—the capacity and the motivation to bring about alterations in the sequences of the procession. Some have proven disastrous, others wise. We will return to this thought from a variety of perspectives, but for the purposes of this discussion, a single example can be offered, and a pertinent one, too, since it involved the creation of an entirely new and significant travel corridor. The city is San Antonio, which has two great tourist attractions: its strikingly beautiful Riverwalk, completed in 1941, and the Alamo, from the nineteenth century. The distance between the Alamo and the Riverwalk at the nearest point is only about a half mile. However, until 1981 there was no easy or pleasant means by which visitors or city residents could get from one place to the other. The way was opened when the Hyatt Regency Corporation agreed to build a hotel that would provide the connector. Within the hotel is an atrium that acts as a public promenade leading from the Riverwalk to a city-built park that ends in a plaza in front of the Alamo. Through this act of cooperation between the public and private sectors, the previous harmful disassociation between the two points of interest was eliminated.

The combination of mercantile and official interests that led to the San Antonio connector suggests still another way of seeing the city: as a vehicle that is constantly being pushed in a variety of directions by those who attempt to influence its future. Those doing the pushing can be agents of the local, state, or federal government; they can be developers, bankers, other business people, community groups, individuals with a grievance, and individuals with a selfless goal for the common good. Alliances, corrupt or pure, can form to achieve the goal, and adversaries may coalesce to prevent its coming about.

When there is a response—and some forces never generate sufficient support to reach that point—the decision-making process that follows has many variations, but they tend ultimately to be governmental in nature and of the sequential character shown in Diagram 5.

The explosion at the top of the diagram symbolizes a focal point that, through some proposed change in its condition, causes a series of actions and counter-actions. As an example, assume that the explosion site is a piece of property on which a businessman wants to build a factory (Sequence A). To gain approval for his venture, he goes to the mayor (Sequence B), who is favorably impressed when the businessman tells him the factory will mean 200 jobs. However, because the neighborhood is zoned residential, a study of the proposal must be made by the city planning commission, which decides the benefits outweigh the drawbacks and gives its approval for the necessary rezoning legislation (Sequence C). Meanwhile, home-owners near the site, who had never paid it much attention before now, are alarmed because they think the factory will drive down their property values (Sequence D). They take their problem to their community association, which agrees with them (Sequence E). To gain support in the battle ahead, the interested neighbors and association officers meet with the district councilwoman (Sequence F), who agrees to oppose the zoning change when it comes before the full city council (Sequence G), where a decision is reached that can set off its own sequence or sequences (arrows).

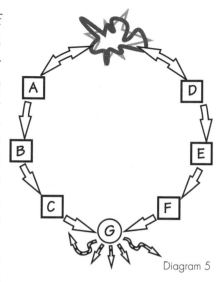

Diagram 5

Disputes like the one between the businessman and the neighbors occur every year in every city, leading to changes in the allocation of space or to prevention of change. (Not all the disputes begin externally; the government may decide on an improvement program in a neighborhood, but the residents don't see it as improving anything, and they fight it.) The history of a city can

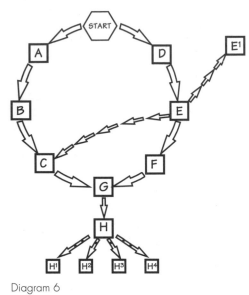

Diagram 6

be seen as a progression of disputes and decisions, some of them insignificant and others of considerable impact on the city's viability as a place for people to live.

The start point in Diagram 6 represents the year of the city's founding. As with the big bang theory of the universe, before then there was no city time, only space. Squares A, B, and C now represent key decisions made about the city during various stages of its existence, while the opposing D, E, and F squares depict counter-ideas that were defeated at these junctures, but that may have had sufficient merit that they subsequently affected or created other decisions, shown by the arrow heading from E to C. As an example, suppose that in the year 1960 a dispute arises over the most feasible development of a significant portion of land in the downtown area. A group of retailers advocates that the land be used as a parking lot; conservationists protest, urging it be planted with trees and resodded for a park. The retailers (C) win and the conservationists (E) lose. As time goes on, it is apparent this decision was an unwise one. The parking lot is an eyesore and has discouraged the residential renewal of the sector, which would have been prompted if an attractive park had been built. In 1980, a similar dispute arises over another sector of the city, and this time the conservationists, pointing to the failure of 1960, win. Alternatively, the city never gets a chance to rectify its 1960 mistake, but the leadership of another city learns from it and adopts the park idea when the same issue arises there, shown by the arrow extending from E to E^1.

As a city proceeds through its spaces and over time, it reaches Sequence G, which we will say is the year 1990. At that stage, a consensus has developed in the city about its future prospects and the goals that are to be met (H). Whether these goals are achieved or not depends on many factors, and because of them and because ideas create other ideas, new considerations (H^1–H^4) manifest themselves, presumably leading to the next point of consensus, and so on.

As is apparent, the constant in the history diagram is the presence of competition. Each individual major issue (be it political, economic, or a question of city design) causes sides to be taken at various levels within the city, with not everyone who is on the same side having the same motivation. Some people who favor a park may do so for purely aesthetic reasons, whereas others might see the park as an opportunity to profit from the building of new homes or apartment houses surrounding it.

Inferentially, the diagram also describes another kind of competition, which derives from two antithetical perspectives about the function and potential of a city.

In the one view, the city is seen as a compendium of random events. Some are dangerous and others benign in their effects on the inhabitants, and all are brought about by individuals either acting separately or, occasionally, in alliances to achieve goals that seem important to them at any given moment. Because of the randomness, the natural drift of any city is toward chaos. To try to prevent the chaos, the government is expected to perform in two ways. One is to impose as much order as it can by trying to make the streets safe and by providing other basic services to the population. Its second activity is to foster, or not prevent, land deals profitable to the parties in the transaction, so that, if the deals work out the way they are supposed to, the government gains new tax revenues to help it better carry out services. From this understanding of the city, it follows that an announced goal may be reached but have no permanence, because the random forces remain dominant. They are like so many arrows, which will always continue to go in miscellaneous directions. Under that interpretation, H^1 through H^4 represent a resumption of the purposelessness that was temporarily interrupted by the enunciation of the goal. Thus, cities merely exist in space, having moments in which they hold the line against chaos and other times when they don't. They are containers for diversity, perhaps, but the container lacks purpose.

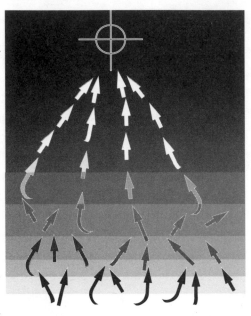

Diagram 7

Competing against this entropic perspective are those who hold that cities have a readily discernible purpose, which is to create a favorable environment for their people; the city's strivings must constantly be in that direction. In this thinking, it is not sufficient that the city's streets are made relatively safe and that adequate services are provided, nor is there an agreement that real estate be developed purely for the immediate advantage of the financiers and the city treasury. Instead, both the physical and governmental ambiance must be such that the aspirations of the citizenry are served, and that participation in the life of the community is eased, not thwarted, by the government's actions. Implementing these goals is a demanding task and one that requires creativity. A single individual can act as instigator. "In a city," Bacon observes, "you need a person who is continuously seeking the forces that are working in the community, pulling them together, continually challenging the people with a bigger concept and introducing brand-new forces as they need to be animated into the city twenty or thirty years later."[2]

Bacon's conception is illustrated by Diagram 7. The focal

point at the top is an idea for the future that the creative force believes is desirable for the city to adopt (as with Bacon's Market Street continuum). Each of the shaded horizontal lines represents the passage of time in years, with the bottom line the first year in which the idea was presented. The arrows depict the random forces within the city, whose existence has been correctly perceived by the entropists. During the early years of the idea's existence, the arrows move in many directions, indicating that, although the idea is now present, some of the forces reject it, others pay no attention to it, and some never will accept it, as shown by the arrows that never move toward the idea. However, as the idea continues to be advocated by the progenitor and is enriched by the feedback its promulgation causes, many of the arrows move toward it. When enough arrows take that path, they don't necessarily form any grand alliance (although that can occur, as we shall see in Chapter Five); rather, primarily the arrows work their way independently to an understanding and acceptance of the idea. Eventually they coalesce around the idea, after which they will pass through it, with the process of coalescence repeated when the next desirable idea is put forward. In Bacon's model, therefore, coalescence is created by the ferment the idea causes, so that it is ultimately freely accepted. Never is it imposed. To attempt to do so at the early stage will fail because there is no consensus, and there is no need to impose it at the later stages since the idea has by then coaxed enough arrows toward it. (If the idea is a poor one, the arrows will ignore it and go along their separate paths.)

According to Bacon's theory, strong and valid ideas for the city's future, once let loose in the marketplace, will have a cohering effect on enough elements in the society to establish purpose. What appeared to be entropic drift has been harnessed, and the city takes on direction. By implication, such ideas could be put in place at the time of the city's founding or at any subsequent moment over the years that follow. In that event, the H-goal of 1990 in the history diagram could have been present in the city since, let us say, 1690, and needs only to be re-recognized and put to work in the context of the needs of 1990.

The impulse toward entropy, however, is a sturdy one. Self-aggrandizing motivations are quite powerful, and even those people who seek a social purpose are regularly confronted by the need to react to a wide variety of random events that can both obscure goals and consume a great deal of energy. The duty to attend to immediate needs is a valid one, too. The budget must be balanced, the potholes filled, the police deployed, the sanitation trucks kept at work. The house that is about to fall, literally or symbolically, must be attended to, even if there is no plan about what to do next. Confronted by these exigencies, it is small wonder we find it difficult to think about what can occur beyond today and tomorrow, and why we lose sight of ideas that guided us well in the past and that could be valuable to use now if only we had the time to remember them. Thus, the very urgency of efforts to fight chaos—by causing counter-measures to be enacted for the moment and nothing beyond—can hasten the movement toward it.

At the heart of the struggle to determine the direction any city will take is the question of how its land is to be used. It can either be treated primarily as a source of profit, to be packaged, bought, and sold, or else, as the holistic perspective teaches, as a resource that in an interrelated manner serves the spiritual as well as the material needs of the people who live upon it. As Bacon observed, the holistic vision is likely to be the expression of a single individual, as it was in the development of three of the four cities that are the subject of the next chapter. In the fourth city, with which the chapter begins, growth was ordained by committee.

2

The Holistic Vision

New York

A visitor to New York, walking from the Battery to Central Park, has the impression of having traveled through two separate cities. One is Lower Manhattan. There, along Wall Street, in Greenwich Village, and Chelsea the topography is varied. Streets cross one another at odd angles, revealing upcoming images with freshness and surprise. Even the cavernous financial district is relieved from impersonality and dullness, due to the slope of the meandering streets and the presence of an occasional old building like a church, with a little park all of its own.

The second city, midtown Manhattan, seems at first to be a complete denial of all that has gone before it. The east–west streets meet the avenues at right angles and, for long stretches, are narrow and dreary in the sullen blankness of their architecture. It is not until we have gotten into the theater district beyond Times Square that the ambience becomes inviting. The avenues, by contrast, are heterogeneous in appearance but, for the most part, offer no sense of going anywhere. They are simply stretching into the horizon.

One daring interruption to mid-Manhattan is provided on Park Avenue by Grand Central Station, the only building that has a relationship to a main artery of travel.[1] Construction on Grand Central, which replaced a previous terminal at 42nd Street and Park Avenue, began in 1910 under the direction of an extravagantly talented engineer named William Wilgus. The problem facing Wilgus was a considerable one. Directly north of the existent terminal, more than sixty acres of railroad tracks obliterated Park Avenue as far as 56th Street; even at that point, where the tracks went underground, the route as far as 93rd Street was pocked by surface openings through which the passing trains emitted blasts of steam and soot. Wilgus developed a plan by which all trains—commuter as well as long-distance—would leave from two underground levels, allowing for removal of the surface and semi-surface tracks. If that had been all that was done, the improvement to the environment would have been marked, encouraging (as was desired) the transformation of Park Avenue north of the terminal into a desirable high-rent thoroughfare. However, the creative notion was far richer than that. Installed was an elegant system of access roads for pedestrians and vehicular traffic around the terminal, so that at no point did the new structure block northern Park Avenue from Park Avenue South. (Unfortunately for the site, that view and much of the sweep of the design has since been obscured by the domineering and ugly Metropolitan Life Building [formerly the Pan Am Building] directly behind the terminal.) In

Schematic drawing of New York's Grand Central Station (c. 1910).

this fashion, the new Grand Central, while admirably serving its prime function of moving passengers, simultaneously created a directional continuum where there had been none before.

A second, and more strikingly humanistic, expression of the use of land in mid-Manhattan is provided by Rockefeller Center. Created primarily by the architect Wallace Harrison, Rockefeller Center was built, beginning in 1931, on a twelve-acre plot between Fifth Avenue and the Avenue of the Americas and between 48th and 51st Streets. Dominating the scene vertically was the RCA tower, which rose seventy floors above the earth but was set back from Fifth Avenue and fronted by a sunken court with a cascade, an open-air restaurant for summer use, and a skating rink for winter recreation. Each of the original fourteen buildings were placed asymmetrically to one another, with the result that the towers offered an ever-changing variety of views as one moved among them, even as the ground-level relationships of space and mass contributed their own sensations. In this way, the entirety became a continuum of vertical and horizontal visual appeal.

Perhaps the most remarkable and suggestive quality of Rockefeller Center is to be found in the way it replicates one of the great joys of cities of medieval Europe: the open piazza in which people can mingle for a variety of purposes—to do business, to relax, to shop. It acts, in that sense, as a challenge to the predominant use of land in American cities, which has been that of public streets lined with private structures. The Rockefeller Center piazza, by contrast, argues against functional isolationism and substitutes for it a vitalizing democratic philosophy of the multipurpose open marketplace, much as occurs with the later Market East development in Philadelphia, but otherwise is rarely seen in America.

Public parks, while admirably serving recreational purposes, all too often exhibit a structural separatism, lacking a connection with the land around them. Such a limitation is not to be found in New York's Central Park, where the life of the city both surrounds and pulsates through it, so that it is at once a refuge from and contributor to the city.

Nearly a half century before work began on Central Park in the late 1850s, the sense of Manhattan as two separate cities had been established by a planning decision. Until then, New York* had grown Topsy-like from its origins at the juncture of the Hudson and East Rivers at the foot of the island; throughout the eighteenth century, the city had remained largely unsettled north of Greenwich Village. Most of the early roads came about as connectors from house to house, from farm to farm, or between trading posts and a fort.

By the first decade of the nineteenth century, New York's population was rapidly growing, its commercial possibilities expanding. In response, a state commission was formed in the year 1807, charged with planning a design that would assure orderly growth of the vast, largely virginal territory above the old city.[2] The street scheme for the second city, approved in 1811, featured a line drawn east to west just north of Washington Square. Streets south of the line would remain as they were, but all save a handful of those to the north and west were to be demolished. The major exception was Broadway, by then firmly established as a significant thoroughfare with houses and places of business along its route. Laid across the terrain were to be nine north–south avenues and 155 cross streets, all meeting at right angles, stopping just south of the old Dutch village of Harlem.

The commission's grid scheme allowed for a bare handful of parks and plazas, few of which were ever built and none of which survived. The planned result, therefore, was to create a city virtually without vistas, without focal points, without amenities. The grid itself was not the problem; the commissioners could have readily introduced attractive variations upon it. No records are available to tell us why they didn't, but we do know a great deal

* At that time, New York City consisted only of Manhattan Island and a small slice of what is now the Bronx, this entity being known as New York County. It wasn't until 1898 that the state legislature created Greater New York, made up of Manhattan and the outlying boroughs of the Bronx, Queens, Brooklyn, and Staten Island.

about the reasons for the popularity of the grid in colonial and post-colonial city planning, and why it most frequently was adopted in an unadorned fashion, as in New York.

Philosophy played a part. In early America, the belief in rationalism, inherited from Europe, was quite strong, and from it was whelped the Americans' fondness for thinking of themselves as a practical people. Out of that perspective, nothing could be more practical or more rational than laying streets at right angles to one another rather than allowing them to wander here and there in a riot of confusion.

The grid, however, was also practical in another way. To lay out a settlement on a grid required only a surveyor's skill, an important consideration in a time when people were anxious to build a new nation as quickly as possible. Moreover, because rectangular lots were more readily measurable than irregular ones, they prevented complaints from shareholders in land development companies that they weren't getting their fair share of the property. The same principle held true when developers sold lots to individual purchasers. These buyers could visualize a piece of land 20' by 30', for example, as they could not one that was 20' at one point, 16.4' at the next, 13.8' at a third, and so on. The ready visualization was important, too. In the early national period, a major portion of the frontier that had opened up was sold sight unseen at auctions held in the eastern cities.*[3] Diagonal and curving streets, circular plazas and parks, all of which sliced land off into shapes

---

* The most important accomplishment of the federal government under the Articles of Confederation was the Land Ordinance of 1785. Its purpose was to establish a national land policy for the United States beyond the East Coast. Colonial charters, written when knowledge of the geography of the country was scant, had given a number of the new states conflicting claims to the western land. The 1785 Land Ordinance solved this problem by making the frontier part of the public domain.[4] Almost all the land was divided into grids, and the expectation was that almost all of it would be used for farms. However, developers quickly became aware that money could be made more quickly by creating towns on maps, which would then be exhibited at the eastern auctions.

undesirable from a sales point of view, were to be avoided in the new towns, just as they were in the New York plan of 1811. The technical considerations reveal the underlying premise of the New York system and others like it: Land was to be packaged for profit-making purposes. The premise was a product of the development of capitalism and contrary to earlier ideas about the allocation of urban space. In the cities of medieval Europe, profit was, at most, an inconsiderable motive. Land there was to be used for the protection of people, as represented by the fortress-like walls that surrounded the cities. Within the cities, significant portions of the land were dedicated to spiritual purposes, as represented by cathedrals and lesser churches, and by plazas across which people approached the physical manifestation of God in their midst. At the same time, the plazas served as spacious connectors to the governmental and commercial life of a city, suggesting that the spiritual and temporal impulses were not in conflict with one another but that each contributed to an interwoven mutuality of purpose for the city and the people who lived in it.[5] An attempt in the New World to apply the medieval principle of mutuality can be found in Philadelphia, to which the New Yorkers looked for the material inspiration of their grid plan.

Philadelphia

When the thirty-seven-year-old William Penn gained a charter for a colony in the New World from King Charles II in 1681, he already had in mind what his capital city would look like. It was to have streets that were straight and wide "so that there be ground on each side, for Gardens or Orchards or fields, that it may be a Green Country Towne, which will never be burnt," hearkening back to the medieval idea of the city as a place of protection for its people.

The site of this urban Eden for Penn and his co-religionists was across the Delaware River from an already existent Quaker set-

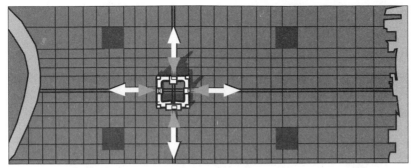

Diagram 8

tlement in Burlington, New Jersey. In 1682, Penn had a surveyor lay out his city on a grid but, unlike in New York, Penn's grid functioned inside quadrants, each of which had a park to assure greenery for everyone. At the point where the four sectors joined was placed a plaza of greater dimensions than any of the parks. (See Diagram 8.)

We don't know if Penn's plan was entirely of his own devising. His inspiration may have come from drawings submitted by architects for the rebuilding of London after much of the city was destroyed by fire in 1666. The London proposal most nearly like Penn's was Richard Newcourt's, which also made use of quadrants and a square in the middle.*[6]

Penn's plan, however, differed from Newcourt's in two key ways. The large middle square in Newcourt's design was apparently intended to be a fifth park. Penn's square, smaller than Newcourt's, was not to be a park but instead the location of the city's government buildings and a Quaker meetinghouse, thereby containing the spiritual and temporal in a single central site. The im-

---

* Newcourt and others were, in turn, responding to a reawakened interest in the ancient world, where the grid had been regularly employed as a fundament of city design. The grid temporarily had been superseded by the meandering streets of the medieval walled cities. The directions the streets took were probably determined by the walls, which were irregular in shape in conformity to the contours of the land, and to where people happened to be living when they were built.

portance of this central location was emphasized by the second way in which Penn's plan differed from Newcourt's. Newcourt's streets were all of the same dimensions. Penn, however, laid out two main thoroughfares, Broad and High (later renamed Market), which were to be wider than the others and which intersected at the central square, causing it to become the axis from which the two main streets radiated east and west, north and south.

The contrast between the cohesive Philadelphia plan and that adopted by New York for development of its "second" city north of Washington Square is illustrated when we compare Diagram 8 with Diagram 9. As we see in Diagram 9, the New York grid, even if it had included Philadelphia's parks, would still have lacked the dominant movement system and structural focus that Penn created by introducing the axis. Note also how readily the New York planners could have added design interest to their

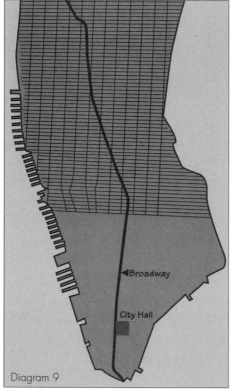

Diagram 9

plan if they had not treated Broadway as an inconvenience but rather exploited its strength by crossing it with another powerful avenue and a plaza or park of some sort at the juncture.

Penn's proposed means of populating the city illuminates his philosophy of the use of land and people's relationship to it. He advertised that purchasers of farm acreage would receive in addition a plot of land within the boundaries of the city, the size depending on the amount purchased for agricultural purposes. In this way, Penn hoped, the settlers would have a proprietary interest in the welfare of the city even as they farmed their lands outside it, a mutuality of purpose that cannot occur when the city and its surroundings are perceived as separate entities. The city's land, therefore, as in medieval times, was not to be exploited for profit, as in New York, but was to serve the common good.

The rural land-sale plan, however, proved difficult to carry out on the scale Penn planned. Perhaps more important, from its very early days the city itself became a beacon for immigrants who had no interest in becoming farmers. Many were attracted solely by the mercantile possibilities of the port. Another incentive to growth, and by no means an incidental one, that had nothing to do with farming was the freedom of religion that Penn offered. Even the Quakers' worst persecutors from the Church of England were welcome. For one reason or another, people came in great numbers. By 1685, just three years after the city's founding, 600 homes had been built, and thirteen years later more than 2,000. By the 1750s, when New York's population was hovering around 10,000, Philadelphia's was more than twice that. Its port had also expanded mightily by then to become the second-largest in the British empire. The value of imports alone reaching Philadelphia exceeded £500,000; by the eve of the Revolution that figure would double.

Not only did the city's population grow, but so did that of the surrounding county, which became rapidly urbanized. (The original city and the county were consolidated into the present city of Philadelphia in 1856.) In most of the county precincts, the grid was again imposed, but not in Penn's imaginative adaptation of it. Instead, street after street followed one another in dreary succession, unrelieved by any squares or parks for the enjoyment of the people, just as in New York.

In this way, Penn's vision of a pleasurably coherent city seemed to have proven incapable of competing with people who saw land solely in terms of profit or who had no ideas, other than in the most rudimentary sense, of what they wanted to do with their city.

Nevertheless, by the second half of the nineteenth century, nearly 200 years after Penn proposed it, his idea for situating the offices of government on Central Square was finally adopted by a popular vote. Until then, city affairs had been conducted out of a building adjacent to Independence Hall. The transfer had a dramatic effect that can be visualized by returning to Diagram 8. Notice how the movement systems created by Broad and Market Streets first appear (the white arrows) to be leading away from Center Square, a result of the absence of any strong focusing structure on it. Once City Hall was placed there, the spokes (shown by the shaded arrows) not only lead from the axis but toward it. The centering function, although without the religious component, had finally been established. A commercial building would not have had that impact. It would have been just one of many of the same purpose, and so would not have had any visual importance. The introduction of the City Hall, by contrast, established the concept of the polis right in the heart of the city. Visitors and residents immediately see City Hall and the strong lines of force (the two major streets) directed toward it, causing it to dominate the commercial life around it. Its tall granite structure informs them—they could not avoid the information even if they wanted to—that the city is not just a conglomeration of mercantile and individual strivings but is intended to be an instrument of service to the people who live within it. That message had been muted during the long period when the site of government was part of the Independence Hall milieu and thereby subordinated to it. In New York, City Hall is separated from the heart of the city where, hence, the commercial function reigns without competition. (See Diagram 9.)

A little less than a century after City Hall reinvigorated Penn's purpose, the power of his design was again made evident by Bacon's continuum from the axis. Over a span of hundreds of years, the arrows had kept moving toward it.

Savannah

Another adaptation of the use of land, even more harmonious than Penn's, sprang from the mind of James Oglethorpe, the founder of Savannah. Oglethorpe, Penn's junior by fifty-two years, was a visionary and a man of social conscience. Like Penn, he came from a wealthy English family; in 1722, he decided to devote his ample leisure time to public affairs. He was elected to Parliament and six years later was named chairman of a committee to investigate London's jails. Oglethorpe was dismayed by the squalid conditions he encountered and was badly shaken when he realized that large numbers of the inmates were incarcerated solely because they owed money.

Oglethorpe interested a number of his influential friends in his concerns, and in 1732 King George II issued him and his partners a charter for the colony of Georgia. To it, Oglethorpe intended to bring not only debtors but other people of little means and few prospects in life, both from England and the European continent. The first contingent of settlers, 114 in number, set out with Oglethorpe for the New World in November 1732.

They landed at Charleston, South Carolina, and proceeded south, where Oglethorpe wrote he discovered "the situation for [our] town upon an high ground, forty feet perpendicular above the high water mark; the soil dry and sandy, the water of the river fresh, springs coming out from the sides of the situation . . . sheltered from the western and southern winds . . . by the vast woods of pine trees, many of which are an hundred and few under seventy feet high." Not everything went well at first, however. As a visitor observed: "Some of the People having privately drank too freely of Rum are dead . . ."

Nevertheless, Oglethorpe pressed forward assiduously and in December of the following year was allotting plots of land to the surviving settlers. His plan is shown in the first part of Diagram 10. In the plan, the shaded areas within the grid represent parks; the open area is the marketplace. (The square outside the grid is a

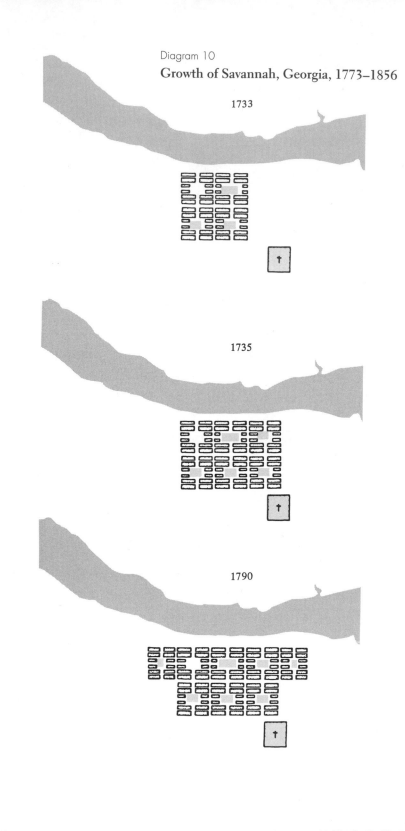

Diagram 10

Growth of Savannah, Georgia, 1773–1856

1733

1735

1790

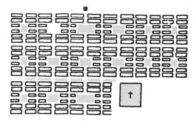

1815

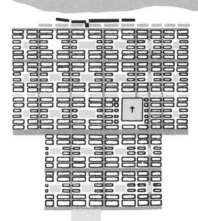

1856

After 1856

cemetery.) In the second part of the diagram, Savannah is shown in 1790, having expanded east, with two new parks. By 1815, expansion had continued to the east and also north from the river. Note the addition (the broken line) of a boulevard just above the cemetery and the black dot just south of the river, which signified the new city hall. Savannah by then had consistently grown in a cellular fashion, the original design simply replicating itself. The result is a very generous and rhythmic use of green space that was not permitted in Penn's self-containing quadrants. In the fourth part of the diagram, depicting the city on the eve of the Civil War, the original single city government building has created a directional movement along the riverfront; south from it, the city has further grown, still obedient to Oglethorpe's design, in the form of a new and larger park that acts as a dramatic signature to those that preceded it. At the same time, boulevards—shown by the horizontal separations of the grid—have been added to the first one, establishing their own consistent signature to the city. The parks remain cells natural to the body, but because each has its own function and distinguishing characteristics, today as in the past, they delight and surprise the visitor who comes upon them, one after the other.[7]

In their desire to create a harmonious, integrated whole, Penn and Oglethorpe had the advantage of being able to create their cities. Imposition of a new design, in whole or part, upon an old city is much more difficult to accomplish, as Bacon found out, but not impossible. An early example of successful imposition comes not from America but from Europe in Pope Sixtus V's plan for Rome, c. 1585.[8] By Sixtus's day, Rome had become a vast, disjointed sprawl of streets and buildings. To combat the fragmentation, Sixtus conceived the idea of constructing obelisks as focal points that would direct patterns of movement among them. (See Diagram 11.) The rhythmic sense of place that today's visitor to Rome senses had its origin in Sixtus's unifying principle.

Sixtus's plan, as with Oglethorpe's and Penn's, shows how an integrated conception can continue to inform and shape an envi-

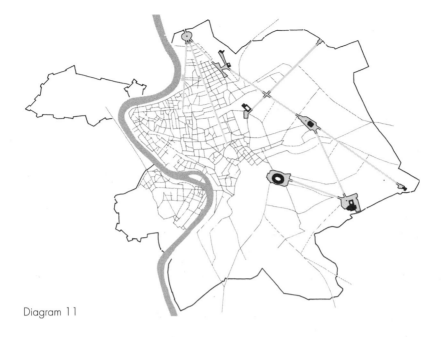

Diagram 11

ronment long after the plan's progenitor is gone and along with him any political power he may have had, as Sixtus did, to carry out the idea. When such a potent design has been put in place, it has the capacity to make the cities that are its beneficiaries amenable to a rewarding and organic growth that gives them the potential of making them more livable for their people. Savannah particularly symbolizes a very nearly perfect continuum of the whole.*

By implication, men like Sixtus, Oglethorpe, and Penn offer proof of Bacon's assertion of the importance of the individual vision in city design. Had Penn and Oglethorpe, that is, not contributed their special genius to the design of their cities, we can

---

* To be found virtually no place else. Oglethorpe's idea, like Penn's, could have been replicated, but because of Savannah's location, relatively few city planners who could have been influenced by it early in American history ever saw it. They did see New York and Philadelphia, and those were the models they adopted, most often concentrating on their worst aspects.

safely assume they would have been laid out on a simple grid, since that was the popular trend of the time; however, we have no basis for assuming that anyone else would have come up with their deployments of space within the grid: the recognition of the role of the axis in one case, of rhythmic cellular growth in the other.

Their contribution can be compared to the role Thomas Jefferson played in 1776. That year the idea of freedom from England was very much in the air—it was a trend—among the American colonists, and some declaration of independence would have resulted even if Jefferson had never lived. But, because he did, the Declaration of Independence of which he was the principal author spoke with such eloquent urgency (his individual enrichment of the trend) that his words fixed not only our national aspirations but those of other emerging nations in the centuries since. In positing an idea for the present, he posited the same one for the future, just as Penn and Oglethorpe did.

Washington, D.C.

In the case of Sixtus's plan for Rome, diagonal communicative lines emerge as the basis for structural coherence. In the New World, no heed was paid to that vigorous ordering of space until the time came for the building of the United States capital, where a complex of diagonals was laid over the basic grid.

In Washington,[9] as in Savannah and Philadelphia, the design that was imprinted upon the land at the time of the founding was holistic, and remained largely so despite subsequent onslaughts upon its integrity. However, unlike Philadelphia and Savannah, Washington was not laid out with the intention of creating an amenable, much less a convenient, ambience for its residents. Its purpose, rather, was to house the government of the United States of America in a manner that would give permanent visual confirmation of the democratic institutions that the struggling new nation was seeking to establish. Washington, therefore, represents a symbolic use of land.

As a result, its institutional center, which extends from the Supreme Court and the Capitol at one end to the Executive Office Building at the other, has a distancing and impersonal quality. We find, that is, much to be admired in that complex but little that is humanly warm and inviting. A sense of intimacy (not unlike that of portions of the original Manhattan) is achieved in Washington principally only in the Georgetown sector west of the White House, with its meandering central avenue, its hills and cozy side streets. But Georgetown really isn't part of the District of Columbia, not historically; it existed as a village prior to the city's founding, and thus was not amenable to incorporation into the grand diagonal plan that is dominant elsewhere.

Just as was true of Savannah and Philadelphia, the creation of Washington came about from the visionary genius of a single person: the French-born Charles Pierre L'Enfant, who, while still in his early twenties, came to America to join the fight for freedom from England. An engineer by training and an artist by avocation, L'Enfant rose to the rank of major in the Revolutionary army, where he came to the attention of George Washington. In March 1791, at Washington's suggestion, his secretary of state Thomas Jefferson named L'Enfant as one of two surveyors for the new capital, which, after several years of debate, was determined to be situated along the Potomac and Anacostia Rivers near the village of Georgetown.

George Washington was already familiar with the area chosen for the new federal district. As a teenage boy, he had assisted in laying out Alexandria, just across the Potomac in Virginia, and in 1790 had visited the District of Columbia site to begin negotiations with property owners for sale of their land to the national government. Jefferson, who also favored the selected location, had drawn up a number of plans for the capital with streets "at right angles as in Philadelphia." He worried, however, about an aspect of the Philadelphia plan that required that all houses be built the same distance back from the street, causing, Jefferson wrote, "a disgusting monotony, all persons make this complaint against Philadelphia," whereas "the contrary practice varies the appearance, & is much more convenient to the inhabitants."[10]

Washington sent Jefferson's ideas and accompanying sketches to L'Enfant, who pronounced them "tiresome and insipid."[11] Jefferson took no open umbrage at this criticism—he was probably aware of the high regard in which Washington held L'Enfant—and in a letter to L'Enfant he wrote: ". . . having more confidence in the unbiassed [sic] state of [Washington's] mind, than my own, I avoid interfering with what he may have expressed to you."[12] With the two most powerful men in the new nation in his corner, L'Enfant may have understandably assumed he was in complete charge of the city's development and that the commissioners who had been appointed to oversee the task would not stand in his way.

L'Enfant set to work with a remarkable burst of creativity. In less than six months, he produced a plan for the city of Washington that, like Oglethorpe's for Savannah, has remained the structural guiding force. As Lewis Mumford has pointed out, L'Enfant's plan was overly comprehensive.[13] It contained too many diagonal avenues, too many circles, leading to a design complexity that was inhibiting in that it made no allowance for growth and adaptation as new needs made themselves evident. Nevertheless, although his design differed radically from Oglethorpe's, just as Oglethorpe's differed from Penn's, L'Enfant's shared with theirs the offering of a vision of a structurally coherent city.

The idea that gave breath to L'Enfant's vision emanated from the major duty that had been placed upon him, which was to establish a setting for the legislative hall and for the home of the President. Convenience suggested they be placed next to one another. L'Enfant's artist's eye, however, was quickly attracted to an elevation known as Jenkin's Hill and, about a mile to the west of it, another lesser elevation. Of Jenkin's Hill, L'Enfant wrote, it "stands really as a pedestal waiting for a superstructure. . . ." On it, he directed that the Federal House, or Capitol, as it became known, be built.[14] The western rise of land was to accommodate the President's "palace," which was to have a "garden park" and a separate building to house executive offices. The palace, L'Enfant decided, was to be connected to the Capitol by public walks along a mall. In this fashion, the executive and legislative branches were kept separate from one another, yet joined, as the Constitution called for. The concept, elegant and simple, was intended by L'Enfant to be and has remained the dominant visual identification of the American capital. Of no less importance was the "garden park," which created a strong line from the President's palace toward the river, directing the eye not just to the city and its monuments but to the natural beauty of Virginia on the opposite bank of the Potomac.

L'Enfant did not remain to see his city built. Cantankerous, arrogant, and self-important, he fell afoul of the District of Columbia commissioners, in a series of disputes about the details of the design and the methods by which lots would be sold for private purposes.

His design for the city, however, by then had been accepted, and it was followed with relatively few changes. Some of Washington's early observers were awed by its beauty, but for many Americans and a parcel of scoffing European visitors, it seemed absurdly grandiose. Neither was it politically correct. Its grand avenues, its circles, its architectural monumentalism—all were too reminiscent of Paris and other French cities as they had taken shape under the autocracy that had been overthrown in a revolution like the one that gave America its freedom. For a nation dedicated to equality and democracy, it was a visual affront, or so it was said.

Philosophically the capital in all its splendor also appeared to be the very antithesis of the rationalism (itself a gift from France) that had helped make the grid such an acceptable mode in city planning. The early, widespread negative reaction to L'Enfant's vision offers one reason it had little impact on the design of other American cities, although the way his diagonals and circles cut into the amount of land that could be sold was probably a more important factor in its rejection by developers. Still, there were a few imitations. An early version for the rebuilding of Detroit after the fire of 1805 was obviously drawn from L'Enfant's scheme for Washington, but it was never adopted, in part due to anti-Washington feelings. To some extent, L'Enfant's ideas were embraced in Madison (Wisconsin), Cleveland, and Indianapolis (which owes much of its present-day attractiveness to them). L'Enfant himself later laid out Paterson, New Jersey, on a diagonal system and helped in the early planning of Buffalo, New York.[15]

Other than for the L'Enfant-influenced cities, as the nation moved westward, the grid remained dominant, and was even encountered by pioneers in the pueblos that had been built by earlier Spanish missionaries and soldiers, suggesting its universal appeal. Had American cities remained uncrowded, within an economy made up largely of individual artisans, the grid, whatever one might think of it aesthetically, would have presented no problems in terms of living conditions. But the factory economy of the new industrialism brought hordes of workers. Because these workers received pittances as wages, even for the most dangerous kinds of employment, they could afford only meager rentals. As landlords quickly realized, that problem could be solved by packing many families into multistory housing; the small sums excised from each renter would make a profitable sum in aggregate, and that is what was done. Soon, in city after city, tenements abutted one another within their confining grids, cramped, poorly maintained, with rudimentary sanitary facilities. Slums were guaranteed.

As the new industrialism progressed, the idea that land was a series of packages to be used individually for the profit of the holders took on a dominating role in the life of cities. But not entirely so. Here and there, some individuals maintained that the city had a richer and more humane destiny to be fulfilled. Their belief had its first significant victory in New York.

3

The City Beautiful

The Industrial Revolution produced a class of self-made million-aires who dramatically altered the appearance of American cities. Some contented themselves with building grand mansions, which might have formal gardens surrounding them for personal enjoyment. Others endowed schools and museums, favoring Greek, Roman, and Egyptian styles of architecture for the edifices.[1] As the decades went on, great business towers, the American version of the medieval cathedrals, also began to appear on the urban landscape.

Politicians built monuments, too. L'Enfant's design for Washington originally met with opprobrium, but the Capitol, built on Jenkin's Hill, was imitated across the land, sometimes with bizarre results. (The doors to the Pennsylvania capitol in Harrisburg are opened by grasping the brass heads of two businessmen subsequently convicted of stealing state money during the construction of the building.) City halls, even borough halls, in this grand fashion memorialized statecraft as an art no less sacred than the accumulation of wealth.

Some of these public and private artifacts proved visually pleasing, adding focus, along with a touch of civility, to the otherwise raw and barren look of the emerging cities. Handsome or ugly, they provided a lesson in civics. They informed the multitudes that if they strived hard and well, they could also expect to rise from mill boy to mill owner, from log cabin to White House.

To the extent that these reliquaries of power had aesthetic values, as well as rhetorical ones, they came in fragments—their very existence, their location and appearance dependent on the whim and taste of the rich and powerful. They did not, and by their nature could not, relate to the need that ordinary people felt to have places of their own for peaceful relaxation, the need that Penn and Oglethorpe had understood. In its nineteenth-century garb, the first striving toward the idea of common enjoyment of the city had its inspiration in the abodes not of the living but of the dead. As Lewis Mumford put it: ". . . in the crowded modern city [of the nineteenth century], the first general exodus to a more desirable dwelling place in the country was the migration of the dead to the romantic Elysium of a suburban cemetery."[2] The earliest of these wondrous resting places was Mount Auburn, outside Boston. Following its opening in 1831, an enraptured visitor wrote: "The avenues are winding in their course and exceedingly beautiful in their gentle circuits, adapted picturesquely to the inequalities of the surface and ground, and producing charming landscape effects from this natural arrangement. . . . Various small lakes . . . of different size and shape, embellish the grounds; and some of these have been so cleansed, deepened, and banked, as to present a pleasant feature in this widespread extent of forest loveliness—this ground of hallowed purpose."[3]

By the 1860s, decorative hallowed grounds modeled on Mount Auburn and New York's Greenwood Cemetery were to be found in or near most American cities and towns. They became attractions for tourists and for a city's working people as well, who visited them to relax, if only for a few hours, as they strolled along the winding paths, as they smelled the flowers and the good green grass, and as they picnicked next to the gravestones. At such times, the visitors could forget the crabbed and increasingly polluted city in which they had their homes, and which threatened them daily with another kind of death, that of the spirit.*

* Pollution came early to American cities, and perhaps to none sooner than Pittsburgh. In 1840, an English visitor there declared it to be "certainly the most smoky and sooty town it has ever been my lot to behold. The houses are blackened with it, the streets are made filthy, and the garments and persons of all whom you meet are soiled and made dingy by its influence."[4]

That the urban dead fared better environmentally than did the living was an irony not lost on some observers. Writing in 1842, Andrew Jackson Downing, asked: "But does not this general interest [in cemeteries as recreational sites] prove that public gardens, established in a liberal and suitable manner, near our large cities, would be equally successful? . . . The true policy of republics," he argued, "is to foster the taste for great public libraries, sculpture and picture galleries, parks, and gardens, which *all* may enjoy."[5]

Among the first to take up Downing's call was the New York City newspaper editor and poet William Cullen Bryant, who in 1844 initiated a campaign to acquire acreage in Manhattan for a great public park while there was still unoccupied land available. In support of Bryant, Downing weighed in with his own scornful assessment: "What are called parks in New York," he noted, "are not even apologies for the thing; they are only squares or paddocks," and the few of them that could be found were, for the most part, in the old Lower Manhattan section of the city.

The campaign launched by Bryant in the *New York Post* succeeded. By 1857, the property that makes up today's Central Park was acquired. Named as its superintendent was thirty-four-year-old Frederick Law Olmsted, who was to become the most influential city and suburban planner of the nineteenth century. A gentleman farmer from Staten Island who had visited England and written glowing articles about its many parks and gardens, Olmsted, assisted by the English architect Calvert Vaux, prepared a design for the park. The terrain he inherited was dismal, but Olmsted had the imagination to conceive of a constantly undulating and variegated park introduced by a formal mall and fountain near the 59th Street and Fifth Avenue entrance.

The amount of work that had to be done was enormous. As Professor David Clow recounts, "Swampy land [had to be] converted to glades, groves, streams, and wide greens. . . . Great rocks beneath the ground were exposed and planted over to look like natural formations. . . ." In the process, the park took on a multi-

View of New York's Central Park, looking south (c. 1870).

dimensional form, in striking contrast to the single-level streets surrounding it. Perhaps most marvelously, the design allowed for four movement channels throughout, none of which intruded on the others—foot paths for pedestrians; carriage drives; bridle paths; and sunken roadways to conduct city traffic. The latter system was the key to the park's long-term survival. Had it not been put in place, Clow notes, Central Park eventually would have been chopped up to make way for highways when the automobile culture made its demands. As it was, almost as if Olmsted had visualized the coming of the automobile, the through-traffic pattern was sufficiently ample and so cunningly situated that there has never been cause to disturb it, and the park has remained whole.[6]

At the time of its opening, and for many years afterward, the pleasures of Central Park were primarily reserved for the members of the gentry. Working people didn't own private carriages, much less have a horse tethered by their tenement to take out riding, and relatively few of them had easy access to the park by public transportation.

Nevertheless, Central Park was an extraordinary achievement, and not only architecturally. The campaign that led to its construction introduced the idea that government has a duty to attend to the aesthetic and recreational needs of its citizens. In the past, members of various ruling classes had bestowed benefactions upon their cities and their people—as Pope Sixtus V did for Rome—but no sense of obligation had been involved. Similarly, the parks with which Penn and Oglethorpe endowed their cities were aspects of their visions of the coherent urban environment, and were not in response to any democratic demand made upon them. In the United States, as Downing had observed, government recognized that one of its functions was to make centers of learning available, not only in the form of schools but as public libraries and museums; such an acceptance of function, however, was quite different from recognizing that citizens also had a right to a sylvan ambience, not for anyone's profit or for a course of practical learning, but purely for their enjoyment. The idea was a deeply humanistic one, and by its acceptance declared a spiritual purpose for the city and its government.

If Central Park had not been such a popular success, its impact might have been much less than it was in advancing the theory that government has a responsibility to make amenable surroundings available to its people. However, Central Park's location was at least as important as its beauty. New York was the nation's largest city. People looked to it for leadership: When New York did something that met with widespread approval, it was likely to be copied, and Central Park was. Within a little less than ten years after its much-heralded construction began, its commissioners were proudly, if not entirely accurately, announcing: "There is scarce a city of magnitude in this country that has not provided, or taken measures to provide a Park for the pleasure of its citizens." Olmsted designed these new elysiums for the living, either by himself or with Vaux, in cities that included Brooklyn (not yet a part of New York), Boston, Rochester (New York), Bridgeport (Connecticut), Detroit, Louisville, and Knoxville.

Olmsted's assignments, however, were not limited to cities; he carried his message of the sylvan ambience into suburbs as well. In Berkeley, California, he designed a village community, based on his naturalistic principles, that later became the site for the University of California. Perhaps his greatest and most long-lasting suburban success was his remarkable design in 1868 for Riverside, Illinois, which emphasized liberal bestowals of green space and curving roads. In his proposal, Olmsted recommended that each Riverside home be set back from the street, and further that "each owner have one or two living trees between his house and the highway line. . . . A few simple precautions of this kind, added to a tasteful and convenient disposition of shade trees," Olmsted went on, in a synthesis of his credo, "and other planting along the road-sides and public places, will, in a few years, cause the whole locality . . . to possess, not only the attraction of neatness and convenience, and the charm of refined sylvan beauty and grateful umbrageousness, but an aspect of secluded peacefulness and tranquility more general and pervading than can possibly be found in suburbs which have grown up in a desultory hap-hazard way. . . . [I]ts character will inevitably, also, notwithstanding its tidiness, be not only informal, but, in a moderate way, positively picturesque, and when contrasted with the constantly repeated right angles, straight lines, and flat surfaces which characterize our large modern towns, thoroughly refreshing."[7]

In Riverside, the altruism that had infused the campaign to build Central Park was absent. Riverside's promoters were out to make money, and they grasped the commercial potential of Olmsted's plan. While its adoption meant they'd have fewer houses to sell than if they were built on a grid, the developers' total profits were greater because of the higher prices they could charge for the "refined sylvan beauty and grateful umbrageousness" they'd be offering to their customers.

The same happy mercantile consequence had occurred in New York, where land values on Fifth Avenue and other streets abutting Central Park rose rapidly following its opening. The connection between greenery and gain, however, as Olmsted's ventures proved, was more readily carried out in suburban than in already densely overcrowded city settings. Although the parks introduced following Olmsted's achievement in New York provided oases where there had been none before, during the last third of the nineteenth century cities became uglier places in which to live, as ever more factories were built, as ever more trains belched their offal into the air, as streets became ever more encumbered with overhead mazes of electric and telephone wires, as the dwelling places of the poor became ever more crowded, fetid, and unhealthy.

Nevertheless, not all the entrepreneurs who had brought these conditions about were satisfied with what they had wrought. Their willingness to support the building of parks was an indication of a new ambition. Now it would no longer be their mansions and their business towers but their cities that would serve as testament to their greatness. When the nineteenth century reached its last decade, that longing took on reality in Chicago.

As with a number of American cities—like much-older Detroit (1701) and Pittsburgh (1754)—Chicago had its origins as a military outpost when Fort Dearborn was built off the shores of Lake Michigan in 1803. At first, Chicago seemed destined never to become more than a tiny village. In the early 1830s, it consisted of a dozen log cabins, two taverns, and a store. There was a good reason that few settlers came and fewer still remained: The nearby mosquito-ridden marshes emitted odors that caused the Indians to dub the site "the place of evil smell." The early residents seemed to agree. The name they gave the village was derived from one of two pungent Indian words, either *chickagou*, which means "garlic," or *shegagh*, which means "skunk."[8]

The odor of the swamps, however, would be overcome by the much sweeter smell of money. Mindful of the economic boom created in New York State by the Erie Canal, Illinois legislators determined to build a canal of their own to transport goods between Lake Michigan and the Mississippi River. Chicago was chosen as the lake terminus, with parcels of land (which were owned by the state under eminent domain rights) to be sold to the highest bidders to help cover the costs of the canal's construction. As news of Chicago's impending commercial importance became known, the population began to swell, reaching roughly 4,000 in 1836, when the English writer Harriet Martineau was a visitor. "The streets," she wrote, "were crowded with land speculators hurrying from one sale to another. A Negro dressed up in scarlet and bearing a scarlet flag and riding a white horse with housings of scarlet announced the time of sale. At every street corner where he stopped the crowd gathered around him; and it seemed as if some prevalent mania infected the whole people. As the gentlemen of our party walked the streets, storekeepers hailed them from their doors with offers of farms and all manner of land lots, advising them to speculate before the price of land rose higher." And it did. Lots often changed hands ten times in a day, with the final purchase ten times that of the first in the morning. As John Reps observed in *The Making of Urban America*: "Most of this value was fictitious since it was not based on cash sales but on purchases with extremely liberal credit. Of course this did not prevent everyone who owned land from imagining himself a millionaire."[9]

The boom collapsed, along with much of the economy of the United States, in the Panic of 1837, and work on the canal came to a halt. By the time the job was finally completed in 1848, the coming of the railroad had made it an anachronism, but one that had served to create a city. By the late 1850s, ten rail lines were running through Chicago, assuring its future as a great metropolis. The population continued to expand in the post–Civil War years, going over the 700,000 mark in the 1880s. The city by then housed great wealth, too. Its business dynasties—including the McCormicks, the Fields, the Montgomery Wards, the Armours, the Palmers—rivaled and sometimes outstripped in wealth and pretention those of the East.

By the late 1880s, Chicago was also well on the way to becoming the nation's center for new ideas in the design of buildings. The path to that status had literally been cleared by the fire of 1871. The extent of its damage had been prompted, in large part, by the city's profusion of wooden houses and stores—many dating back to the 1830s—that were so closely packed together that the flames jumped easily from one to the next. The bitter experience of the fire succeeded in bringing home to Chicagoans the realization that a city's structures cannot be considered solely as discrete entities on the landscape, but rather that their proximity and safety in construction must also be considered. For the first time, building regulations and zoning codes became matters of importance, and not only in Chicago. Other cities, recognizing that their helter-skelter growth could open them to the same tragedy as Chicago's, followed suit with their own ordinances.

Within ten years of the fire, the rebuilding of Chicago had been largely accomplished. Its entrepreneurs provided the money, but of no less importance was the fortuitous presence in the city of a cadre of extraordinarily skilled architects.

One of them, William Le Baron Jenney, introduced the steel-cage framework that made buildings much less likely to collapse if on fire, reducing the number of deaths and limiting the probable spread of the conflagration. However, probably the best known of the Chicago School of architects,[10] as they became known, was Louis Sullivan, who created bold, abrupt buildings relieved by emphatic vertical lines and carefully calculated ornamentation in a modified version of the Beaux Arts style.* (Sullivan's office assistant, Frank Lloyd Wright, would go on to become more famous than he, but Wright was never primarily a city architect.)

In 1890, John Root and his partner, Daniel Burnham, were named the consulting architects for the World's Columbian Expo-

---

* The Beaux Arts School of Paris was the recognized world center for architectural thought in the late nineteenth century and retained its primacy well into the 1920s.

sition to be held in Chicago to celebrate the 400th anniversary of Columbus's arrival in America. A major role was also played by the revered Olmsted, then in his seventies, who chose Jackson Park, facing Lake Michigan, as the location for the exposition's great attraction, the city of the future. At Olmsted's suggestion, a series of canals were constructed; these added a charming, placid touch and were embellished by dramatic reflecting pools. Burnham, who became the principal architect following Root's death in 1891, invited his colleagues of the Chicago School—with the exception of the disapproving Sullivan—to contribute their ideas. Burnham also engaged the services of the most popular sculptor of the time, Augustus Saint-Gaudens, to select the artists who would execute the various statues and obelisks and design the fountain.

Despite the massive egos involved, the discussions among the planners seem to have been remarkably harmonious, perhaps in large part because the independent-minded Sullivan wasn't a participant (though he did design the Transportation Building for the exposition). Nearly without exception, the various halls were designed in the neo-Classic modes then favored by the Beaux Arts School. When completed in 1893,* the buildings gave the appearance of marble but—because they were never intended to have a life beyond the fair itself—were made of stucco laid over steel frames. The disagreement among the planners concerned the colors to be painted over the stucco. When no resolution to that dilemma could be reached, it was decided they would be painted no color at all—they would be white, hence the White City, by which name that portion of the Columbian Exposition came to be known.

Although the alabaster appearance came about by happenstance, the White City was aptly named. Black workers had been deliberately excluded from its construction and also from the building of the exposition midway. Exhibits were arranged in a manner to depict the rise of civilization. Farthest from the White

* A year late. The exposition was supposed to have opened in 1892.

City were displays depicting "savage" American Indians and black Dahomeans (of what was then French West Africa). As visitors neared the White City, the exhibits extolled the "superior" contributions of the Aryan race. While it was true, according to the orthodoxy accepted by the nation's propertied classes, that all whites were superior to all people of color, the Aryans or Teutons or Anglo-Saxons—the three words were used interchangeably—were the most superior. Middle and Eastern Europeans, including Jews, and the "darker" Mediterraneans were, in the words of the artist Frederick Remington, "rubbish" fit for extermination by the Aryans if they caused trouble. They did. From them came the ethnic base of the labor unions that were then giving problems to the upper classes. The White City itself may have felt the wrath of Remington's "rubbish." Less than a year after the Exposition closed, most of the White City was leveled by a fire allegedly set by strikers against the nearby Pullman Company.[11]

The Columbian Exposition and the White City that was its centerpiece expressed the ideological values of its promoters. To the architects who built it, however, the White City was to be a dramatic vision for the future. Its intent was expressed by Burnham when he said: "Make no little plans for they have no power to stir men's minds," and there was nothing little about the White City. Indeed, never had so many buildings on the heroic scale been put together in one place. The effect could be considered one of overwhelming beauty or overwhelming vulgarity (which was Sullivan's contention), but in either case, it deliberately bore no resemblance to any real city, past or present. It represented an ideal that was to inspire those who saw it.

It proved to be a success, too. At the opening of the White City, spokesmen from Chicago's business establishment extolled its virtues, and more than 21 million people from across the nation came to see it for themselves. Their appreciation was given voice by a businessman named Clarence G. Nicholson, who was so impressed by his experiences that he wrote a book in longhand about all he had seen. Onto the hundreds of pages of his tome, he care-

White City, Columbian Exposition, Chicago, 1893.

fully pasted pictures of the sights, intending his volume as a bequest to his heirs so that they might know of the greatness that had existed for that brief moment in time. At one point, he notes: "We pause before some of the exquisitely modelled figures near the portal and are more than delighted with the appearance . . . and cannot help but feel that the architects must have been imbued with a heaven born inspiration to have executed a building as stands before us now." A writer for *Harper's Magazine* gushed: "The fair! The fair! Never had the name such significance before. Fairest of all the World's present sights it is. A city of palaces set in spaces of emerald, reflected in shining lengths of water which stretch in undulating lines under flat arches of marble bridges and along banks planted with consummate skill."[12]

Louis Sullivan saw no heaven-born inspiration. Instead, he saw an illness. In his autobiography (1924), he traced the influence of the White City over a thirty-year period, concluding: "The virus of the World's Fair, after a period of incubation in the architectural profession and in the population at large, especially the influential, began to show unmistakable signs of the nature of the contagion. There came a violent outbreak of the Classic and the Renaissance in the East, which slowly spread westward, contaminating all it touched. . . . Thus, Architecture died in the land of the free and the home of the brave—in a land declaring its fervid democracy, its inventiveness, its resourcefulness, its unique daring, enterprise and progress. Thus did the virus of a culture, snobbish and alien to the land, perform its work of disintegration, and thus ever works the pallid architectural mind. . . ."[13]

By the time Sullivan launched his invective, 233 cities across the nation had begun or completed White City–inspired programs. Some were quite limited in scope—perhaps a Greco-Roman civic center intruding on the land in the manner that Sullivan deplored. Other plans, however, were far more extensive. Significant studies of municipal needs took on reality in the form of landscaped parks, parkways, boulevards, and the like.

In the City Beautiful Movement, as it was now formally called, L'Enfant found exoneration. Burnham and other urban designers returned to his diagonal streets and traffic circles, although Burnham was more directly influenced by the later French planner Georges Haussmann, whose sweeping alterations of the street plan of Paris began during the Second Empire of Louis Napoleon.

One city to which Burnham turned his attention was San Francisco.[14] He proposed its grid street pattern be eliminated and replaced by grand avenues proceeding on diagonals, connecting to markets, plazas, and traffic turn-arounds. The drawings he submitted were destroyed in the fire that followed the earthquake of 1906, and the old grid was reinstated, apparently because it was the quickest and easiest way to proceed. Whatever the reason, the decision was a wise one. The grid, by its very modesty as a system, serves well the contours of San Francisco's landscape—its hills and valleys—and intrudes on none of its many splendid vistas. Burnham's diagonals would have come into conflict with and tended to overwhelm all that natural beauty.

In 1909, shortly before his death, Burnham also developed a new plan for Chicago, again on the L'Enfant-Haussmann model; it was widely acclaimed, and portions of it were actually carried out. One proposal was for a half-crescent loop that would enclose the central business district, isolating it from the rest of the city. Another called for the extension of Jackson Park southward along Lake Michigan; in front of the park, a grand boulevard was to be laid out on which would be situated Chicago's cultural and civic centers, isolating them from the rest of the city.

Unlike almost every other beautification plan of the period, in Chicago Burnham took the problems of rapid transit into consideration, and even briefly turned his attention to the slum problem. For that, however, he offered no remedy, instead contenting himself by declaring: "Chicago has not yet reached the point where it will be necessary for the municipality to provide at its own expense . . . for the rehousing of persons forced out of congested quarters; but unless the matter is taken in hand at once, such course will be required in common justice to men and women so degraded by life in the slums that they have lost all power of caring for themselves."[15]

The slums weren't taken in hand, and neither did Burnham's proposals consider ill effects that might be caused when one of his diagonals cut across an existent, stable neighborhood, separating and destroying it. His view of the value of community—so different from that of Jane Addams, then hard at work preserving community life at Chicago's Hull House—would be adopted with passionate ignorance by Robert Moses in New York a generation later.

Burnham's scheme for Chicago was sponsored by the merchants' Commercial Club, which may explain the emphasis on monumentalism and the general disregard for human concerns. Indeed, considering who was paying him, that Burnham mentioned the need to solve the slum problem at all can be seen as an act of courage on his part, even if he was careful to lay the responsibility not on the businessmen but on the "municipality."

The extent of the power of Burnham's backers can be seen in *Wacker's Manual of the Plan for Chicago* (1912), which they

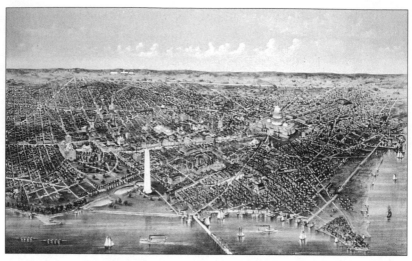

Washington, D.C., 1892. A century after L'Enfant completed his design, his brilliant and simple concept of a connector between the legislative (Capitol) and executive (White House) functions of government remains powerful.

caused to become required "study in the Schools of Chicago." Every youngster thereby was exposed to boosterism and glorification of business in the guise of learning about Burnham's wondrous plan. In a grim piece of irony, the text extolled Haussmann as the greatest city designer of all time,[16] neglecting to mention that one reason he proposed tearing down the narrow streets of Paris was in order to give Louis Napoleon's soldiers a better chance of not being ambushed as they gunned down opponents of the government.

That Chicago's plan was to be implemented without any input by its average citizens was by no means unusual. In city after city, whether the goal was building a new auditorium or completely redesigning the city's streets, the proposals came from—and the architects and planners were hired by—groups like Chicago's Commercial Club.[17] Money handed over by taxpayers directly or indirectly eventually paid for the construction, but that was usually the only role they played.

The new City Beautiful Movement also extended to Washington, with somewhat happier results than in Chicago.[18] In 1902, Burnham and others, including Olmsted's son, were commissioned by Congress to restore and perhaps improve L'Enfant's vision for the city, which had undergone its share of desecrations. Perhaps most egregious was the fate that had overtaken the mall between the Capitol and the White House. It had been cut across by railroad tracks, and Congress had given approval for the construction of a terminal on the site, to replace the sheds that already were there. (See tracks and sheds intruding on capital mall in illustrations on page 56). In the context of the time, nothing could have been less surprising. Railroads were all-powerful; they regularly bullied cities into submitting to their demands for right-of-ways (which were free of taxation at that).*

As it happened, the tracks and sheds on the mall were owned by a Burnham client, the Pennsylvania Railroad, then one of the largest corporations in the world. Burnham approached its president, Alexander Cassatt (now remembered, if at all, as the brother of the Impressionist painter Mary Cassatt) and prevailed upon him to remove his tracks from the mall and to transfer the site of the terminal to an area north of the Capitol, where it was built; in due deference to the railroad's might, the terminal covered more space than the Capitol itself.

Aside from removing the trains from the mall, the most significant contribution of Burnham and his colleagues was the establishment of an axis from the White House on which the memorials of Thomas Jefferson and Abraham Lincoln would be built. These edifices were to give a dramatic new focus to the city. However, they also caused a loss in their deviation from L'Enfant's elegant conception of a vista extending south from the White House "down the

---

*The courts were among the best allies the railroads had. In one case in the latter part of the nineteenth century, a fire negligently started by railroad company employees in a freight yard cost lives and destruction of homes nearby. A jury's verdict on behalf of the people who brought suit was reversed by the judge on the grounds that paying damages would result in an unfair financial imposition on the railroad. The verdict typified the contemporary attitude of those who held positions of power or who were beholden to them (as many judges were): The railroads had been the key to America's economic power, and the cost of injuries they caused was to be borne by the injured.[19]

Potomac with a prospect of the harbors" and the Virginia hills beyond. L'Enfant's expression of urban design as outreach in this way had connected the city to the river as an embodiment of regional force; it had made the Washington plan environmentally cohesive. The man-made structures, no matter how handsome they were, destroyed the continuum and had an enclosing rather than a liberating effect on space. (See illustration on page 56.)

The City Beautiful Movement was not entirely lacking in a social conscience. One of its most prominent leaders, J. Horace McFarland, focused his attention on the slums. He traveled the country taking photographs of deplorable living conditions that became the props for thousands of lectures. The praise he received as a crusader was widespread, the results he achieved virtually nonexistent. What he discovered was that it was relatively easy to gain support for building a beautiful parkway—there was profit in that for contractors—but tearing down tenements was a different matter. They were profitable for their owners, who were almost invariably politically well-connected.

McFarland's failure to gain support for his proposals speaks to the inherent nature of the City Beautiful Movement. Its goal was never to create a beautiful city—if it had been, slums would have had to go—but rather to create beautiful parts of a city. The appearance of the object to be installed was its value, not its role (aesthetically or sociologically) as part of the total environment.

The City Beautiful Movement did not have a long life. Even as Sullivan was engaging in his critique, it was about to be overtaken by a new force, born in Europe in the 1920s. It too was dedicated to beauty and it too to monumentalism, but of a different sort.

The progentior of the new order was Swiss-born Charles Edouard Jeanneret, who had adopted the name Le Corbusier. Along with his ideological ally and contemporary, Walter Gropius, who founded the Bauhaus, Le Corbusier developed what came to be known as the International or Modernist school of architecture, and from it emerged new ideas about planning the urban environment.

In 1922, Le Corbusier, then thirty-nine years old, unveiled his ideas through his manifesto, *The Radiant City*. In its pages, he called for a reconstruction of Paris far more radical than anything Haussmann had produced for Louis Napoleon. Although Le Corbusier's plans were never adopted in Paris, they excited interest there, throughout Europe, and in the United States as well.[20]

To show the problem he meant to cure, Le Corbusier began with drawings of the existent center of Paris, emphasizing its profusion of low-built, crowded housing, which had nearly eliminated open space and parks. His next renderings show the congestion swept away and replaced by skyscraper apartment buildings to house the population displaced by the razing of the neighborhoods. Because people would now live in the air rather than take up great amounts of land with their living quarters, the skyscrapers could be surrounded by plazas, making for a more airy and pleasant, sun-stroked environment. Access to this new vertical city would be by expressways shooting across Paris, an extravagant version of Burnham's proposal for Chicago.

In Le Corbusier's sketches, the apartment houses are built on pillars. Above them rise floor after floor of identical window grids. The style rejected the ornamentation and structural complexity of the architectural past.

Le Corbusier and Gropius weren't the only ones challenging the Beaux Arts tradition. So did the American architect Frank Lloyd Wright, but he also rejected Modernism, with its preachment of the self-contained structure that had no affinity to the habitat in which it was placed. To Wright, "the house should not be on the hill but of the hill."[21] The difference could not have been sharper: Wright's buildings were in love with the land; Modernism issued a bill of divorcement from it.

The Modernist style—with its dedication to cleanness of line and pure functionalism in everything from a spoon to a skyscraper—can be compared to the achievements of another figure of the 1920s, George Gershwin. He proved that non-classical music could be successfully and enthrallingly placed in containers not previously thought suitable for it. By contrast, the Modernists showed that the same craftsmanship used to build a White City could be employed to create daringly different containers. Gershwin was exciting, the Modernists were exciting. All were a part of the reaction against tradition that was the creative mark of the 1920s. Icons were to be struck down in architecture, music, painting, fiction, poetry, and dress. All the social taboos of the pre-war world were renounced.

That which begins as liberation from the past, however, has a way of becoming a dialectic of the present. By the 1930s, having gained widespread acceptance in the United States, the Modernists were hunting down deviationists. Anyone who didn't adhere to their orthodoxy in every particular was considered a betrayer of the movement, and an overt opponent was particularly likely to be vilified, as architect Eliel Saarinen was. The Finnish-born Saarinen's pivotal assertion—that the harmony of mass and space does not stop at the lot line—was particularly inimical to the Modernist dictate that the individual building is the only thing that counts because it alone is "pure architecture."[22] Saarinen, who had created an Olmsted-like continuum for his Cranbrook School of Design in Bloomfield Hills, Michigan, was relentlessly ridiculed as a man out of fashion. Edmund Bacon, who became a Saarinen student following his return from China in the mid-1930s, remembers that many of Saarinen's own protégés called their mentor "Pappy," in the same way that up-and-coming young Mafiosos derisively dismiss their old-timers as "Mustache Petes."

Even more powerful than Le Corbusier was Gropius, who, upon joining the faculty at Harvard, caused the university to cease teaching the history of architecture, lest the students be contaminated by earlier ideas and thereby question the one and only true architectural church, of which Gropius was the pope. No longer were architects to labor lovingly over renditions of fine buildings, illustrating them with shadings and Chinese watercolor washes to show the details of their surroundings. Instead, they were to think of rectangular holes in space. The new rule, Bacon recalls, was: "If it looks nice, it's wrong."

Realizations of the Modern style can be seen in cities across the United States. The high-rise public housing projects that became common in the 1950s have their genesis in Le Corbusier's Radiant City. The barren plazas and window-grid architecture of the World Trade Center in New York sprang from the same doctrine. A particular revelatory example came to fruition in Cleveland when, in the 1960s, the city's officials wanted to revitalize the Eighth Avenue district and turned to a Le Corbusier disciple, I. M. Pei, to solve their problem. At a cost of $29.5 million, the result was Erieview Plaza, a skyscraper complex set far off the avenue, reachable by traversing a wide and empty plaza that acts as a wind tunnel, driving gusts up to 60 miles an hour across it from off the lake. Erieview, in this fashion, not only became uninviting for anyone to approach but also separated itself from the very sector it was supposed to save, leading to its further deterioration.[23]

By rejecting the core idea of the continuum, Modernism sought to discard the sense of urban texture that can be found on old streets with their myriad of shop fronts and house facades. The Avenue of the Americas in New York City offers an example of this effect. Along it, sterile Modernist structures completely destroyed the sense of placement and movement from one interesting visual experience to the next that the street had provided. Or, as Clow has put it, Modernism introduced an "Age of Sensory Deprivation."[24] To the extent that happens, the identity of a city becomes lost and with it the sense of orientation within one's surroundings.

Regardless of any inroads the Modernist architects might have made by the sheer power of their ideas, they could not have achieved their great success had they not satisfied those who paid the bills. The Modernists advised their clients that should they insist on cornices, arches, towers, and like frills, they'd be considered philistines. Since no one, and especially a philistine, wants that label, a certain amount of coercion was involved. However, the lesson was also one the clients were willing to receive, reckoning that, by omitting the ornamentation, their buildings would become cheaper to construct. After all, under the new dispensation, all that had to be done was build a rectangular box, as many stories high as was required, and then snip it off at the top as if with a giant pair of scissors. An architect might not even be needed for the interior planning, as happened with the skyscrapers that are a major feature of Pittsburgh's Golden Triangle. For them, the floor spaces were laid out by a real estate agent; only when his chore was done was an architect hired to construct the frame around the floors.

In the vertical grids, we see the same appeal at work that the horizontal ones had in the planning of city streets. They were practical and economic, and didn't require anyone to do any creative thinking. As long as aesthetic concerns were irrelevant, the principal skill that was required was that of the engineer. That, in the end, was the singular contribution of Le Corbusier and Gropius: They removed the art from architecture and made of it a technology.

The economies in cost offered by the Modernists took on a new desirability when the stock market crashed in 1929 and brought on the Depression of the 1930s, but that was not the only reason for their growing influence during that era. Even those who maintained their fortunes (perhaps particularly they) were resented by the masses who had taken their investment advice and now were broke. Anticapitalist sentiment, as a result, was on the rise. It caused a milieu in which it didn't seem prudent to build new and ornate palaces, for either personal or commercial use. Such indulgences could be taken as deliberately provocative paeans to greed, and some concern was expressed that mobs might riot against them. (The plutocrats' fear of the communists was as strong as the communists were weak.) The spare and the functional, on the contrary, fit the tenor of the times, and that the Modernists did offer. Whether, in fact, such a popular mood about architecture existed—indeed, if there was any mood—is questionable. One grand monument to family wealth and privilege built during the Depression, Rockefeller Center, was enthusiastically accepted, probably because it welcomed people into the kind of beautiful and harmonious setting that the Modernists fulminated against.

The American Depression, during which Modernism made its first great advances, was also a time when public works altered the face of American cities, when better housing for the poor finally became an issue on the national agenda, and when, for the first time in their histories, cities no longer looked to themselves but to Washington for help with their problems.

4

Federalism and the City

During Herbert Hoover's four years as President, which ended in March 1933, unemployment rose from 1.8 million to 15.8 million, with the unemployment rate rising toward one in every four.[1] By 1933, a thousand families a day were finding themselves out on the street, having lost their residences to foreclosures.[2] City and state governments, which were teetering on the edge of bankruptcy, could do little to provide assistance. In Toledo, as just one example, the municipal allotment for the poor was 15¢ a week.[3]

When Franklin Roosevelt and his New Dealers succeeded Hoover, they found themselves facing a task that was both enormous in scope and simple in duty. They had to find ways to put people back to work, they had to stop the foreclosure drains or towns and cities would become ghost communities, and they had to find ways to build housing that the poor could afford. Since the housing problem was at its worst in the cities, that's where the greatest concentration of effort was focused, beginning with the Home Owners Loan Corporation (HOLC), which was designed to stem the foreclosure flood by permitting mortgages to be refinanced at reduced rates.[4] As useful as the HOLC thrust was, by its nature it was not geared to getting the construction industry back on its feet. If that occurred, millions of jobs could be created. An early attempt to energize new home starts was undertaken when the Federal Housing Administration (FHA) was created in 1934. Its goal was to encourage building in the private sector by insuring mortgages and by making loans available for construction (and also for repairs to existent housing) at long-term, low-interest rates. To an extent, the FHA succeeded in doing just that, but as Jewel Bellush and Murray Hausknecht pointed out in *Urban Renewal*: ". . . the FHA program did little or nothing to alleviate the housing situation of blue-collar people or the lower middle class, because FHA regulations discouraged the issuance of mortgages on low-priced homes and rental properties," where the chances of default by the builders was too great if they couldn't maintain sales or occupancy rates.[5] (Trying to sell private homes in these neighborhoods was a risky proposition, too; people who might be attracted to buy in them often lacked the means to make the down payment.) As a consequence, although the FHA was responsible for creating activity in the house construction business, and jobs thereby for the unemployed, during the Depression (and for many years afterward) the home buyers it primarily helped were of the middle class, with a sizable portion of the new building taking place in the suburbs.

Since "middle class" in the 1930s meant white, the policy was racist and quite deliberately so. The FHA *Underwriting Manual* for 1938 notes that "if a neighborhood is to retain stability, it is necessary that properties shall continue to be occupied by the same social and racial groups." The manual suggested that restrictive covenants be written to keep out "inharmonious racial groups" and helpfully provided a model covenant for those who couldn't write their own.[6]

But the New Deal was nothing if not multipronged. One of its efforts was to provide housing for the poorest of the poor, who were the FHA pariahs. The first step in that direction was the establishment in 1933 of the Public Works Administration (PWA), under the aegis of Harold Ickes, the secretary of the Interior Department. The ideological framework of the program that Ickes was to introduce had its origins in late nineteenth-century analyses of the sociological meaning of slums.* Not only were the New

---

* The sociological perspective developed around the same time as the City Beautiful Movement but separate from it. Although linkages can be found between the two efforts—as in the case of McFarland's slum clearance agenda—the City Beautiful's emphasis on aesthetics was a subject of secondary interest, if that, to the sociologists of the nineteenth century and later.

Deal policies formulated out of this thinking, but it has continued to affect decision making ever since.[7]

Of early influence were the socialist teachings of the English writers Beatrice and Sidney Webb, but the seminal event in the United States was the publication of Jacob Riis's *How the Other Half Lives* (1890), which shocked the public conscience as few other books ever have. Riis described an inner city teeming with walkup tenements, some ten stories high, each filled with dens of human misery. Outside them, juvenile gangs were found on virtually every corner. But it wasn't only juveniles who formed into gangs. In the "Little Italys" of one major city after another, hoodlums set up homegrown versions of the Sicilian Mafia, crafting a government of fear that was more powerful than the elected government.

Drug addiction in the slums, which was to become a hallmark of life in the inner cities later on, was not epidemic in Riis's time. More common was alcoholism, largely among men, and some observers decried it as the plague of the poor. While these reports were exaggerated (to serve as fodder for temperance forces), the corner saloon had become the focus of life for many inner-city men.

The saloon, as Riis saw it, was only the most visible symbol of the negative social structure of slum life. Unless, he said, strong and immediate steps were taken, the crime, the alcoholism, the prostitution that was also widespread—all would not only persist but worsen over the generations. Continued brutalization of life, he warned, would lead to a brutal people.

Riis and his followers believed that the tenements themselves represented the core problem. Replacing them with more healthful buildings, they argued, would improve morale and with it the character of the poor. As a result, the poor would become better workers, and there would be less drunkenness to disrupt the productivity of the assembly line: Increasing wages wasn't the answer to the poverty problem; bettering living conditions was. This curious assumption, that income and housing were somehow separate issues in dealing with the poor, was to show great persistence throughout the twentieth century.

The influence of the Riis-inspired slum reformers waned substantially in the 1920s, but before then, in a number of cities, they were able to pass laws that restricted the high-density population of slums, and to make rental and home purchase prices more affordable. They also encouraged plans for emigration of the poor to garden-type complexes (a notion very popular in the pre–World War I era),[8] few of which ever came to fruition; the few that did rarely proved affordable for subsistence-level families.

The diaspora of the poor from the slums, which Riis urged, ignored his own insight (shared by settlement-house workers like Jane Addams and Lillian Wald) that the slum neighborhood also contained vital unifying forces that could be harnessed for the common good. The problem was that as the relocation proceeded, necessarily on a piecemeal basis—it was impossible to knock down whole slums at one time—the people of the old slums who possessed those positive values and the capacity to instill them in others would be dispersed, too. With communal ties and friendship webs broken, people would become strangers to one another in their strange new land, and some critics wondered if what had been disrupted could be put back together.

Ickes took up the call of the Riis reformers during the lifetime of the PWA Housing Division Program. Its purpose, he declared, was to "eradicate and rehabilitate slums [in order to] demonstrate to private builders, planners, and the public at large the practicability of large-scale community planning [which would] furnish decent, sanitary dwellings to those whose incomes are so low that private capital is unable to provide adequate housing within their means." (In one way, Ickes parted company with the Riis reformers. Their concern was solely with people who lived in slums, whereas Ickes, recognizing the effects of the Depression, also saw public housing as suitable for families who had never lived in slums but who lacked, temporarily anyway, the means to buy or rent a home of their own.)[9]

In his statement, Ickes was apparently trying to placate the realtors and the home-loan businesses, which feared that public housing would take customers from them. Instead, government was going to help only those people with whom private capital couldn't deal profitably, yet simultaneously "demonstrate to private builders" how they could make a profit. Ickes next announced that he hoped the "practicability" of the new housing projects would "encourage" states to take over the "construction and operation of public housing programs."* This message was also a political sop; at the time, governors and other state officials were expressing concerns about the New Dealers trampling on their prerogatives.

Regardless of his public utterances, Ickes had no interest in turning control of the PWA over to anyone.[10] For him and his President, the agency represented a potent political tool. Foes could be punished by withholding housing funds, thereby preventing them from handing out construction contracts on which they would get kickbacks. By the same token, political friends— those who produced big vote totals for Roosevelt and the Democratic Party—could be favored. This introduction of politics to the slum-housing equation caused Robert Weaver (later the nation's chief housing official under Presidents Kennedy and Johnson) to worry that the favored politicians would engage in their own brand of favoritism: Whites would get housing, blacks would not.[11]

Despite or because of all these machinations, PWA quickly built fifty low-rent projects serving about 22,000 people in more than thirty cities. Compared to the need, however, the accom-

---

* The land itself was to be made available through condemnation under eminent-domain laws that were passed in many states for the specific purpose of slum clearance. The eminent domain proceedings provided income to owners of inner-city real estate that otherwise was virtually unsaleable in a Depression economy.

plishment was a meager one. Inner-city blight was rapidly spreading. A 1936 study by James Ford, for example, described 40 percent of Manhattan "as bearing strong slum characteristics."[12] Nationally, 5 million new or rehabilitated units was the requirement, according to one estimate. Nevertheless, from these first experiments in public housing, Ickes had cause to feel encouraged. Projects in Atlanta, Cleveland, and Chicago particularly seemed to prove that slums could be replaced by affordable good housing for their previous tenants. But elsewhere a warning bell had been sounded about a problem that would never be completely solved. An example was New York's Knickerbocker Village on the Lower East Side. When the price of obtaining the land and the construction costs were accounted for, it was necessary to charge rents of $12.50 per month per room, nearly quadruple the rate that had been in effect in the slum it replaced. The result was that the old tenants couldn't possibly afford to live in the new homes and ended up elsewhere in the remaining slums, bereft of any community connections they may have had, just as the early opponents of slum clearance had feared would happen.[13]

This signal notwithstanding, public housing for the poor seemed to be the only choice in an economy in which private initiatives on their behalf remained virtually nonexistent. Roosevelt sounded the necessity to address their problems in his dramatic second-term inaugural speech in 1937, when he spoke of "one third of a nation . . . ill-nourished, ill-clothed and ill-housed." Roosevelt's rhetoric may have been persuasive to the public, but it was the landslide size of his reelection that counted politically. His opponents, including those who viewed public housing as a socialist scheme right out of the Kremlin, were on the run, at least temporarily.

In the immediate wake of his triumph, Roosevelt was able to secure the passage of the Housing Act of 1937, which transferred the PWA functions to the newly created United States Housing Authority (USHA). As the PWA had, the 1937 act emphasized the need ". . . to remedy unsafe and unsanitary housing conditions and the acute shortage of decent, safe and sanitary dwellings for families of low income." No longer was there talk of demonstration projects or of the role of state government. The achievement of the goal, rather, was to be the exclusive responsibility of the federal government.

That was the pronouncement, but not the practice. The regulatory language actually sharply restricted the federal role. USHA was to lend money to local agencies that would be entirely in charge of how it was to be spent, after they had obtained the necessary USHA approval for site planning, building costs, and rents. Thus, if the locals decided, as they frequently did, that the housing was to be for whites only, that would be the population served. Weaver's worries about racism under the PWA had found their realization under USHA.[14]

In practice, USHA also added one more fragment to an already fragmented effort. It became one of seven federal agencies that, by the late 1930s, had a piece of the housing action. Frequently the agencies worked at cross-purposes, in part out of ineptitude, in part out of ignorance of other programs, and in part out of turf rivalries. A contemporary observer, Charles Abrams, described what too often happened: "USHA, for example," he wrote, "would approve the clearance and rebuilding of a slum area, only to find that FHA had made loans for the modernization and repair of some of the obsolete buildings [marked for removal by USHA], while HOLC propped up values by buying mortgages at par." USHA, that is, wanted prices kept low so it could assemble land cheaply, while HOLC wanted to help mortgage lenders by keeping prices high. Meanwhile, Abrams went on, "FHA policy, not integrated with USHA policy, encouraged developments in peripheral areas, thus drawing the population from the central area and accelerating blight . . ."[15] as the hitherto high-density sections were left with unoccupied and frequently vandalized shells.

But even if there had been no bureaucratic in-fighting or in-efficiency at the federal level, even if merit had been the sole criterion when the local decisions were made, the safety net created by all these agencies had made the real estate entrepreneurs and the lenders, not the public, the primary beneficiaries. When taken as an entirety, Abrams pointed out, the formula "for providing new homes [other than public housing] was fashioned so that builders needed no investment to venture and lenders assumed no risk in lending."[16] Although the policy did help create jobs, and some new and renovated dwellings, by the eve of World War II—despite all the New Deal efforts—the amount of safe and adequate housing in the United States had declined since 1929.

Recognizing the failures, a number of humanistic city planners and architects had, by the late 1930s, launched efforts to encourage owners of multifamily slum dwellings to rehabilitate them voluntarily by means of offering them loans at low rates. Neither the owners nor the financial institutions that held their mortgages, however, showed much interest in the idea. For the owners, it was more profitable to allow the property to remain as it was, milking it for whatever rentals could be obtained until such time as the economy turned around and buyers reentered the market. Presumably the new owners would take care of whatever fixing needed to be done. In practice, that rarely happened, since they bought multifamily slum properties for the same reason as had the previous owners.[17] As well intentioned as the owner-entrusted rehabilitation idea was, it failed, for the same reason that New Deal housing programs for the poor had: The underlying emphasis was on improving the cash value of the land and not the value of the lives of the people who lived on it.

Meanwhile, as the 1930s neared their end, public housing was becoming increasingly controversial. The obvious failures of USHA—a great deal of money going out, but very few projects going up—had something to do with that, but the most significant attack came from the National Association of Real Estate Boards[18] and its allies in the building-and-loan associations, neither of whom showed any gratitude to the New Deal for all the help it had given them. The reasoning that led to their enmity expressed itself in a number of cities, but in none perhaps more illuminatingly than in Flint, Michigan.

Flint in those days had a population of about 200,000. It was a company town, with General Motors as the company. Four of its divisions (Chevrolet, Buick, Fisher Auto Body, and AC Sparkplugs) were located in Flint, and virtually everyone who lived there, directly or indirectly, was economically dependent on GM. By 1937, the company was becoming increasingly worried about its corporate image. The widespread poverty in the city wasn't part of that concern, and neither was the sit-down strike then in progress that had captured national headlines and led to demands by GM that the governor evict the strikers. GM's corporate image problem, rather, as perceived by its chief executive, Harlow Curtice, was that, in a city dedicated to the automobile, railroad tracks ran across the main street and unsightly traffic jams were commonplace as motorists fought their way to the plants that were situated one at each of Flint's four corners.

Eliel Saarinen, whose Cranbrook School of Design was nearby, was asked for his assistance in solving the traffic problem. Saarinen wasn't interested in becoming involved but did recommend one of his students, twenty-seven-year-old Edmund Bacon. GM proved agreeable to that proposal, as did Bacon, who was placed on the staff of the newly formed Institute of Research and Planning, which was dominated by the city's business establishment.

Flint, Bacon quickly discovered, had a sizable upper-middle-class residential center but except for it, the city's appearance was that of a speculator's haven, much like Chicago in the 1830s. Subdivisions were staked out, and lots were being sold, often without having paved roads, water, or sewage systems in place. The Depression had added its own despairing twist to the scene. Thousands lived in tar-paper shacks and lean-tos, their water wells adjacent to and contaminated by outdoor privies.

The political situation was tense. Each day the strikers' wives, wearing red bandannas (they were called "the red brigade"), trudged to the GM plants to pass food through the windows to their husbands, while national guardsmen stood by waiting for the order to shoot the men down. Bacon recalls, "I'd sometimes stand on the hill looking down at the Chevrolet plant where the murders were to occur. Only at that distance was the view safe. I remember when I tried to walk down the street toward the plant, a militia man put the point of his bayonet to my stomach, and told me I was not allowed there." He was allowed, however, to attend the annual Beaux Arts Ball, at which the rich people of Flint cavorted: "The theme that year was Dickens, and the women in their crinolines and the men in their waistcoats sat down on the floor in derision of the strikers and booed Governor Murphy as he stood at the podium because he had refused to give the order to kill." (Murphy courageously continued to stand up to GM; the lethal order was never given, and the strike ended with the workers victorious.)

Bacon began his work for the institute by conducting a traffic survey. Helped by federally paid workers, he clocked the comings and goings of every car that passed through the city. Based on that information, he designed new street routes and published a report that was met with such acclaim that the Flint Junior Chamber of Commerce named him its man of the year for 1937. His star was about to descend as rapidly as it had arisen.

His interest in helping the poor did him in. While the strike was still going on, he had begun to turn his attention to the subdivisions. To his shock, he learned that the families who appeared to own these homes did not, with rare exceptions. Rather than hold mortgages, they were required to "buy" their homes on contract. That meant they didn't gain a penny in equity until the entire contract was paid off, in ten or fifteen years, and if they missed a single month's payment they lost the house.* Inability to pay was common, not only because of Depression-caused unemployment but also seasonally, during the two to four months each year that GM laid off all its workers while it designed the following year's models. The next family in line would get the house or, once GM retooled, the original owners might, but because of the lapse in payments they would have to start a new contract. Sold over and over again, the contract houses, in effect, were cash cows for the builders, much more profitable than they would have been if they had rented them to tenants, since then they would have been responsible for upkeep.

Because the developers were part of the city's business establishment and enjoyed close relationships with the GM executives, they and their shoddy subdivisions were largely immune from criticism. One bank president, however, had never approved of what he saw as exploitation by the developers. In him, Bacon found an ally; this led to the creation of a Citizens Housing Council, which included on its rolls a number of automobile workers. The meetings that followed marked the first time in Flint's history that laboring men and members of the gentry had sat down together in a room to discuss any problem.

The immediate goal of the council was to find ways to house those who had been evicted from the subdivisions and others who lived in the tar-paper shacks. With that purpose in mind, Bacon went to Washington, where he obtained a $3.5 million USHA public housing grant that was to be spent to bridge the gap between the amount tenants could afford to pay in rents and the cost of financing the construction.

When Bacon returned with the money, he naively expected he would be treated as a hero, just as he had been following the

* This practice was not limited to Flint. Nearly thirty years later in Chicago, it became a civil rights issue. There, almost all the "contract" buyers were blacks who wanted to buy homes to escape the slums. After nearly five years of protests, in 1970 the local real estate industry backed down and contract sales ceased.[19]

completion of his traffic survey. Not so. The real estate developers and their allies reacted in horror. As they saw it, every family that was able to get into public housing was one less family they could exploit as customers, either in tenements, shacks, or subdivision contract housing.*

They acted swiftly. Bacon's friend, the banker, was told if he wanted to keep any of his business depositors he'd better dissolve the housing council. He did. Three other members of the council — a doctor, a lawyer, a schoolteacher — were threatened they would be smeared as "reds" unless they backed down.

Neither Bacon nor his remaining allies, however, were ready to give up. Defying his employers at the institute, Bacon helped organize a referendum to place on the ballot the question of whether the USHA grant should be accepted. As Bacon recalled those days: "We still had sympathizers among the rich people who supported us financially, but to get their contributions, I'd have to go to their back doors and the money would be handed out to me that way; they didn't want to be seen with me." Bacon's group got the necessary signatures for the referendum; he assumed that, since 95 percent of Flint's population was working class, victory was assured and the public housing would be built.

But the realtors and their allies at GM had only begun to fight. They controlled the Flint *Journal*, which denounced public housing and urged a "No" vote. Over the radio, a campaign was waged in which listeners were falsely told that, if they voted for public housing, their children's schooling would be cut back by eight weeks each year. On the floor of the city council, Bacon was denounced as a communist. The referendum lost.

Bacon was fired, but not publicly. His bosses at the institute found it embarrassing to admit they were getting rid of the very

---

* The year played a role, too. By 1938, the economy was on an upswing, and realtors could now envision renting and selling sizable amounts of property, as they couldn't have even a year earlier.

man they'd just spent the previous year praising. Therefore, they put out the story that their "highly respected planner" had resigned to take a position elsewhere. Bacon, whose Quaker heritage had taught him never to become involved in public controversies, agonized over whether he should expose the lie. His answer to himself was a letter he wrote to the *Journal* revealing that he had been dismissed and why. The newspaper asked him to retract the letter. When he said he wouldn't, they refused to publish it. Bacon's defeat was complete, and so was that of the poor of Flint, who remained, and would continue to remain, as before, under the thumb of GM and its minions.

It was not only in Flint that public housing was in trouble. By the late 1930s, opposition, fanned by the National Association of Real Estate Boards and its powerful and well-financed allies, was growing across the country. Racist fears of blacks moving in with whites were exploited. In some places, the red-scare tactic was quite effective. Most Americans considered communism evil; therefore, so were all its ideas, including social planning, of which public housing was portrayed as an example. However, since most Americans also supported Roosevelt and his New Deal planning programs, the allegations of communism could be of only limited effectiveness, and the same was true of the racist ones (at least as long as public housing remained segregated, which was the policy at the federal and local levels). In Flint, not only were the vast majority of the voters working class, but they tended to be liberal to left-wing in their political sympathies; neither were they likely, it would seem, in the wake of the strike to be in a mood to accept the advice of the GM-dominated establishment when it told them to oppose the referendum. Nor could bigotry have been a factor; the city was nearly all white, which meant so would be the public housing recipients. With this as the voter profile, if there had been any city in the country that should have embraced public housing, that city was Flint.

That it didn't makes clear the underlying reason for the antipathy, which had to do with the way most Americans felt about themselves and their country. Even during the Depression, even among those who were having a hard time themselves, the belief in rugged individualism remained strong. If you had bad luck, you turned it around with hard work; you had some get-up-and-go; you pulled yourself up by your bootstraps. In America, the strong succeed, the weak fail, and who wanted to be thought weak?

Out of these assumed verities of the American experience, a scenario about poverty that fit the Depression milieu took form. The New Deal's opponents helped it on its way, but it was also perhaps a natural and necessary evolution. Featured was a majoritarian concept of the deserving and undeserving poor. There was no need to define the undeserving. Everyone in the majority knew who they were: shiftless blacks, "backward" white hillbillies, riffraff like the migrant workers portrayed in Steinbeck's *Grapes of Wrath*, and those who, in the words of one commentator, "are living in shacks and hovels because God made them unable to earn more."[20] The deserving poor, by contrast, were all those white, hard-working Americans who had gotten along fine under capitalism until the Depression came along. Unlike the undeserving, their poverty wasn't their fault, and they therefore properly had available to them government programs like the HOLC and the FHA to help them recover and resume their rightful place in society. They were, that is, not only the poor who deserved help but also the temporary poor, and they were not likely (nor were they encouraged) to have fellow feeling or even much interest in the undeserving poor. Spending taxpayer money on social programs for the undeserving—like public housing—became, out of that psychology, an easy posture for the deserving to oppose. The distinction between the deserving and the undeserving was one against which the New Dealers offered no serious contention. At times, instead, the New Deal went along with the underlying philosophy, as in the FHA's instructions on how to draw up racial covenants. Nevertheless, taken as a whole, the New Deal marked a resurgence of the nineteenth-century belief of Downing and his supporters that government must try to be the benefactor of its citizens and not merely serve as an instrument to be exploited by the most adept strivers in reaching their personal goals.

As George Reedy pointed out in his study of the Irish in America, the public protector role taken on by the federal government during the Depression substantially weakened the ties that people had felt toward their local governments, and this was particularly true in the cities where the major New Deal effort was concentrated.[21] The ultimate personal impact of the New Deal in that regard, however, was to expand citizen assumptions about the role all forms of government should play. As a result, city politicians found themselves expected, and often by legislative mandate required, to carry out social service programs they had never offered nor been expected to offer in pre–New Deal days.

The various New Deal housing programs had an effect on this revolution in expectation, but they were of such a scattershot nature—and met with such opposition—that they did not significantly change the physical appearance of cities, and directly affected the lives of only a small number of their people. Of much greater impact in that regard was the Work Projects Administration (WPA), which wasn't a housing program.

The WPA burst across the American scene in 1935 with an energy in keeping with that of its administrator, Harry Hopkins. His mandate was to put people to work, and to do so he cast his net much wider than did programs like the PWA, in which employment was an important but secondary goal. Within just a year, the WPA had a staggering 70,000 physical improvement efforts under way, every one of them putting people back to work.[22] Some, like building dams, took place in rural areas, but cities and towns were the principal targets. In them, parks were built and firehouses and schoolhouses and playgrounds, jails, police stations, hospitals, sewage plants, water plants, subways, streets, bridges. In San Antonio, as just one example, it was WPA workers who drained the river and built the walkway that has remained one of the most beautiful places in any city of the nation.

Bacon remembers how "WPA officials would approach city after city asking—practically begging—the politicians to come up with public improvement programs that could be put into action virtually immediately, so that people could be put to work." Bacon's traffic study in Flint met Hopkins's very broad definition of public improvement, and for it he was given ninety WPA employees. The popular stereotype of the period of eleven WPA workers standing around watching a twelfth lean on a shovel was not entirely without its basis in fact. Even so, the sheer volume of jobs handed out could have human benefits, as explained by Melvin Daus, a New York Parks Department official: "In the Thirties, the [playground WPA workers were] young guys . . . all college-educated. There were no other jobs available then. We were trained in working with young people, supervising them, giving them help. And . . . there were so many supervisors—there were two or three at even the smallest playgrounds—that we could really get involved with kids . . . be around so that if one of them needed someone to talk to, he had someone."[23]

However, not every project got funded, at least not immediately. Construction plans had to be approved by Army engineers, who established uniform specifications. (This is why so many of today's city playgrounds, for instance, look so much alike.) Only the cheapest materials could be bought, no ornamentations. Because it was well adapted to frugality, the Modernist style was favored.[24]

At the beginning, the WPA did not so much go to cities as they came to it. From all over the nation, mayors would regularly trudge to Washington to meet with Hopkins. One city that was always prepared was New York.[25] Its grand vizier of planning, Robert Moses, was a Republican and a bitter foe of Roosevelt, but because he did his homework, there was never any basis for turning down his ideas, whether they were for the Triborough Bridge, a park, or the $2 million Orchard Beach bath house, which, thanks to

Moses's persuasiveness, was very un-WPA-like in its appearance, featuring classic colonnades and terra cotta tiles. By 1936, one of every seven dollars in WPA funds was going to New York.[26]

Although in New York, everything was cleared with Moses— he often held Republican mayor Fiorello H. La Guardia in thralldom—elsewhere in the country political bosses were likely to dominate the decision making. Thus, if the sewer commissioner had more clout than the streets commissioner, then it would be sewer projects that got the most money. Public need was less important than empire building.

Even so, sewage disposal systems were improved; children did get physically improved schools in which to learn and more places to play; the cities' people got parks, improved public transportation systems, and public buildings (like the fire stations) they badly needed. In these ways, the appearance of American cities changed more rapidly under its new federal patron than at any time in their history. Extraordinarily valuable goals were met: People got jobs, public services were vastly bettered, and the nation's infrastructure was repaired.

The structural effect the WPA programs had on the cities was uneven. It could hardly have been otherwise, dependent as the agency was on the thinking of politicians about their practical (and self-aggrandizing) wants. When the local idea was a good one, a continuum could be created, as with the San Antonio Riverwalk, that changed a city's way of thinking about itself. But most often the result, even when admirable goals were being fulfilled, was the addition of visually uninteresting and unrelated structures to the city's landscape. At times, projects were built simply because the money was available, and they were stuffed into whatever space was available for them with minimal benefits for the citizens. It was not, however, only Hopkins and the New Deal that were changing cities in the 1930s. So was the automobile.

Speaking at the Town Planning Council of the Royal Institute of Architects in London in 1910, Daniel Burnham had turned his attention to the automobile. "The use of horses in a great city," he declared, "is near its end, because motor vehicles are becoming very cheap and will soon be [even] more economical . . . and with the passing of the custom of using horses will end a plague of barbarism which we still live in. . . . [T]he government can dispense with the army of cleaners. . . . The air and streets of our cities of the future [because of the automobile] will be as clean as our drawing-rooms; and the people living in sweeter conditions should be better citizens, should they not?"[27]

As unduly roseate as was Burnham's prognosis, he was quite correct in understanding—and he was not alone in his awareness—that the automobile would have a revolutionary impact on American society. Like the railroad, it offered a rapid means of transportation. But unlike the railroad, where one was herded in with strangers, the automobile offered a sense of individual control of one's destiny.

No longer need the traveler, who had to get somewhere at a speed faster than a horse could provide, be dependent on the train's schedule, no longer dependent on the skill of the engineer, no longer limited to the path of the railroad tracks. In the automobile, one could go hurtling through space, putting space behind one, meeting new space, at a pace that the horse and carriage never permitted. And besides, the car, unlike the horse, never got tired; as long as it had gas, it could go on forever (in theory). The drivers and passengers were masters in these private boxes,* determining where they went and whom they saw. The car didn't produce freedom, but it represented it.

---

* Privatism seems as deeply imbedded in American character as is its close kin, individualism. Nineteenth-century entrepreneurial privatism, which Sam Bass Warner and other scholars have studied, had at its core a peculiar combination of frontier mythos (in the form of rugged individualists like Jim Bridger) and Social Darwinism. Yet the contrary communitarian principle has never been silenced. It can be found in the "commons" of New England villages, in the wagon trains that settled the west (which Bridger roamed), in Jane Addams's Hull House, and in the civic associations that are to be found in every city today.

During the three decades that passed between Burnham's speech in London and the beginning of World War II, the automobile's impact upon the landscape became substantial. For it, new wider roads had to be built and paved. By the late 1930s, superhighways, like the Pennsylvania Turnpike and several Long Island parkways, were already in existence or nearing completion.

For the cities, as Bacon learned in Flint, the coming of the automobile meant that traffic-flow systems had to be changed because the newly congested streets and their criss-cross patterns had never been designed to accommodate that form or quantity of locomotion. But that was not all. Automobiles changed the physical appearance of cities, as parking lots for them began to take up large amounts of urban space, and the same was true for the filling stations and repair shops that provided a new means of making a living for many more Americans than the horse-and-wagon business ever had. The architecture of houses began to change, too: By the 1920s, a common selling point to buyers of newly built homes was that they had their own garage.

By the 1920s, too, it was apparent that the automobile was going to facilitate the movement of people from the cities to the suburbs in numbers that had never been feasible before. The impact of the automobile-engendered suburbanization on cities was not, however, to be seriously felt until after World War II, and then in multiple ways.

In sum, the cities of America on the eve of World War II displayed a fragmentization on several levels. The City Beautiful Movement, which called for a pleasing urban ambience, had been dismissed as a romantic absurdity, and replaced by Modernism's insistence on pure functionalism, in which no functional piece was related to the next. The traditional relationship of people of the cities to their local government had been replaced by the federalism of the New Deal, yet the New Deal itself had a fragmenting effect, as it thrashed about offering one conflicting urban housing program after another. Under the indefatigable Hopkins, the WPA alone gave a clear and consistent signal of government acting on behalf of people, but even its efforts, by the nature of the structure of the program, were fragmented as it cooperated with local politicians eager to enrich their own little kingdoms. And all this while the automobile was changing the appearance of cities and their suburbs far more dramatically than anything the WPA did, in ways more suggestive of chaos than of any well-conceived purpose.

Nevertheless, a very strong and coherent idea about the purpose of cities—their present moment in time and their future—was about to emerge in Philadelphia, where Edmund Bacon had returned after his disastrous but valuable learning experience in Flint.

5

A New Vision for the Old City

By the eve of World War II, most large cities had planning commissions as part of the executive branch of their governments.*
The duties of these commissions varied from place to place, but
generally included: assisting in the preparation of the capital improvement budget; proposal of locations for public works programs; undertaking population density and traffic flow studies; and
recommending which sectors of the city should be zoned residential, which commercial, and which were to have mixed use.

In practice, however, the early planning commissions had very
little or no real power. They acted largely as rubber stamps for the
proposals of the dominant business and political interests in their
cities. The only significant exception was New York's planning
commission. Enacted as part of a new home rule charter passed in
1938, it was administered by seven paid commissioners whose
terms were arranged so that the mayor, in any single four-year
term, would not be able to control the majority of the appointments. The commission was to direct New York's growth by developing a master plan for land use and a six-year capital budget for
municipal improvements, which became law unless overridden by
a two-thirds vote of the city council.

Rexford Tugwell, a former professor of economics, who had
been an early brain-truster of the New Deal, was the first to head

* An offshoot of the City Beautiful Movement, city planning, as a profession, was then still quite new. The American City Planning Institute did not
come into existence until 1917, and the first courses in city planning were inaugurated that year at Harvard University.[1]

the commission. Tugwell proposed an imaginative program that contained restrictions on the amount of new building and featured a greenbelt system to create open spaces in the city's neighborhoods. Tugwell quickly met with opposition, led by Mayor Fiorello La Guardia and Parks Commissioner Robert Moses. La Guardia feared that the planning commission's independence, which seemed such a fine idea to the reformers who had initiated it, could create a political power base to rival his own. Moses saw a different threat. "It [the comprehensive plan]," he told a newspaper, "reflects the program of a socialistic, planned economy whose aim is to reconstruct the entire city and with it our economic and political systems. [The people] would rather have Tammany back, with all its evils, than be in the hands of the Planning Reds."

After months of rancorous hearings in 1941 on the comprehensive plan, Tugwell resigned in despair and La Guardia named Moses to the commission. Thereafter, the body became and largely remained his.

Around the time Moses joined the New York planning commission, he wrote an article in which he asserted that it wasn't enough for a planner to know what the public ought to want; such a person, he stated, must also "concern himself with educating public opinion and building up the support which would allow him to finish his work." Moses's recognition that the planner must also be a teacher (an insight he never seriously attempted to put into practice) was not accompanied by any thought that the public should be permitted to contribute to the decisions.[2]

Just such an idea was emerging in Philadelphia around the time Moses wrote his article.[3] It did not come, however, from the city's planning commission, which was weak even by the standards of the time. The commission employed one man who spent years doing all manner of worthy technical research to which no attention was paid, not by the business establishment, not by the public, which barely knew there was a commission, and not even by the commission's own board, which met just once a year, and then only long enough to pass a resolution to pay the employee's salary. Such boards and commissions were not uncommon in Philadelphia (or elsewhere for that matter). Their only discernible purpose was to provide gentlemen of good families a credential of public-spiritedness, without requiring them to come up with a single idea, much less a program for action, to improve the public or its spirit.

Contributing to the municipal malaise in Philadelphia was a history of political venery extending back to the second half of the nineteenth century. The corruption within the dominant Republican Party enjoyed the support of the Pennsylvania Railroad, which was the most powerful business entity in the city. An unwritten agreement existed between the "Pennsy" (as the natives called it) and the political bosses. Under its terms, the politicians were to vote for legislation the Pennsy considered important and were never to mention the railroad's disinvestment from Philadelphia at the expense of its growing investment in New York. In return, the bosses continued to receive their contributions from the Pennsy and its allies, and were allowed to have their own way in the buying and selling of municipal contracts, all the while filling City Hall with patronage hacks whose principal qualification was their willingness to work the polls on election day and commit whatever frauds might be deemed necessary.

Although the business establishment as a whole displayed no interest in containing political corruption, elements within it did want to influence policy beyond (but not in contention with) the interests of the Pennsy. The principal means for carrying out that purpose was the Public Affairs Committee, which had begun as a reform body within the Republican Party in the early 1900s. Because of its members' financial standing, the committee was able to exert influence not just on Philadelphia issues but on state matters as well. Officials at both levels were summoned to the committee's off-the-record meetings at the Princeton Club in downtown Philadelphia, where, as a 1940 summary of proceedings put it, the committee offered "suggestions [that] are sometimes taken, and in this way the Committee can prevent mistakes being made which once they are made can only be corrected with a great deal of trouble."

It is probably fair to say that more than 99 percent of Philadelphia's voters, whose lives were affected by these private decisions privately arrived at, had never heard of the Public Affairs Committee.

The movement toward citizen participation in planning the future of the city had its genesis in a failure. In 1939 Walter Phillips, a twenty-seven-year-old attorney from an upper-class family, had joined a movement for a new city charter under the impression that the citizenry was yearning for good government. When the matter was put to a vote, it was resoundingly defeated by the Republican organization, with most of the support coming from tiny enclaves of privilege in Germantown and Chestnut Hill. However, no sooner was the election over than the resilient Phillips was contemplating how its result could be overturned. The vehicle he hit upon was the synergistic one of bringing together civic-minded young people from various walks of life. By forming an organization to analyze the city's problems, the members, he hoped, would be in a position to act with unity when— some ten to twenty years hence—the time arrived for them to replace the present establishment. If, while they were waiting, they came up with a project and had some success with it, that would be good, too, since that way their weight would be felt and their potential for leadership recognized. But creation of the network was the principal purpose.

To get started, Phillips drew on his own circle of friends, including those who had been active within the defunct charter movement, and expanded from there. Within a month or so, he had sixty-six favorable responses. The first meeting of the City Policy Committee, as Phillips's organization decided to call itself, was held in late January 1940, also at the Princeton Club. Those who attended met Phillips's goal of diversity. Represented were the fields of banking and law (the stalwarts of the Public Affairs Committee) and, in addition, broadcasting, labor, architecture, city planning, and politics, among others. The City Policy Committee also included women—not many of them, just six, but that was six more than the Public Affairs Committee had.

The city planner that Phillips brought on board was Edmund Bacon, who had returned to his hometown in 1939. He had not done so eagerly. Despite the fiasco in Flint, Bacon had found Michigan to be a vibrant place to live and work, a hotbed of social activism, and a center for intellectual giants like Saarinen who, for Bacon, had exciting ideas about how to create richer lives for the people of the cities. Philadelphia, in dreary contrast, seemed to him beyond redemption.

The ascetic-looking, Harvard-educated Phillips, with his high-pitched voice and visionary's zeal, however, could be persuasive to a fellow visionary like Bacon. He also gave the unemployed Bacon an eminently practical reason to return. He secured for him the job of managing director of the Philadelphia Housing Association, and it was while there that Bacon would learn a second and pivotal lesson in politics that helped determine his own goals for the city and how to go about obtaining them.

The Philadelphia Housing Association, and its counterparts in other major American cities, had its origins in the theories of late nineteenth-century reformers like Riis and the English Octavia Hill Association, which also had branches in the United States. While the Octavia Hill groups were principally interested in building new homes for slum dwellers, the Philadelphia Housing Association focused on rehabilitating existent buildings and dealing with health hazards. (Philadelphia, by the late 1930s, still had many privies and in the South Philadelphia area, some people kept pigs that fed on municipal garbage dumped in their backyards.)

In carrying out its function, the housing association dispatched inspectors in response to citizen complaints about conditions in their neighborhoods. Because it was a private agency, the association had no enforcement powers, and was limited to documenting and reporting the situations to city officials for them to act upon—or not act upon, which was frequently the case, allegedly because they lacked the funds to do so. The problem, officials explained, lay in the city's inadequate abatement fund. Under its provisions, the city was empowered to make needed repairs on a property when the owner didn't, with a lien then placed on the property. To Bacon the answer was obvious: Increase the size of the abatement fund. With that worthy thought in mind, he appeared before the city council urging a doubling of the abatement appropriation to about $500,000. To his delight, the council accepted his proposal. Reality did not smack Bacon in the face until he called on the city's housing commissioner with the good news that he could now rehabilitate twice as many deteriorated and abandoned buildings as before. The commissioner, it turned out, had no intention of spending the extra money. He had a web of political supporters among the city's slumlords and was not about to offend any of them by putting liens on their properties, just because he could now afford to do so.

Since the commissioner was part of the Republican Party hierarchy, it was clear to Bacon, on reflection, that the Republican council never would have passed his ordinance without consulting with the commissioner. That meant members of the council knew all along that the additional money it appropriated was not going to be spent or at least not in ways that would embarrass their friends in the real estate business. The new law, he realized, had been passed only to placate the housing association, which was something of a favorite charity of socially prominent Philadelphians of a civic-virtue turn of mind. In Flint, Bacon had had similarly well-placed backers for public housing, who, like their counterparts on the Philadelphia Housing Association board, had proven ineffective. So had he, twice now. In Flint, it had been the

powerful real estate interests backed by GM who had been the authors of his defeat; in Philadelphia, it had been the powerful politicians, knowing their backer, the Pennsylvania Railroad, would not
be concerned about slum conditions, who had outwitted him and
his well-intentioned board of directors. Never depend, Bacon concluded, on the kindness of strangers.

On further thought, he realized that was also the position in
which the average people of Philadelphia constantly found themselves—dependent upon the whim of the powerful and the corrupt. One step, among many, that was required, he decided, was
to create an agency for them that would be free of political en-
tanglements and undue influence and that would dedicate itself to
bringing about a city that was a better place for people to live.

At the second meeting of the City Policy Committee, Bacon
made a speech outlining his idea for a planning commission
which, like New York's, would be an integral part of the municipal
government and have the authority to initiate and carry out programs for the city's total physical development. No task could be
more important for the City Policy Committee to adopt, he urged,
than to work for the establishment of such an agency. Phillips and
the others responded enthusiastically, and Bacon's proposal was
adopted. Phillips, whose vigor on the city level rivaled that of
Harry Hopkins nationally, quickly got to work. Along with other
committee members, he brought on board as allies the Junior
Chamber of Commerce, the Lawyers' Council on Civic Affairs,
and the Mortgage Bankers Association, whose officers could see
value in a regularized means of developing capital improvement
projects without constant political interference. The new, enlarged group, which called itself the Action Committee on City
Planning, therefore, was one that had some clout. Impressed by
the alliance's components, Mayor Robert E. Lamberton, a personally honest old-family Republican gentleman, asked the group to
submit an enabling ordinance for a new City Planning Commission. The prospects looked bright.

The content of the ordinance became the next issue. Even before Lamberton was approached, the members of the Action Committee had agreed that the old commission was to be swept away in its entirety, not only because it never did anything but because a handful of rich amateurs should not be in a position to unilaterally determine a city's planning, even if they had the resolution to try to do so. The new body, rather, must be professionalized and headed by an activist, informed board that was responsible to the electorate. Left unanswered at that point was the crucial question of how to give the commission the power it needed structurally to carry out its ideas.

Advice came from the graybeards of the Public Affairs Committee. They had taken a fatherly interest in the upstart youngsters of the City Policy Committee who were, for the most part, from the right kind of family. Bacon might be something of a wild-eyed radical, but he was, after all, a Bacon, whose ancestors had come over with William Penn, so he couldn't be too unsound. The same was even more true of Phillips who, unlike Bacon, was listed in the Social Register. In those circumstances, it made sense to tutor these youths, so they'd know the proper and gentlemanly way of doing things when their time came. The advice the graybeards offered was: Your planning commission must have direct political power, because if it doesn't, no matter what else you do, it is doomed to fail. Therefore, adopt the New York system, in which your opponents require a two-thirds vote of the city council to overturn any recommendation you make. That's muscle.

The youngsters, as youngsters should be, were impressed by the wisdom of their elders and about to agree. Bacon meanwhile had invited a man named Robert Walker, who had written a book on planning, to address the City Policy Committee. Walker's view was the opposite of the graybeards'. The main effect of political power, he declared, is to politicize the group that holds it. In a system like New York's, he pointed out, because of the constant fear of the veto, the commission makes its planning decisions based on what it believes the city council will accept and not what it should accept. To get the necessary votes, its proposals are likely to be weakened by compromise. Even should it avoid a veto, Walker warned, such a commission's power exists only on paper.* If the mayor or his minions want to circumvent the capital budget the council has passed, that will be done, just as had happened when Bacon's abatement authorization was never spent.

A viable planning commission, Walker said, is one that devotes itself to developing ideas. Ideas are the true power, he hypothesized. Go to the community with them. Listen to the community. Be willing to incorporate its ideas into your ideas. That's how you arouse enthusiasm and the broad-based public support that translates into a power that politicians have to listen to.

For Bacon, Walker's speech coalesced the intuitions and understandings he had been garnering from his experiences in Flint and with the Philadelphia Housing Association. Phillips was excited, too. To him, Walker's insights moved away from the elitist approach to problems that Phillips had learned to mistrust—he didn't consider his City Policy Committee elitist—and, as with Bacon, he found them congenial to the ideals of liberal democracy he had imbibed, along with so many others, from the programs of the Roosevelt administration.

Walker's advice carried the day. The proposed ordinance was written without reference to the New York system. The commission it created was to have as a purpose to create community understanding and acceptance of the need for long-range planning. At its head was to be a nine-member board of experts, supported by a technical staff whose jobs were protected by civil service, an unusual requirement in patronage-laden Philadelphia. The principal planning instrument was to be a six-year capital budget (as in New York) to be passed each year. The first budget would cover the years 1942 through 1947, the second 1943 through 1948, and so on. (Six years was the time chosen in both

* Unless, of course, it has a Robert Moses, who hadn't yet succeeded Tugwell in New York. But even assuming someone like Moses would be a positive force for Philadelphia, there was no way to predict or encourage his emergence.

cities because four seemed too short and five too reminiscent of Stalin's plans in the Soviet Union.) The ordinance called for a first-year budget of $60,000. It was submitted to Mayor Lamberton. He died before any action could be taken.

Under the protocol of the Philadelphia charter, Lamberton was succeeded by the president of city council, a ward-heeler named Bernard "Barney" Samuel. He lived on Shunk Street, and when Phillips and Bacon approached him to support the new planning commission, he erupted: "You tell me what I can do at Third and Shunk? No way!" The commission appeared to have died with Lamberton.

Its proponents, however, were not ready to give up. If Samuel wouldn't sponsor the bill, then it would have to be done by a city council member. Because Bacon and Phillips were Democrats, the chances were virtually nil they would get anyone on the Republican city council to introduce their bill. On their behalf an influential Republican friend of Bacon's approached council president Fred Garman, who agreed to submit the ordinance but only "by request," a signal to the other council members that he didn't care what they did about it. Unless he pushed it, the ordinance would die in committee. Nevertheless, that was better than not having it in committee at all.

To apply pressure, Bacon and Phillips turned to the Chamber of Commerce, hoping it would follow the lead of the Junior Chamber of announcing its support. The senior (and much more important) Chamber, however, came out strongly in opposition to the planning commission.

With the usual avenues of influence in the city now closed, Bacon recalled Walker's advice: Go to the people. Bacon put his Philadelphia Housing Association staff to work. Citizens' organizations across the city were contacted, ranging from the T-Square Club to the Busy Bees of Mayfair. Bacon, Phillips, and others met with them. Few of those to whom they spoke had any idea what a planning commission was or might accomplish, but when the proposal was explained, their response was almost always positive.

Walker was right, Bacon recalls thinking; there is a collective consciousness that slumbers most of the time but can be aroused when confronted by an idea of merit.

Within a matter of months, eighty groups had approved the planning commission, and, at the urging of the proselytizers, had dispatched letters to the city council. They arrived by the hundreds. Bacon: "Our goal was to have a pile of letters an inch high on every councilman's desk," and they just about succeeded. The impact was sufficient, that, early in 1942, Garman ordered public hearings on the ordinance. The Busy Bees were there to testify, so were representatives of unions, people black and white, poor and rich, from all sections of the city.

The opposition was led by George Elliott, the executive director of the Chamber of Commerce, who played the old Bolshevik riff. He declared the proposed commission was the dirty work of a bunch of dangerous red radicals, who were "threatening life as we know it." While reaching his peroration, Elliott observed Edward Hopkinson, Jr., arriving. So did others. A hush descended on the ornate chamber. Hopkinson was as close to a deity as Philadelphia had. From a first family—one of his ancestors had signed the Declaration of Independence—he was the chief executive officer of the mighty Drexel Company, which advised the almighty Pennsylvania Railroad.

A few weeks earlier, Bacon, who didn't know Hopkinson but had read he was the most powerful man in the city, had paid a visit to him to discuss his ideas on how Philadelphia might spend its surplus. (In those days, as incredible as it might now seem, many cities had more money than they knew how to spend.) Bacon, who knew Hopkinson was scheduled to make a speech to the Republican Women's Club, suggested he tell his audience that a sound way to allocate the surplus was through a vitalized city planning commission, which Bacon went on to describe. Phillips made a separate visit to Hopkinson for the same purpose. Neither could be certain of Hopkinson's response.

They learned it when Elliott of the Chamber of Commerce,

assuming Hopkinson backed his anti-planning views, asked Hopkinson to replace him on the rostrum. Hopkinson, a man of few words, told the council he thought the planning commission was "a good idea."

It passed. Unanimously. Apparently what Hopkinson wanted, Hopkinson got. The truth, however, was not that simple. Although Hopkinson's approval of the commission was important, it was so only in the sense that it made it easy for the council members to do what they were already inclined to do, though not out of idealism but the realities of politics.

As Councilman Clarence Crosson, who, rather than Council President Garman, held most of the votes in his pocket, told Bacon and Phillips: "I was completely opposed to this thing until I came to this hearing. In my thirty years on City Council, I've never seen such testimony with such a wide cross-section of secular, religious, ethnic support, and that's why I'm supporting this program one hundred percent."

By that he meant he knew how many votes eighty community groups represented. He knew something else, too. It was a scary thing for politicians to vote against the wishes of their masters, which was why it was a good and considerable source of relief to have Hopkinson's approval, but the political fact that both the councilmen and their masters understood was that a politician can serve the master only if he keeps getting elected.

The events of that long-ago time in Philadelphia offer an illustration of Bacon's model (they helped inspire his understanding of it) of how a vital idea that is posited about the future can draw toward it, like so many arrows reaching a target, otherwise diverse elements in the society. The acceptance of the vital idea, however, marks only the beginning of its history. Once it has been formally accepted, it may lose (or appear to lose) sight of the purpose that drew the arrows toward it. If it takes on the form of a government agency, as the Philadelphia Planning Commission did, its tendency will be to respond to the priorities of the system rather than the outside forces that made its existence possible. This process is not necessarily wrong or anti-democratic in all its respects. A mayor, for instance, as the chief elected representative of the public, should have input concerning the decisions of a city planning commission, and the legislators, who have to fund the commission's capital improvement budget, would be remiss if they showed no concern about what they are approving. Nevertheless, the new agency, as part of this process, is likely to begin to perceive that its legitimacy arises from the government system and not from the outsider forces that made its existence possible. An article that appeared in the *Journal of the American Society of Planners* put this understanding well: "The *first*—and most important—[duty of a planning commission] is to develop an appreciation of the position and feelings of the legislators. . . . Just as a good doctor must develop a 'bedside manner,' a good planner must develop what we might call a 'cigar-smoke sophistication.' "[4] (Italics in original.) In this milieu, the commission, by definition, will come to see the outside community and its spokespersons as secondary sources of influence, at best. If the commission is ever going to dictate policy—run roughshod over anyone—it will be the outsiders and not the inside enablers who will be the target.

The effectiveness of the agency is also likely to diminish as its administrative apparatus becomes increasingly complex, and as its goals become cloaked in a bureaucratic language that the insiders alone can interpret. When that happens, the initiators no longer have a grip on what the agency is trying to accomplish. At most, they perform an *ex post facto* role in which they point out failures that, because of the attention drawn to them, will not be repeated.

As the absorption process matures, an outsider-inspired agency like Philadelphia's planning commission can become indistinguishable from an agency that was devised internally as a population-control device. The discouragingly similar histories of the outsider-inspired Environmental Protection Agency and the insider-authorized HUD suggest as much.

The outsider-inspired agency is also likely to soon suffer from the inattention of its sponsors and their supporters. A subject that seems of critical importance at one moment in time, like a planning commission, can become lost sight of in the next moment as new events, new problems, new causes emerge. Very often, too, the outsiders, feeling they have accomplished their altruistic duty, turn back to their private lives, renewing careers they interrupted while they devoted their efforts to the public-interest movement. (This is the major difference between the outsider and the professional politician. For the outsider, establishing public policy is an interest that can be temporarily all-consuming but it is never visualized as a way of life; for the politician, creating policy is her or his full-time job.)

When an agency, through absorption or inattention or some complex set of factors, becomes unresponsive to the needs that brought it into existence, we must not be quick to mark either it or its initiators as failures. To begin with, although this is frequently done, it is improper to view events solely in terms of their conclusions as they appear to be at the time we are studying them. It is necessary to also evaluate the actions of the agency during earlier periods, of either brief or long duration, in which it carried out its mandated goals enthusiastically and imaginatively, thereby possibly creating effects that have continued to be influential long after the enthusiasm and imagination are gone. These effects may not be limited to the agency's mandated goals; they can, to return to Bacon's line of force bouncing off City Hall, ricochet in many directions, causing new ideas and conceptions to enter the public dialogue.

Neither can the apparent conclusion of an event always be considered its final conclusion. Time has a way of going on, and what seemed permanent at one moment becomes temporary at the next. Thus, when an agency is perceived to be ineffective, but the need that brought it into existence continues to be perceived as important, heirs to the initiators will announce themselves and, learning from the example of their forebears, revitalize the agency or else create a replacement for it. As long as the initiating idea remains forceful, this process will continue to repeat itself so that the various points of apparent failure can actually prove to be the energizing moment for the next success. An idea for the future is always an idea for the future.

As it happened, the initiators of the Philadelphia Planning Commission and its supporters were aware of the dangers of losing their mandate for change. After the city council authorized the commission, the eighty-five organizations that by then made up the coalition transformed themselves into the Citizens Council on City Planning, with Walter Phillips as president. To prevent absorption, the citizens council acted to forefend efforts to exert political influence on the commission's actions. To prevent public inattention, the council took it upon itself to explain the commission's proposals to the citizenry, seeking support for those it approved and drumming up opposition when it disapproved. In this way Bacon's speech to the City Policy Committee in 1940 set in motion events that led to a remarkable exercise in participatory democracy.

The citizens council, as the voice of the people, continued in existence for a number of years, but by the early 1950s it had largely ceased to play a role in the city, due not so much to inattention as to the assumption its job was done. That belief was brought about when the administration of the entire city government came into the hands of a group of liberal reform Democrats—Phillips was one of their leaders—who promised the kind of good government that would make a citizens' watchdog group unnecessary.

During its years of greatest activity in the mid to late 1940s, the vigor with which the Citizens Council on City Planning worked to establish community-oriented planning helped set the stage for the creation of an ideological antithesis to the White City of 1893: the Better Philadelphia Exhibition of 1947.

Three years earlier, the architect Oskar Stonorov, Phillips, and

Robert Mitchell, the executive director of the Philadelphia Planning Commission, had gotten together for drinks while attending a planning convention in Chicago. During the course of their conversation, Stonorov suggested and the other two agreed that a jump-start for planning in Philadelphia following the war would be a public exposition along the lines of the exhibits showing the world of the future that had been a great attraction at the New York World's Fair in 1939. Bacon, at the time, was serving in the Navy in the South Pacific, and Stonorov wrote him to enlist his support. In between battles, Bacon got to work, making a series of drawings for a time-space machine that would depict in overlapping plastic frames how the city had developed from William Penn's day.

When Bacon returned from the war, he joined the planning commission staff, but his principal energies were devoted to the Better Philadelphia Exhibition. He served as its principal designer, along with Stonorov, who was also the director. (Bacon and Stonorov were close personally but poles apart philosophically. The Russian-born Stonorov had gone to Paris to become a pupil of Le Corbusier and was a firm believer in Modernism, while Bacon came out of the humanist tradition of Saarinen and the Cranbrook Academy to which Modernism was opposed.)

Also deeply involved in the project were Phillips and Edward Hopkinson, Jr., who had become chairman of the planning commission. Hopkinson used his considerable weight to obtain contributions from Philadelphia businesses and made sure the exhibition would have the financial support of the city government as well.[5] However, just as occurred with the founding of the planning commission, a grassroots involvement proved significant. The Citizens Council on City Planning, which by now numbered 114 organizations, acted as co-sponsor, energizing a sense of excitement at the community level.

To provide a site for the exhibition, Gimbel's Department Store cleared two floors out of its building, which showed both the company's civic virtue and its business acumen: More than 385,000 visitors entered the store during the two months of the exhibition, and many remained to shop there.

No city before had attempted anything remotely on the scale of the Better Philadelphia Exhibition, and none has since. Perhaps the most remarkable quality of the exhibition was its inviting accessibility. Stonorov, Bacon, and their colleagues wanted their displays to be readily comprehensible, dramatic, light, and amusing, in accordance with the goal of involving the public with the whole idea of planning as something that meant a great deal to them personally. As a result, the exhibits not only included turntable models showing the center-city business district (as it was and could be) but focused on individual neighborhoods, and on placement of schools and playgrounds. It even showed folks how they could make their personal lives more pleasant by suggesting simple and inexpensive ways to do over their backyards.

Neither was the exhibition for adults only. The organizers also reached out to the schools. The magazine *Architectural Forum* described what happened: "Of all displays, the least elaborate was perhaps the most popular. . . . This was an exhibition by school children, showing what their neighborhoods would be like if they had a hand in planning. The program was introduced [in 1946] as an experiment in 15 schools. Its success has made it a regular course of study in every school in the city. . . . The Board of Education [was] delighted with an opportunity to teach children how to integrate themselves into society. . . . The children, for the first time actively involved in community life, [were] filled with a new importance. Their surveys of local conditions have taught them more about the neighborhoods than their parents know, [and as a result] have helped arouse interest at the adult level."[6]

Forty years later, Bacon, having been asked to lecture on city planning at one of Philadelphia's inner-city middle schools, provoked the same enthusiasm by having the youngsters photograph their neighborhood. The pictures allowed them to see their surroundings in a way they didn't on a day-to-day basis, and the classroom became filled with the sound of children exchanging ideas of how they'd like to see things change. Just as with the school children of 1947, these boys and girls became aware, for the first time, of the relationship of their environment to themselves. However, save for Bacon's lonely venture, city planning has long ceased to be considered a fit subject for children to study in Philadelphia's schools, and such programs exist across the country in few if any places. It's now considered solely a subject for professionals. In this way, a creative means to give children—and the adults they will become—a sense of the wholeness of their city and impart to them a sense of right of participation in making it the way they would like it to be has been sadly lost.*

A number of the proposals by the Better Philadelphia Exhibition for the revitalization of the downtown, including the Independence Hall mall, were quite good and later carried out, but the solution offered for the central business district's worst eyesore was completely lacking in imagination. This was the area directly west of City Hall on Market Street. There, many years earlier, the Pennsylvania Railroad, in a display of the same corporate arrogance that led it to lay tracks across the mall in Washington, had constructed a terminal adjacent to City Hall and, leading from it, a wall that carried trains traveling between New York and Washington. Quite apart from the noise and pollution and the spread of soot that the trains riding on it caused, the Chinese Wall, as Philadelphians called the structure, cut its portion of the downtown in half, hiding from view the attractive Benjamin Franklin Parkway, the Art Museum, and the verdant reaches of Fairmount Park beyond.

The Better Philadelphia Exhibition designers assumed that the Chinese Wall (which continued on Market for about four blocks before veering northward) would be razed. Everyone had

* The active role played by the Philadelphia children in 1947 contrasts with the passive acceptance of Burnham's plan asked of Chicago children in 1911. The Chicago children, at least, however, were exposed to the idea that the design of their city could have an effect on their lives.

Model of Philadelphia at the 1947 Better Philadelphia Exhibition: View of downtown east as seen from the 30th Street Railroad Station and the Schuylkill River.

been assuming this since the opening of the 30th Street Station, which was outside the downtown area. To replace the Market Street portion of the wall, the exhibition offered a squat department store that the city's leading real estate developer had been thinking of building, although not necessarily at that site. The department store was to be abutted by a miscellany of office towers that followed no logical sequence and that, if constructed, would again block the view of the parkway.

Bacon, meanwhile, had been inspired by the possibilities of the site to conceive his Penn Center plan. When he submitted it to his colleagues, they, led by Stonorov, rejected it out of hand. It was much too fanciful. The practical idea—one that would also generate more contracts for architects—was the hodgepodge of office buildings and the department store, and that was what was shown at the exhibition.

Nevertheless, taken as a whole, the Better Philadelphia Exhibition met its goals, and bountifully so. It educated the Philadelphia public, adult and child alike, about the need to create a more habitable, visually pleasant city. For Philadelphia, the exhibition was also a much-needed booster shot. The city had long been a national laughingstock, the legendary "corrupt and contented" den of iniquity of Lincoln Steffens's description, and now it had mounted this ambitious and successful display under the auspices of, as an awed *Architectural Forum* described it, the best city planning commission in the country. Businesses that would never have given Philadelphia a thought as a place to locate now might be likely to do so. The effect of the exhibition was also by no means localized in another sense. As word of its marvels spread, people came to see it from across the United States, as well as from abroad, and, just as visitors to the White City had done more than fifty years earlier, they took home with them ideas of how they might improve the conditions of their cities, too. Only this time, the emphasis was on the humane city, not a city of grandiose temples.

It was this underlying theme that gave the Better Philadelphia Exhibition its importance in its own time and that continues to provide a conceptual touchstone for the present and the future. That lesson was printed on the wall that the visitors saw just as they were leaving. The words were Lewis Mumford's: "The final test of an economic system is not the tons of iron, the tanks of oil or the miles of textiles it produces: the final test lies in its ultimate products—the sort of men and women it nurtures and the order and beauty and sanity of their communities."

The Political City

The experience of the advocates of the Philadelphia Planning Commission suggests that a political apparatus adopts a new idea for the city's future only when its promulgators (who could be officeholders or candidates) succeed in developing a climate of public consciousness in favor of it. A city's political system, that is, cannot be relied upon to act as an initiator of change, since its only purpose is to gain and maintain control of the government. Ideas for change have significance—they are electioneering instruments—but those that appear likely to threaten the control goal will be shunted aside.

This portrayal of political action as the result of laying pressure on the players and simultaneously alleviating their fear of change describes a basic tenet of political dynamics, but it lacks nuance. Politics is also a matter of attitude. Voters develop attitudes about what the political system (and hence government) is supposed to do for them, and politicians develop attitudes about what they are supposed to do for voters and for themselves. The result in any city is a continually shifting social process, in which the political workers affect one another, and affect and are affected by those outside their organizations.

The attitudinal relationship between the governed and the governors in cities had its genesis in the 1830s. Prior to that time, party politics, displaying sharply divergent ideologies (attitudes) were very much part of the national scene and had been since the presidency of George Washington, but municipal governments, by and large, were in the control of gentlemen, who saw holding office as a form of *noblesse oblige* and often a handy means of influencing legislation that could affect their commercial well-being. As Chancellor Kent of New York wrote in 1835: ". . . the office of assistant alderman [roughly comparable to a councilman of today] could be pleasant and desirable to persons of leisure, of intelligence, and of disinterested zeal for the wise and just regulation of the public concerns of the city."[1]

By Kent's day, however, the spirit of Jacksonian democracy was already at work. It led to white males gaining access to the vote in great numbers as long-standing property restrictions were removed. At the same time and for the same reason, a marked increase took place in the number of offices thought suitable for election rather than appointment.[2]

Politically ambitious men were quick to perceive how these changes could work to their advantage. By organizing the newly enfranchised voters under their banner, they could seek the best electoral posts for themselves and could reward followers with nominations to the lesser ones. The principal recruitment centers in many cities were volunteer firefighting brigades, along with other working-class social organizations, like the Society of Saint Tammany in New York. Members were frequently street toughs spoiling for a fight and could be counted on to keep the opposition away from the polls, but they and their more law-abiding allies had in common that they saw themselves exploited by the privileged class. They were eager to join ranks behind a man who spoke to their aspirations, and many of the leaders were, in fact, themselves of humble origin. William Marcy Tweed, for example, whose name would become synonymous with political corruption, was a lowly chairmaker's apprentice who got his first step-up in politics by joining a New York City fire brigade. Social caste had also played a role in determining political allegiance on the national level, but it is only in the cities that we see a nearly exclusive reliance by the newly emerging political bosses on the us-versus-them attitude as the lever for seizing power.

As important as the Jacksonian reforms were in setting the stage for big-city political machines and the relationships that would develop with their voter base, a catalyst of at least equal impact was the potato famine in Ireland. The hardships it produced led to the emigration of close to 2 million Irish to the United States between the mid-1840s and the eve of the Civil War (nearly 200,000 in 1851 alone).[3] The living conditions the immigrants faced in the East Coast cities at which they disembarked were terrible. The lucky ones found backbreaking and low-paid work, often as stevedores; others led a literal hand-to-mouth existence, picking their food from garbage cans, their clothes out of trash bins.[4] Because the Irish were Catholics, they were also victims of religious bigotry at the hands of the native-born Protestants. Cartoonists like Thomas Nast stereotyped the Irish as subhuman creatures with receding foreheads and chins, and heavy-cast, animal-like features.[5] (Nast's drawings of the Irish bear an uncanny resemblance to the depictions of African-Americans when, some years later, they came to be perceived as threats.) Not surprisingly, considering their circumstances, many of the potato-famine wave of Irish immigrants turned to crime.

For the new breed of populist city politician, however, the Irish did not represent a threat but rather a potential cornucopia of votes. The model, which would be replicated with only minor variations elsewhere, was established in New York. There, the Society of Saint Tammany, which, unlike the individual fire brigades, was city-wide in scope, proved to be the organizing locus. The Irish would come to dominate Tammany, just as they would other big-city machines, but that didn't happen all at once. Fernando Wood, elected in 1854 as Tammany's first mayor, was a Protestant, as was Tweed, who became chairman of the Democratic Party in New York in 1859 and Tammany Grand Sachem* in 1863.[6]

---

* The Society of Saint Tammany was founded in 1789, named after a legendary Lenape Indian chief of New Jersey. As with other fraternal organizations, Tammany soon developed a hierarchical system. Initiates began as "Hunters" and worked their way up to "Warriors," with the ultimate goal to become a "Sachem" (chief); the pinnacle was that of "Grand Sachem," who presided over the "wigwam" or hall, hence Tammany Hall.

For the impoverished masses, Tammany was their only friend. From Tammany, they received coal when they could not afford to heat their homes and food when they were hungry; it was Tammany that saw to it they were not dispossessed when they fell behind on their rents. Tammany would pay for funerals and might pay for weddings. An immigrant could be set up as a saloonkeeper, with his hostelry becoming the Tammany political club of its neighborhood; if a peddler was loyal to Tammany, he was not bothered by the police just because he did not have a proper license. The police carried out Tammany's orders, too, since it was through Tammany they got their jobs, as did the city's firemen. When, in the post–Civil War period, new immigrants arrived from mainland Europe, Tammany (by then under Irish rule) performed the same services for them.

For each wave of immigrants, the same simple contractual arrangement applied: We (the machine politicians) help you, and you in return vote for us. The underlying nature of the relationship, however, and its repercussions were not simple, but multifaceted in their effects on the cities and the people who lived in them.

The career of State Senator George Washington Plunkitt (1842–1924) exemplifies the relationship on one level. From his throne, the bootblack stand in Tweed's New York County Courthouse, Plunkitt lectured his cronies on the marvels of the machine, and reminisced about grand sachems like "Honest John" Kelly, the soapstone cutter who replaced Tweed in 1871; Charles Murphy, a onetime horse-car driver; and Richard Croker, who got his start as a strong-arm man. One of those who attended on Plunkitt was a New York reporter named William L. Riordon, who in 1905 published a little book bearing the title *Plunkitt of Tammany Hall: A Series of Very Plain Talks on Very Practical Politics.*

Plunkitt's yarns are never less than engrossing, and should be required reading for students of political science, but he is particularly pertinent on the subject of self-enrichment as the proper, even ethical, reward of a life of serving the people. As he explained: "Yes, many of our men have grown rich in politics, I have myself. I've made a big fortune out of the game, and I'm gettin' richer every day, but I've not gone in for dishonest graft — blackmailin' gamblers, saloon-keepers, disorderly people, etc. — and neither has any of them who have made big fortunes in politics. There's an honest graft, and I'm an example of how it works. . . . Just let me explain. . . My party's in power in the city, and it's goin' to undertake a lot of public improvements. Well, I'm tipped off, say, that they're goin' to lay out a new park at a certain place. I see my opportunity and I take it. I go to that place and I buy up all the land I can in the neighborhood. Then the board of this or that makes its plan public, and there is a rush to get my land, which nobody cared particular for before. Ain't it perfectly honest to charge a good price and make a profit on my investment and foresight? Of course it is. Well, that's honest graft."[7]

The Wall Street insider traders of the 1980s adopted the Tammany Hall philosophy as explained by Plunkitt, as did, during the same decade, the Mafia in Atlantic City, which gained knowledge of where casinos were to be built, bought the land cheap, and sold it high.

Nevertheless, there was a difference. Neither the Wall Street insiders nor the Mafia had any motivation beyond their own avarice. The machine politicians, on the contrary, had an idea of public service. While it is true they recognized that the favors they bestowed on their constituents — whether it was a patronage job or a bucket of coal — was the reason they wouldn't be turned out of office, they also, for the most part, enjoyed helping people. No doubt doing so gave them a sense of power, but there also must have been a genuine quality to their generosity or else they would not have put in the extraordinary hours they did in displaying it. Riordon recounts a typical day in the life of Plunkitt, which begins at 2 A.M., when he "was aroused from sleep by the ringing of his doorbell and found a bartender, who asked him to go to the police station and bail out a saloonkeeper who had been arrested for violating the excise tax." Plunkitt did so, returned to bed at three and

was up again at six, when he heard fire engines going by and has-
tened to the scene to "give assistance to the fire sufferers, if
needed." His last function of the day, at 10:30 P.M.: "Attended a
Hebrew wedding reception and dance. Had previously sent a
handsome wedding present to the bride."[8]

The reciprocity that Riordon describes had an added dimension, based on the initiating us-versus-them attitude. That dimension was recognized by the social worker Jane Addams in an article
she wrote for the *International Journal of Ethics* in 1898. She begins by telling how the ward leader in her Hull House district bestowed his favors: ". . . When others are spending pennies, he is
spending dollars. . . . [At a church bazaar] where anxious relatives
are canvassing to secure votes for the two most beautiful children
who are being voted upon, he recklessly buys from both sides, and
laughingly declines to say which one he likes best . . . [spends] five
dollars for the flower bazaar, the posies, of course, to be sent to the
sick of the parish. The moral atmosphere of a bazaar suits him exactly. He murmurs many times, 'Never mind; the money all goes
to the poor. . . .'

"Indeed," Addams went on, "what headway can the notion of
civic purity, of honesty of administration, make against this big
manifestation of human friendliness, this stalking survival of village kindness [in the otherwise unkind city]? . . . The reformers
give themselves over largely to criticisms of the present state of affairs, to writing and talking of what the future must be; but their
goodness is not dramatic; it is not even concrete and human. . . .

"The question does, of course, occur to many minds: Where
does the money come from with which to dramatize so successfully? The more primitive people accept the truthful statement of
its sources without any shock to their moral sense. To their simple
minds, he gets it 'from the rich' and so long as he again gives it out
to the poor, as a true Robin Hood . . . they have no objections. . . .
The next less primitive people of the vicinage are quite willing to
admit that he leads 'the gang' in the City Council, and sells out
the city franchises; that he makes deals . . . that he guarantees to

steer dubious measures through the Council, for which he demands liberal pay; that he is, in short, a successful boodler. But when there is intellect enough to get this point of view, there is also enough to make the contention that this is universally done . . . that such a state of affairs is to be deplored, of course, but that is the way business is run, and we are fortunate when a kind-hearted man who is close to the people gets a large share of the boodle; that he serves these franchised companies who employ men in the building and construction of their enterprises, and that they are bound in return to give jobs to his constituency. Even when they are intelligent enough to complete the circle, and to see that the [graft] money comes, not from the pockets of the companies' agents, but from the street-car fares of people like themselves, it is as if they would rather pay the two cents more each time they ride than give up the consciousness that they have a big, warm-hearted friend at court who will stand by them in an emergency. The sense of just dealing comes apparently much later than the desire for protection and kindliness. The Alderman is really elected because he is a good friend and neighbor."[9]

As Addams realized, the "friend at court" machine politicians gave their constituents an illusion of power that made them much less prone than they otherwise would have been to become rebellious about their condition in life. In that way, the machines performed a valuable placating function for the propertied classes and for themselves as organizations.

They also shared with capitalists an interest in keeping the poor poor. For the capitalists of those days, low wages meant high profits. (It hadn't yet apparently occurred to them that better wages meant more expendable income to buy capital's products.) For the politicians, the lower classes were their largest voting bloc, and if their economic situations improved substantially they'd be less dependent on the many friendly aldermen and less likely to vote the machine's way.

This is not to say that the machine never promoted upward mobility. It certainly did for men like Plunkitt, who had begun his life in dire poverty, son of an immigrant Irish family, and who had but three years of schooling. The patronage jobs that the Plunkitts handed out provided, at the very least, economic security for those who previously didn't have it. Patronage also strengthened the machine as its job-holders recruited friends and members of their families to become party loyalists. In this way, patronage constantly shored up the party's voter appeal, and made it much less dependent on wealthy contributors to finance campaigns than is true of today's city parties. In fact, politicians like James Curley of Boston based their electoral success almost entirely on portraying themselves as friends of the downtrodden in their endless battle against the exploitive capitalists. There was a measure of sincerity in this opposition, but that did not stop the politicians from accepting bribes from the supposed enemies or from entering into crooked deals with them.

Indeed, advice that they do just that was offered by Matthew Quay, the political boss of Pennsylvania, who thrived in the era immediately following Tweed. As Quay saw it, the reason for Tweed's downfall was his failure to give the business community a share of the spoils. Once the capitalists were in on a corruption scheme, Quay pointed out, they were not going to blow the whistle on the machine for what it was doing in some separate enterprise, lest the malefactions in which they were involved come to light.[10] (Quay practiced what he preached, too, entering into corrupt business arrangements with millionaires like P. A. B. Widener, the racehorse king. The son of a preacher, Quay died a millionaire in 1904, a time when, as Brooke Astor put it, a million dollars meant something.)

Relationships between the machines and the business leadership varied a great deal from city to city, and could also change from time to time. By the early years of the twentieth century, in Pittsburgh the Mellon banking family had brought the Magee machine to heel, much as in Philadelphia the Pennsylvania Railroad had the Vare organization in its pocket. In other cities, like New

York and Boston, the situation was much more fluid: today a battle, tomorrow an alliance, the third day an apparent battle that masked an under-the-table deal. The only constant was the shared attitude toward the mass of the citizens. They were there to further the interests of capitalist and politician.

During their heyday between the Civil War and World War II, the machines, however, were hardly entirely negative forces upon their cities. They often carried out public works projects that made cities more pleasant, as well as healthier, places for their people to live. Moreover, they represented, when it was in their interest, a restraining force upon the worst elements of the business community. The machine's welfare system had some advantages, too, which have largely been lost by the civil service bureaucracy that replaced it. Under the machine, because of the votes they could offer, the poor did not perceive themselves as valueless, nor were they seen that way by their benefactors; the opposite is true in the modern welfare model. But there is something more: The humane quality of the old system—Plunkitt's wedding gift to the Jewish bride—has been replaced in the new by sets of impersonal rules that even the most compassionate of social workers must abide by. The new system no doubt is more equitable, since people are eligible for help without having to rely on a good-natured politician. But paradoxically it is also more unfair. Welfare recipients, for instance, are not permitted to hold a job on the side to help them get by. They can be arrested and sent to prison, under some circumstances, if they do, and they will be punished with loss of benefits if they dare try to save money to further their education. That kind of thinking would never have occurred to Plunkitt or to Addams's alderman; if it had, they would have rejected it as monstrous.

The amount of corruption that the machines practiced as a unit, or that they permitted among lieutenants like Plunkitt, did not play a significant role in their decline. When the amount of stealing became scandalous, reform movements might succeed in throwing the rascals out, but as long as the intimate relationship between the machines and the voter mass remained in place, the setbacks were temporary and usually (as with Tammany Hall) of short duration.

The intimacy was disrupted, fatally so, by Franklin Roosevelt, who initiated the current era of city politics. Ironically, Roosevelt never saw himself as an opponent of the machines. On the contrary, he recognized and relished their capacity to turn out huge margins for Democratic* candidates, and he rewarded their bosses with patronage largesse. Tammany Hall, even with the Republican La Guardia as mayor, always did well for Roosevelt, and so it was rewarded; Frank Hague in Jersey City may have done best of all, so that, regardless of the personal despisal in which Roosevelt held him, his machine thrived during the Roosevelt years, as did Crump's in Memphis and that of the Pendergasts in Kansas City. (Roosevelt could be ruthless, too. When Boston's Curley did poorly for Roosevelt at the polls, he paid the price in jobs he didn't get.)

Nevertheless, Roosevelt's activist response to the needs of city people during the Depression sounded the death knell of the machines. Although a few, like Chicago's, persisted well into the second half of the twentieth century, the machines' mass base of support had been eroded by the economic safety net the federal government was now providing. Conceivably, if that is all that had happened to the machines, they might have become reinvigorated following the Depression, when support programs like the WPA ended. But that was not to be. Inadvertently, Roosevelt's policies also opened the way for the development of orbiters — individuals

---

* Almost all of the machines were Democratic. Republican machines that flourished from time to time in cities like Pittsburgh and Cincinnati, as well as in Philadelphia, were identical to the Democratic ones in their operation, their corruption, and their benevolence. The machine's party label could be determined, as it was in Philadelphia, by the affiliation of its first boss or by particular local conditions. Elsewhere, for the largely Catholic big-city masses and their largely Catholic political leaders, it was sufficient that the wealthy were Protestant and Republican for them to adopt the Democratic banner.[11]

and voter blocs that had their genesis outside the metropolitan Democratic parties, but which, as the moon affects the tides, influenced political decision-making.

The unionists came first. For many years, they and the machines, Democratic or Republican, operated at cross-purposes. The unionists wanted to organize the poor out of their poverty; the machines liked the situation just as it was. The generally unfavorable climate for unionism in the cities did not change significantly until 1935, when the Roosevelt-supported National Labor Relations Act (Wagner Act) was passed, granting the unionists their long-sought goal of collective bargaining rights. Until then, union membership could be dangerous for a worker. Murders of strikers were not uncommon, yellow dog contracts (to keep out unions) were, and unionists were regularly the targets for other reprisals by management. The Wagner Act would not bring an immediate end to the perils of the workers—as the sit-down strike in Flint later amply proved—but in effect it had legitimized unionism, which meant the timid were likely to join as they had not before. But the most important fact about the Wagner Act was that, through it, Roosevelt had unequivocally announced himself and his party to be the friend of the laboring man and woman, giving them and their leaders, at long last, a political home in one of the two mainstream parties.

A second event of 1935 was hardly less significant. That year, John L. Lewis led the United Mine Workers out of the American Federation of Labor (AFL) to form the Congress of Industrial Organizations (CIO). Under vigorous leaders like Walter Reuther of the United Automobile Workers, the CIO became a vast organizing tool of non-trades employees. Infused by a left-leaning philosophy, which an irate Lewis did not share, the CIO was far more militant than the AFL. Its organizers spread throughout the country, preaching a gospel of social action and of unity against the capitalists.

Often they were not welcome, and nowhere, as civil rights attorney David Kairys has pointed out, "was their reception more hostile than in [Democratic] Jersey City. . . . The CIO planned to distribute literature on the streets and host outdoor meetings, but permits for these meetings were denied by [Mayor] Hague." He seemed to be acting on sound Constitutional grounds, too. Ever since 1894—in an opinion written by Oliver Wendell Holmes, then of the Supreme Court of Massachusetts, and subsequently upheld by the United States Supreme Court—use of public spaces for speeches could be prohibited by local authorities. Hague, Kairys goes on, "had firmly allied himself with the manufacturing and commercial establishments. He made it clear that labor organizers were not welcome in Jersey City, and many were cast out of town, usually to be put on a ferry to New York. Local businesses were promised that they would have no labor troubles while he was mayor; his response to the CIO was: 'I am the law.' " The CIO brought suit against Hague, and in 1939 the United States Supreme Court overturned the 1894 ruling, observing that: "Wherever the title of streets and parks may rest, they have immemorially been held in trust for the use of the public and . . . have been used for purposes of assembling, communicating thoughts between citizens, and discussing . . . questions."[12] As a public-interest movement, unionism's establishment of the right to free speech in America, even when government authorities opposed it, may have been its single most important accomplishment that moved beyond the boundaries of its own beneficiary class.

Although there were exceptions to the far left and a few to the right (like Lewis), union leaders and particularly those of the CIO otherwise saw themselves as ideologically allied to the liberalism expounded by the Democratic Party under Roosevelt. Nationally, some union leaders like Sidney Hillman obtained executive positions in the New Deal. But, in or out of office, their counsel was courted, their approval sought. A certain amount of self-interest was involved. The unionists wanted a continuation of the favorable atmosphere for organizing workers that the New Deal provided, and the New Deal wanted their votes. But the underlying spirit was one of genuine cooperation since New Dealers and unionists, by and large, perceived fundamental human rights issues the same way.

Not all efforts by the unionists to affect political decisions involved joining forces with the Democrats. In New York in the 1940s, garment trade unionists, led by Alex Rose and David Dubinsky, created the independent American Liberal Party. ("American" was later dropped from the title.) Dubinsky and Rose wanted to avoid aligning unionism with the corrupt Tammany Hall machine, seeing alternative possibilities in a city in which progressive Republicanism, as embodied by Mayor La Guardia, was not extinct. The Liberals, therefore, embarked on a policy of endorsing those candidates from either party who came closest to meeting their ideology. Although the Liberals remained very much a minority party in terms of registration, they were recognized by Republican and Democratic candidates as an important swing factor whose endorsement was to be valued; the result was that, in order to achieve it, candidates were likely to move in a liberal, pro-union direction. The Liberals' endorsement of Republican John Lindsay in 1965 has been credited as the reason he was elected mayor that year.[13]

Other than in New York, however, with very few exceptions the unionists sought to work within and work upon the local Democratic Party. By the late 1940s, their political impact had become widespread, and for good reason. The union leaders could generally deliver their members' votes (about a third of the nation's non-agricultural workforce by then was unionized), were capable of getting out large election-day forces, and, as their coffers grew more full from membership dues, were funding candidates individually who met their criteria.*

In most instances, the financial clout was sufficient to assure that favored candidates would be endorsed by party leaders, of whom, as time went on, a substantial number were themselves

---

* Today's Political Action Committees, or PACs, had their origin in the labor union movement.

union officials. To the extent that this occurred, the difference between independent orbiter and organization became blurred. However, the unions never entirely lost their orbiting function. Should a non-endorsed Democratic candidate meet their favor, that person would be funded in the primary election, and (more rarely) a union might punish the Democrats by supporting a Republican or two in the general election.

As has frequently been observed, the union influence on cities did not stop at elections. The winning candidates, either because they were ideologically in tune with the unionists or felt beholden to them, geared their policies in ways that, at a minimum, didn't run counter to union needs. In city after city, municipal unions gained ever more favorable contracts, in terms of wages and benefits. Decisions on which capital improvement projects would be funded at times were reached by the local politicians based on how many jobs they'd provide union workers rather than on the value a project might have for the city as a whole. (The argument might be raised, with merit, that the same decisions would have been reached to benefit contractors, not unions, and often were; contractors can also be major campaign contributors.)

What has been less frequently noted is that mayors with a great deal of political acumen will be able—when it is to their interest—to thwart the influence of unions (or any other orbiter), typically by employing co-option as a technique.

A master at this skill was Richard J. Daley of Chicago. Throughout his tenure as mayor, which extended from the 1950s into the 1970s, Daley made it a policy to name union leaders to boards and commissions that had little or nothing to do with their union roles. The head of the janitor's union was named to the Police Board; that of the plumber's union to the Board of Health; the man from the electrician's union to the Board of Education; the clothing workers union had a representative on the Library Board, while the head of the Chicago Federation of Labor and an official from the Teamsters helped run the city's poverty program. By accepting these largely honorary positions, the unionists became highly visible members of Daley's team, giving the impression he was running a union town when, in fact, he was running a Daley town. The constraining web of favoritism with which Daley surrounded the union leaders did not stop at the public showcases he provided them. He also regularly handed out patronage jobs to the sons of union bosses, which made them more reluctant than ever to cross Daley when they might disagree with him. Since all this occurred in a context of vast construction programs, which offered tens of thousands of jobs to the rank and file, any social concerns that the union leaders might have regarding Daley's racist policies and his destruction of working-class neighborhoods (to make way for all that building) were thoroughly muted.[14]

As the last years of the twentieth century arrived, unions continued to play a role in urban politics, most noticeably in the big old northern cities where their strength had been and remained the greatest. But, by then, their influence just about everywhere was on the wane. To some extent, they had been weakened by their own success as negotiators of wage and benefit packages for their members. Because of them, millions of working-class Americans entered the middle class, and the notion that they were engaged in a struggle to create a more just society—which had been the fervent hope of both the New Deal and union activists like Reuther—began to seem quaint, if not irrelevant. They had obtained their just society, monetarily anyway. Even in voter totals, union influence in the cities declined as more and more members moved to the suburbs. An ideological schism also began to exhibit itself between leadership and the rank and file. The commitment of the CIO to equality of job opportunity (which had been so vital when the issue was between union and non-union workers) took on a threatening cast to the existent white membership as it saw job competition arising from the minority populations of the inner cities. Liberalism was all good and fine, but not when it threatened the wallet.

Trust in union leadership weakened substantially in the 1980s. As more jobs fled abroad, as more foreign-made goods entered the country, as leveraged buyouts added to the unemployment rate, no longer were the wage-and-benefit packages improved with each contract; instead, they were generally worsened. If the union leaders could no longer carry out their prime purpose of protecting jobs and benefits, there was less reason than ever for the rank and file to listen to their advice, or even remain in the fold. By 1992, the unionized percentage of the non-agricultural workforce had declined to about 16 percent.[15]

Nevertheless, the remaining rank and file, through the dues it paid, continued to underwrite the political goals of the union leaders. That leadership might no longer be able to deliver many votes, but the endorsements (often contrary to the increasingly conservative thinking of the membership) remained eagerly sought by city candidates because of the PAC contributions that accompanied them.

Well before the 1980s arrived, a second body had begun to orbit and then penetrate the big-city Democratic Party structure. It, too, could trace its origins to the New Deal. Its members were black.

When Franklin Roosevelt became president, approximately 70 percent of the nation's blacks lived in the South, where, because of Jim Crow laws, very few of them were permitted to vote. That was never the case in the North, but black voters there had never done the Democrats much good since they remained loyal to the party of the Great Emancipator. As a result, the Democratic machines saw no need to include them in their job provision or charitable activities, and the white Republicans ignored them, too. In the 1930s, Roosevelt's liberal policies and the message he got across that he wanted to make life better for everyone rapidly brought the northern black vote over to the Democratic camp. Progress was much slower in the South, where blacks who were registered tended to remain Republican, no doubt largely because the Democratic Party in the South was in control of and assiduous in carrying out discriminatory statutes and customs. Even as recently as 1960, by which time the civil rights movement had made progress in enrolling black voters in the South, the Republican candidate for President, Richard Nixon began his campaign with substantial black backing.*

By 1960, however, the overwhelming majority of the blacks who lived in the northern cities were Democrats, if they were registered at all. There were lots of them, too. The post–World War II migration to the North by blacks was in the millions, and the Democratic Party chiefs in the cities where they arrived welcomed them, sought to register them, and sought to help them get housing and get on welfare. The goal was to control this new voter force, and in city after city the Democrats did just that, establishing their own version of the plantation system, in which the overseers were either white ward leaders or Uncle Toms, many of whom held patronage jobs.

That accommodation ticked along peacefully enough until the early 1960s, when the civil rights movement turned its attention to the inequities of life for blacks in the North. Leadership independent of the Democratic Party soon emerged. Clergymen played a major role, just as they had in the South. Not all the organizing that took place, however, had direct electoral goals in mind. A great deal of the emphasis was placed on laying pressure on employers to open jobs to blacks, as exemplified by the Rev.

---

* He lost it on the eve of the election when his opponent, John Kennedy, phoned Coretta King, wife of Dr. Martin Luther King, Jr., to express his sympathy after her husband had been held without bail on a chain gang following his arrest on a traffic ticket charge. Kennedy's gesture united the civil rights leadership behind him.[16] The effect, however, was felt less in the South than in the North, which had many more registered black voters, who cast their ballots for him in unprecedented numbers. In tightly contested Illinois, their support for Kennedy arguably won him the election. That the phone call could have such an impact speaks to the low level of expectation that blacks had of all white politicians at the time. (Even a few kind words were surprising.) But it also speaks, just as the history of the planning commission in Philadelphia does, to the importance of outside pressure to force a political action. Had there been no viable civil rights movement in 1960, and King or any black man had been treated the same way, there would have been no call to his wife, and Kennedy might not have been elected President.

Jesse Jackson's Operation Breadbasket in Chicago. In most cities, the first overtly political activity had as its purpose to wrest the wards from the overseers. That effort entailed developing candidates and trying to force them on the party's white leadership or fighting incumbents when the party refused to endorse the insurgents. The degree of the accomplishment of the black orbiters can be found in a single statistic: In 1966, there were no black mayors in the United States; twenty-five years later, more than 300 had been elected. Of the five major cities, only Chicago didn't have a black mayor, and it had previously had one in Harold Washington, who died in office.

As had been true of the unionists, the black orbiters (some of whom were also union leaders) could at times be indistinguishable from their city's Democratic Party. However, also like the unionists, by no means all of the black influencers were directly involved in party activities. The politically powerful clergy was particularly likely to retain its separatist advise-and-consent role. Meanwhile, others moved in and out of the ranks, depending on whether their goal of the moment was to confront the white wing of the party or ally with it against a common foe.

The third orbiting group to which the New Deal gave birth consisted of white middle-class liberals. Their ideological roots can be found in abolitionism and in the perceptions of urban reformers, like Riis and Addams, who conceived that government had a moral duty to make good on its announced intent to provide liberty and justice for all.

In a political party sense, early liberalism had no home, any more than unionism did. The progressive policies of Theodore Roosevelt had given liberal thinkers cause to lean toward Republicanism, and many subsequently were attracted to the new internationalism, designed to assure world peace enunciated by Democrat Woodrow Wilson. But it wasn't until Franklin Roosevelt became President that the liberals gained a political party to call their own. Roosevelt also gave American liberalism a political definition it had hitherto lacked. Again, the National Labor Relations Act was the primal document. Its premise that a workable arrangement could be created between management and labor through collective bargaining, if true, meant that capitalism was not inherently exploitive. Rather, capital required only checks on its power, which the moral government could (and should) bring about. The just society, consequently, was feasible without changing the economic system—as left-wingers thought was necessary—nor was a major overhaul of government institutions required. Modern political liberalism thus began as a philosophy of fine-tuning to create equity, and has never substantially moved from its natal position.

As this precis of liberalism in its New Deal formulation indicates, it need not have ethnic or occupational bounds. As a set of beliefs, it can and has appealed to a broad constituency. The liberal orbiting group, however, is quite specific. It consists of whites from middle-class to well-to-do backgrounds, like Edmund Bacon's friend Walter Phillips. Their influence, which has been considerable, emanates from two sources. First, because many are affluent and have access to other affluent people, white liberal politicians have been in a position to finance their own campaigns and force their presence on the Democratic Party for that reason alone. Secondly, their ideas have often enough been sufficiently compatible with the black and union orbiting groups that they have been able to create multiple and frequently quite effective electoral alliances with them. Although disputes within the troika have been many and at times divisive, the overall effect has been to give the city Democratic parties something they never had in the days of the machine: a consistent ideology that, in programmatic terms, is defined by such positions as opposition to racism, favoring of contracts let out on non-discriminatory terms, and a sense that it is important to develop initiatives that will improve the conditions of the poor, in part by expanding social and health-care services. The orbiters may, like the machine politicians, have their own self-advancement in mind—hungry for influence, hungry for office, hungry for power—but they have created a fundament of social policy principles for the city.

Espousing the principles, however, has proven to be easier than carrying them out. One reason is the disagreement among the orbiters about which programs are desirable; another, a diminishing urban revenue base that calls for curtailment rather than expansion of social services; a third, the immediacy factor (the constant daily crises that make it difficult to think in the long term); and a fourth, still another orbiting body that has its own impact on politicians and their decision making.

This is the orbiter that has always been present, the city's business and financial establishment. Although certain of its leaders can be far-seeing and may even be in general accordance with the philosophy of the other three orbiting bodies, the business thrust essentially is toward land-packaging. In the business view, social betterment schemes are to be evaluated in terms of their impact on profit; they are not to be adopted solely because they may someday lead to a more equitable society or because they allow their advocates to feel good about themselves for proposing them.

For good or ill, the counsel offered by the primarily Republican business and financial establishment is not one that is readily ignored by the Democratic politicians with whom they deal. An administration that doesn't have the alliance of the investment community will be in dire straits in obtaining the financial support it needs to carry out its programs and obtain the necessary loans to keep the city functioning. The politicians will also be reluctant to oppose the land-packaging, since such developments, if successful, will presumably give them the revenues to carry out their social programs. Moreover, in very pragmatic terms, crossing the business establishment is a dangerous course of action for any politician, since it cuts off a fecund source of campaign contributions.

To this point, the image drawn of today's big city Democratic Party is that of a piece of rope constantly changing shape and direction as various outsider forces push and pull at it. But if that is the only image offered, it is a misleading one, since it is also true that city parties continue to carry out many of the functions that were theirs in the days of the machine. In most cities, ward structures, as before, principally determine who will fill vacancies in city council, state legislative posts, and most minor city-wide offices. Moreover, in cities in which judges are elected, the Democratic Party endorsement remains eagerly sought by lawyers who pay large amounts of money—$50,000 to $60,000 is not uncommon—to the party in order to receive its backing. (The lawyers recognize that voter interest in the judiciary is low, and the ward structures will usually be able to turn out enough votes to assure victory.) Party leaders, too, are the ones primarily in charge of redistricting following the decennial census, drawing the new boundaries in ways that will further the opportunities of favored candidates. (As an illustration, assume that Hispanics are becoming a voter force in a council district held by a black or white; after the redistricting they are likely to find that instead of an emerging majority in one district, they are now relatively insignificant minorities in two.)

The principal weakness of the push-pull image, however, is that it has omitted the greatest inherent strength of a political party, which is that it is a party. As such, it carries out important social and socializing functions. The party as a party can most vividly be seen on election night, as poll workers hurry to ward headquarters, tally sheets in hand, for a time of mutual congratulation or commiseration. Alternatively, as the returns come in, they may wend their way to the hotel where the head of the ticket is invariably holed up in a suite with advisers. In either situation, and regardless of who wins or loses, people who share an interest are getting together. In joy and gloom, fellowship is present.

Unlike some party-givers, the politicians as hosts welcome outsiders. Few campaigns are so impoverished in their appeal that they don't attract at least a few newcomers to electioneering, and if these individuals remain involved beyond a single campaign, a socializing process takes place in their lives.

At the beginning, the neophyte may not be clear about who is a party "regular" and who is an orbiter (or, for that matter, who is an orbiter who also wears a regular's cap, like the union boss who doubles as a ward leader), but he or she is likely to find the experience a pleasant one mainly because most politicians are likable people. They tend to be convivial, and a substantial number of them—a reason they were attracted to politics in the first place—genuinely enjoy helping people, just as George Washington Plunkitt did. The newcomer may also be shocked to find that professional politicians, whom he or she may have previously dismissed as ward heelers and ignoramuses, are, in fact, for the most part highly knowledgeable about local issues, often more so than the newcomers are. But this is as it should be: Just as when one enters the widget business, one has to learn about widgets in order to succeed, so must politicians learn about people and their problems if they wish to succeed.

As the newcomers become more and more immersed in the political world, they discover that under the outward conviviality are hatreds, jealousies, and conspiracies in plentitude. But that realization doesn't prevent the socializing from going forth and even adds spice to the adventure as the newcomers enter into alliances that form and re-form, so that yesterday's opponent may become today's best friend. It is here we see the insinuating attraction of the political world: What may have begun as an outsider opportunity to promote one's ideology and favorite issues has become transformed into a continuing insider experience.

Of all outsiders, none were as alienated from the urban political process for as long a time as were the blacks. Both because of the gains they made during the civil rights era and those they failed to make, many of the activists became convinced that in order to make the political system respond to them they would have to become part of it.

Election to office did provide a direct influence on legislation they had previously not had, but it also brought with it a blunting effect. From the outside, the white establishment could be perceived in monolithic terms as the enemy, but once the activists were on the inside, that posture was difficult to maintain. The enemies now became human beings, and frequently very pleasant and convivial ones, who assured the activists that they also favored civil rights; in fact, many did. Moreover, even the most militant of the black activists soon realized that to get their programs through they had to work with the whites, supporting white-engendered programs to get support for their own. The party leadership played its own significant role. It may have opposed the activist when he or she first ran for office, but generally would endorse that same person for reelection and provide campaign funds as well. In this way, the leverage the activist had gained by the first election was balanced (and sometimes more than balanced) by the leverage the party gained by assuring reelection after reelection. It is difficult to continue to see as an enemy an entity that is constantly helping you.

But other factors in bringing about the transformation were more important and more long-lasting. For a sizable number of the black activists, election meant that for the first time in their lives they were earning a good income. Their constituents remained poor, but they were now in the middle class and would remain there as long as they continued to hold office. It was natural they would become aware of and appreciative of the middle-class way of life and want to maintain it. Here we see the dilemma that poor people, regardless of race, encounter: When they succeed in electing one of their own to office, that person ceases to be one of their own.

But most important of all is the mainstreaming. Let us suppose that a young black man who has gained a reputation as a vibrant leader of his inner-city community is elected to city council. He comes to his new task with an agenda he wants to press on behalf of his people. However, simply by the fact that he is now a council member, he finds himself confronted for the first time by the intricacies of municipal finance, and by a whole series of decisions to be made on legislative proposals that have little or no direct bearing on his agenda. He learns that business interests—which he hitherto may have considered purely oppressive—must be encouraged to invest by the awarding of tax breaks. He also learns that his own programs may not be realistic. No one will say they oppose them, but unless the city is put on a sound financial footing (as with the tax breaks for business), there will be no money to fund what he wants. When he reaches that view, he is no longer seeing the city through the eyes of his constituents, as he did before he was elected, but instead has accepted what he has been told are the proper priorities in the proper order for the city as a whole. At that point, he is still a minority member, but he has adopted the majoritarian attitude and has been mainstreamed. His constituents may wonder what has happened to the firebrand they first elected, and some will accuse him of selling out. But in his eyes he hasn't sold out; rather, he perceives himself as having advanced from a parochial to a global view.

What we see in the councilman is a developing pattern of domination of him by majoritarian ideas (the importance of a sound economy in which banking and other business interests thrive, leading eventually to a trickling of benefits to his constituents). He didn't have to be black for that to happen to him. However, as a black person, he was readily prone to labeling as someone who represented only a single interest, which gave him a motivation to prove the label false. In recent years, as the black presence in urban government has expanded, the single-issue labeling has begun to disappear, but the mainstreaming effect has not. The same majoritarian principles apply, so that a minority-dominated city council of today is not likely—for better or worse—to perform much differently from the majoritarian white councils of the past, and the same holds true for black mayors. (The long career of Thomas Bradley as mayor of Los Angeles offers a case in point.) If anything, out of their remaining concern not to be labeled, the black officials may act more in accordance with majoritarian attitudes than did the previous white-dominated bodies.

The black urban experience in America provides a broader exemplification than does the mainstreaming of the councilman of the effect that majoritarian assumptions have on outsiders. Until about the 1840s, unemployment was relatively rare among the free blacks of the northern cities. Black sailors rode the seas, black stevedores manned the docks. For them, incomes were not good even if they were steady, but others did well. Catering provided a good income for some. James Forten made a fortune as a sailmaker, and the Amherst–educated Robert Purvis owned a sizable amount of valuable real estate. Blacks were also involved in the entertainment business, and not in Stepin Fetchit roles, either; one of the nation's most popular bands of the early nineteenth century was led by a black man, Francis Johnson, who was also an accomplished composer of music.

The arrival of the Irish immigrants marked the beginning of widespread black urban poverty. White bosses fired the Negro stevedores and sailors, and replaced them with Irish immigrants, both out of bigotry and because, in some instances, the Irish were so desperate for work they would accept lower wages than the blacks had been paid. Nevertheless, black, urban middle class persisted. By the post–Civil War period, it included merchants like William Still (author of *The Underground Railroad*), funeral directors, doctors, teachers, and a sizable number of ministers. In many instances, the success achieved by certain families proved to be trans-generational, with names that were prominent in the 1870s still prominent today (much as has occurred in white society). With some notable exceptions, however, members of the black middle class were not zealous in demanding better housing or jobs for the less-fortunate members of their race. They were widely considered accommodationists (the kernel of the accusations that were to be made against the councilman) who imitated the manners and material goals of the whites. It was as if by becoming as white as possible, by causing as little trouble as possible for the master class, they would be spared the worst forms of bigotry that could cause them to lose the precarious perch they had obtained.

The civil rights movement markedly enlarged the size of the black middle class and made it more heterogeneous occupationally, but that did not stop the same allegations being raised against it. On the contrary, such criticisms became more vocal, and because they were usually initiated by black activists, white liberals felt free to adopt the same view, shaking their heads in dismay over the black middle-class desertion of the black poor.

We might accept the denunciation of the black middle class as valid if the white middle class was held to the same standard. But it has never been, for a good reason: Because of its social dominance in the United States, the white middle class has been able to write the rules of conduct and applies to itself only those that are convenient or self-congratulatory. Under this rubric, members of the white middle class, for instance, are to be praised when they help the white poor or even the black, but they are neither required nor expected to do so. The black middle class, however, is said to fail in its duty to its poor when it doesn't.

By promulgating high standards for outsiders, the rules-writers create an insidious climate of opinion that is so pervasive that even some members of the outsider group—who readily recognize overt forms of bias against them—buy into the ideological underpinning. Women, thus, have long accepted the male idea that Caesar doesn't have to be pure but his wife does. And well they might, since purity, after all, is an admirable quality; one really can't argue against such high-mindedness. Similarly, it is difficult to argue that the black middle class shouldn't attempt to succor the black poor, so that the premise there—what is privilege for us is duty for you—is also lost sight of. The rules of conduct, by setting impossibly high standards for outsiders (absolute purity of self, complete self-sacrificing duty to others) and low standards for insiders, set in motion a dynamic whereby the outsiders are constantly vulnerable to feelings of inadequacy, in their own eyes as well as those of the insiders. That's how domination works; to the extent it succeeds, domination tends toward entropy by narrowing the opportunities for the expression of ideas that, if given free rein, could lead to a more holistic society.

By extension, the theory of dominance also applies to those within a city who, lacking insider status, attempt to urge upon the majoritarians a more favorable ambience for people through changes in the city's physical design and its political institutions. Such individuals, in effect, are seeking to change the vocabulary of the city, but in so doing they must constantly confront the vocabulary of the dominant rules-writers. As Edmund Bacon learned throughout his life, outsiders like him are charged with being radicals or starry-eyed visionaries, which (in the rules-writers' vocabulary) means they are unrealistic, a terrible thing for any American to be. (Never mind that no one can define "unrealistic." It's the emotional content of the word, not its meaning, that counts.) Faced with these accusations, the recipients are expected to conclude that they are doomed to failure unless they accept the realistic assumptions of the rules-writers. Bacon says that if he had listened to the vocabulary of realism, he would never have accomplished anything in his life. But many do listen. Daniel Burnham did. When he presented his plan for Chicago, he knew it neglected and even impinged upon the problems of the city's poor; further, he recognized it was vital to the city's future that solutions be found. Given his awareness of green-tract alternatives to tenements, he could have incorporated them into his plan, but he did not, apparently because (based on his own hedging language, quoted in Chapter Three) he understood that this kind of approach would not be acceptable to his rules-writers. Because he capitulated to their premises, his plan was considered realistic.

In the political socializing context, "realism" is the key to the entire grammar of action. "Of course," said the rules-writers, in effect, to the councilman, "we all want change, but we have to be realistic about it." He and those like him, not wanting to be thought unrealistic, accept the language, losing sight of the fact that if their "un-realism" should succeed, it would become the new realism.

Political reform movements, the subject of the next chapter, are also in the rules-writing business, which means they develop a vocabulary, too. One of their favorite words is "integrity," and it can be quite the trickster where the public good is concerned.

7

Good Government

The political reform movements that dot the history of American cities have been premised on a belief that Lincoln Steffens described in *The Shame of the Cities* as "an ancient superstition . . . that we shall devise some day a legal machine that will turn out good government automatically."[1] The reason we can't, according to William Penn, is people. "Governments," he wrote in 1682, "like clocks, go from the motion men give them, so by them they are ruined, too. . . . Let man be good and the government cannot be bad; if it be ill they will cure it. But if men are bad, let the government be never so good, they will . . . warp and spoil it to their turn."[2]

When Penn's and Steffens's reasoning is taken together, it would appear that reform efforts will always be futile because they are headed by fallible humans who create fallible mechanisms; worse yet, because of the same fallibility, we have no way to guarantee the constant supply of "good" people who can make the flawed mechanism work to its optimum capacity. However, even within the context of this discouraging thesis, an argument can be advanced that reform efforts are valuable since they have the capacity to improve—not perfect—the engine of government in a manner that will make it exceedingly difficult, if not impossible, for a succeeding generation of warpers and spoilers to run rampant. Moreover, and much more important, because the reformers have established ideals of official behavior that the public has embraced, the trend will be toward longer periods of relatively good government and shorter ones of bad.

This optimistic view of reform is countered by another that asserts that such movements have failed to have any but the most meager positive effects on cities; the reason they haven't has nothing to do with quixotic searches for a magic formula or with any lack of "good men" to conduct the search. Their fatal flaw, instead, derives from their equation of good government with clean government. Consequently, the reformers' ideas for change are not primarily directed to making the city a more enjoyable and fulfilling place for its people to live; instead they only attempt to insure that integrity in office will replace venality. That goal may be a worthy one to achieve, but the assumption implicit in it is a false one: Honesty, by itself, is no guarantor of competence or intelligence or of the ability to conceive the kind of coherent vision that a city needs to thrive.

It may be, however, that the two analyses are not quite so mutually exclusive as they seem; with that possibility in mind, we turn to the movement toward good government that Edmund Bacon's friend Walter Phillips helped lead in Philadelphia. In both its successes and its failures, its fine insights and its flawed ones, its acceptances and its rejections, it encompasses virtually every aspect of the reform genre. It begins, typically enough, with knights in shining armor in hot pursuit of the dragons of corruption.[3]

When reform came to Philadelphia, its victory was widely attributed to the work of white, upper-class liberal orbiters, and there is a certain amount of truth to that view. Its three most prominent leaders—Joseph Sill Clark, Jr., Richardson Dilworth, and Phillips—were all well-to-do WASP gentlemen, and they were well matched by representatives from the affluent Jewish community, like Lessing Rosenwald of Sears, Roebuck and the author Emily Sunstein.

The upper-class liberals, however, did not act alone. Although they did not organize at the community level in any significant way, as the policy committee had done, their base of support was a fairly wide one, ranging from labor union leaders to a handful of representatives from the black middle class. One of their best finds was Leon Shull, an adept political organizer who came from the Jewish labor movement in New York City.

At the beginning of 1947, the year in which the reform movement surfaced, its prospects for success were not good. Both the city and the dominant Republican Party were firmly in the grip of an oligarchy that called itself the Band of Brothers. The most equal of the brothers in the Orwellian sense was Philadelphia sheriff Austin Meehan, but not far behind him were William Meade, who controlled the Delaware River wards, where he could turn out 20-to-1 vote margins, and the Hamiltons, who actually were brothers and presided over much of the city's middle-class northwest section.

Pitted against the incumbent mayor Barney Samuel in the 1947 election was attorney Richardson Dilworth. He had presented himself to the Democratic City Committee as their candidate and gained endorsement when he promised to finance his own campaign. A major figure in the history of American cities, Dilworth proved to be a colorful and indefatigable campaigner. He spoke, it seemed, on every street corner in the city, even venturing into Meade territory. On one occasion, Dilworth spoke in front of Mayor Samuel's house, pointing out that the block contained, in addition to the mayor's abode, a brothel, a police station, and a wide-open gambling operation. Dilworth observed that the combination suggested a great deal of what was wrong with Philadelphia. By election day, he had named 128 Republican office-holders, including judges, as corrupt. The newspapers weren't impressed by his allegations. The *Inquirer* derided Dilworth as a wide-eyed radical whose election would destroy the city. Samuel won. The machine-controlled vote was still large enough to assure that result.

Opposition to the Band of Brothers and their predecessors was nothing new. A series of attempts, going back to the nineteenth century, had been made to reform the Republican Party from within, and all had failed. On the other side, the Democratic Party bosses had long shown little capacity for combat, in large part because they were fed enough scraps from the Republican table to keep them bloated and passive. A different tack was adopted by the liberals in 1947. Their goal was to establish an organization that would act as a political force independent of both parties.

They began with a purge. By the end of World War II, a tenuous alliance of reformers called the National Citizens Political Action Committee (NCPAC) had come into existence in a number of cities. It consisted, for the most part, of a mixture of liberals and leftwingers, with a strong labor union input. It was in the union component that the divisions were strongest. With the Cold War dawning, liberal unionists were eager to rid their movement of those they considered communists, and they succeeded. (Many of the NCPAC leftists went on to become active in Henry Wallace's Progressive Party campaign for the Presidency in 1948.) In Philadelphia, the cleansed NCPAC was transformed in 1947 into a chapter of the newly created Americans for Democratic Action (ADA).* Clark was named its first chairman, with Phillips hovering in the wing. The ADA, which endorsed Dilworth that year, would provide much of the leadership of the reform era that was to follow.

Size was never the Philadelphia ADA's strength. At its zenith, it only had a little over a thousand members. What it did have was commitment. (Phillips alone was enough to assure that.) But it also had another characteristic that would prove useful in the years immediately ahead. Because enough of its leaders came from the same social milieu as the Republican gentlemen who dominated the city's business establishment, the grounds were present, regardless of idcological differences, for alliance.

In 1947, however, the businessmen were not yet in any mood for alliance. Cautious and conservative, they viewed Dilworth and his liberal supporters as anathema. Who could guess what crazy ideas they might come up with, what roadblocks they'd put in the way of business (especially with their union allies), if they were

---

*For many years, to be accepted into ADA membership, one had to sign a loyalty oath.

elected? As for the charges of corruption, they remained of little concern to the business leaders. The Republican Party would carry out their interests, and that was all that counted.

The proposals for comprehensive city renewal offered by the Better Philadelphia Exhibition the same year sparked little interest on the part of the business establishment. Edmund Bacon recalls that the attitude was either dismissive or patronizing. For average Philadelphians, however, the exhibition had a marked political impact. They long had had no reason to be proud of their city, and the exhibition roused them from their apathy by speaking to them in specifics of the good city of the future. The exhibition, therefore, without ever mentioning politics, helped prepare the public for the need to have a government committed to bring that future about. Dilworth's allegations of corruption against the incumbent administration, which were being made at the same time as the exhibition, further set the stage. Bacon's model of coherence was coming into place, the idea posited, ready to draw the arrows of energy toward it.

Another arrow took on force from the event that precipitated the downfall of the Republican machine. It was set in motion, also in 1947, when the city's firemen asked for a raise. That seemed an innocuous enough request, and one that gained support since firemen, unlike most other public servants in Philadelphia, were held in high regard by the citizenry. Mayor Samuel, however, was opposed to the firemen's demand, which meant the Band of Brothers was, too. The expressed concern was that if the firemen were granted their increase, other city employees—this was in the days before unionization of municipal workers—would want one, and there allegedly wasn't sufficient money in the treasury for that.

The real worry appears to have been that reformers like Dilworth and the ADAers would seize on the firemen issue to raise questions about the city's hiring practices, which didn't bear even a cursory examination. For decades, salaries of city employees had been kept low in order to create the maximum number of patronage jobs out of the available money pie. The policy had not been adopted out of any sense of thrift, but from the realization that the more patronage employees there were, the greater number of loyal party voters and election-day workers. Undoubtedly, some of these employees put in a full day's labor for a half-day's wages, but many more had other jobs and showed up at their city offices only part of the time or not at all, save to collect their checks. Still others engaged in whatever chiseling schemes struck their fancy, comfortable in the knowledge that the bosses and the law enforcement agencies they controlled would keep their eyes closed to what the party loyalists were doing to supplement their meager incomes. The business leaders must have known that the pay-scale made it nearly impossible to attract significant numbers of competent employees to city government, but that had never seemed a problem to them.

Samuel, recognizing that the voters might not believe his unsupported statement that the treasury lacked sufficient funds to grant raises, announced the appointment of a blue-ribbon commission to look into the matter. Blue-ribbon panels are a hoary but frequently very effective means by which politicians try to defuse an issue that makes them uncomfortable. The Samuel panel was typical in that everyone named to it was of undoubted integrity. Samuel, therefore, could not be charged with attempting a cover-up, and the press, figuring the problem was being taken care of by these public-spirited citizens, would turn to other stories. The blue-ribboners, in fact, were every bit as honest as they were purported to be, but—and here is one reason these schemes work— they were also selected because they were so busy with their own affairs they'd have little time to give to the investigation. Thus, they might take years to reach a finding, which was desirable since, by then, interest in the subject would have waned and few, if any, questions would be raised about how they had reached their conclusion. Samuel had every expectation the findings would be what he was looking for, due to the second criterion for choosing members of a blue-ribbon panel: their lack of political sophistication. Not understanding how government worked, they could be spoon-fed information; they wouldn't know what they weren't receiving or what to ask for next.

Of the fifteen persons who agreed to serve, Samuel made no mistake about fourteen of them. The fifteenth ruined him and the Band of Brothers.

He was Robert K. "Buck" Sawyer. Despite his dashing nickname, Sawyer was a conservative Republican economist employed by the privately funded Bureau of Municipal Research. Proceeding in a seemingly casual way, Sawyer requested one document after another; since they came from a variety of offices, no one in the administration seemed aware of exactly how much information he was compiling. From his findings, he stitched together a pattern of pervasive corruption and embezzlement in the Department of Public Supplies, the Water Bureau, the Fire Marshall's Office, the Department of Public Works, the Police Department, and the Office of Receiver of Taxes, where he unearthed a printed rate card showing the amount each employee was to extract from a citizen for services, legal or not.*

As Sawyer's investigation continued, he (and his increasingly interested compatriots) began to worry that Samuel would get wind of what was being learned and disband the panel before it could finish its work. To make sure he wouldn't dare do that, Sawyer leaked his material to the City Hall bureau chief of the Philadelphia *Bulletin.* In the wake of the headline stories that followed, an official of the Amusement Tax Office committed suicide, leaving behind a note implicating fellow employees in an embezzlement scheme. Three other suicides came in quick order, including that of the chief of the police vice squad, who took his life one step ahead of indictment.

Their eyes pried open by Sawyer, members of the business es-

*The rate card may have been necessary. The auditors in the Tax Office probably would have had difficulty figuring out the math themselves. The employment application of one listed as his previous experience "basketball player" and as position held "forward."

tablishment finally realized that the den of thieves and incompetents in City Hall couldn't possibly be trusted to help bring about the badly needed commercial revitalization of the downtown. The employees would steal every brick they could lay their hands on, and those they didn't steal they'd probably lose. With that grim realization in mind, the businessmen organized their own reform body, which they called the Greater Philadelphia Movement (GPM). Sawyer was named its executive director. The GPM, however, was not geared for political action; the ADA was. In 1949, Clark was elected city controller and Dilworth city treasurer. Clark's office allowed him access to city financial records, and he made the most of the opportunity. By 1951, thirty-six city officials had been charged with graft, as had three Republican ward leaders; the suicide total had reached six. That year Clark, riding a crest of popularity, became the Democratic candidate for mayor; Dilworth was slated for district attorney. Both won in November by roughly a 120,000-vote margin.

As all this was going on, the GPM had not been idle. Its backers had influence in the Republican-controlled state government, and in 1949 succeeded in gaining passage of the First Class Cities Act. It permitted Philadelphia, for the first time in its history, to raise revenue without prior approval by the state legislature. From the business view, the provision was a key one, since it meant that ordinances necessary to bring about business-favored building projects could be passed without delay and without having to worry about possible veto by rural assemblymen, who often opposed anything Philadelphia wanted. Of greater long-range importance was language that would allow Philadelphia to choose its own form of government, which is what the Philadelphia reformers, led by the ADA and the GPM, set out to do.

In the document they produced, we see limned the strengths and weaknesses of political reform movements when their goals, worthy in themselves, are limited to replacing dishonesty with honesty, inefficiency with efficiency, and favoritism with equality of opportunity in government jobs.[4] Under the new Home Rule

Charter, integrity was to be assured by two changes, the second of which would also bring about equity in hiring. The first idea, a novel one, rose from the recognition that every mayor is subject to constant pressure by the chiefs of the agencies of the executive branch. Not only did each of them consider his agenda to be the most important (which meant none were concerned about the city as a whole), but it was also at the agency level that historically most of the corruption had occurred. It seemed, therefore, a good idea to insulate the mayor as much as possible from these streams of influence, both the corrupt and the self-serving. That way, the mayor could make decisions with magisterial objectivity. To bring this goal about, the charter called for the appointment of a managing director who would be a non-political public servant, probably with experience as a city manager.* All agency heads were to report to the managing director, who would evaluate their requests and forward them to the mayor with his recommendations. In short, because the managing director was non-political and hence (theoretically) non-corruptible, his very presence would discourage corrupt and political activities. (Over the years since 1951, managing directors in Philadelphia have ranged from being highly skilled professionals to the mayor's political lackeys.)

The second change was the conventional one of introducing civil service throughout most of city government. The principal exception were city council employees. (The courts were part of the state system, so the city had no authority to change their hiring practices, which had been and have largely remained based on patronage.) For nearly a century before the Philadelphia liberals

---

*City manager was a relatively new profession that was enjoying a vogue of popularity at the time, and the GPM contingent had proposed that such a person become the chief executive of Philadelphia, with the mayor relegated to largely ceremonial duties. The ADA liberals objected; they thought the mayor should be the accountable public official—accountable to the voters, that is, and not the business community, as they feared a city manager would be. The idea of the managing director was developed as a compromise between the two positions.

came along, good-government theorists had been advocating civil service as a means of assuring a better quality of public employee. Because, unlike patronage workers, they would be hired and promoted on merit, they presumably would have an impetus to be faithful, diligent, and (above all) honest.

The Philadelphia liberals, however, had an additional reason for favoring civil service. Hitherto, city government employment had largely been closed to blacks. The few jobs they held, doled out by the all-white Republican leadership, were, with only a handful of exceptions, on the janitorial level. That would no longer be so in the executive branch of government under Clark. Neither did his vigorous leadership in enforcing equal-opportunity hiring stop with city jobs. The example he provided caused the Gas Works, a privately managed public utility, to reverse its biased hiring policy, as did the privately owned Philadelphia Electric Company. Clark and other city leaders like him opened the way, through civil service, for the rise of hundreds of thousands of African-Americans from poverty to the middle class, long before such trans-class migrations became a national goal of Lyndon Johnson's Great Society in the 1960s.

Although machine politicians, for self-interested reasons, had always opposed civil service, not all their arguments against it as a governmental method can be easily dismissed. Clark's reforms of the police department provide a case in point. At the beginning, the establishment of the civil service there brought about positive changes. Officers could now be seen actually patrolling their beats at night, rather than sleeping in the back rooms of stores whose owners paid them to protect their property. Because Clark restored integrity and named as his commissioner a man of known rectitude, the department for the first time was able to attract young men (no women in those days) who saw police work as a means of public service. College-trained officers appeared, and the quality of detection of crimes improved. Beating of suspects, which had been commonplace, became much less frequent. Yet, twenty years later, with all the Clark reforms still in place, the Philadelphia police had become notorious nationally for their brutality, and by the 1980s the level of corruption in the department rivaled, and may have exceeded, that of New York in the days of the Knapp Commission and Serpico.

Civil-service protection in the police department has also proven troublesome in Los Angeles. In 1933, alarmed about corruption at the very top of the department, the city instituted civil-service coverage for the chief as well as officers below him. The protection made it practically impossible to fire an incumbent commissioner, so that he was unaccountable to the public and elected officials, as he wouldn't have been if he'd been a political appointee. (The appointment system was finally readopted in 1992.) Neither, any more than in Philadelphia, did civil service do much to protect the Los Angeles citizens from police brutality. In 1990, more than $11 million was paid out to recompense victims, a figure some cities hadn't then reached in their entire histories. We might wonder which was worse: the patronage-based police department or the one based on civil service.

But perhaps police don't provide a fair basis for judging the merits of civil service. Police officers are open to temptations in dealing with the public that other civil-service employees (or patronage employees, for that matter) are generally not prey to. Nevertheless, the Philadelphia experience with its cops, like New York's and Los Angeles's with theirs, suggests that some forms of misconduct by government workers bear no relationship to the employment rules. Moreover, even if we grant that civil-service workers are more honest than patronage employees (a doubtful proposition), their integrity can be compromised precisely because of the merit system under which they operate. As part of that system, each civil-service worker gets a regular job performance evaluation, which has its useful purposes; however, the threat of a poor evaluation, with its impact on salary and career, can silence an employee who has doubts about departmental policy or who otherwise might report instances of corruption. When that happens, civil service diminishes the quality of citizen services that its very presence is supposed to insure. The great virtue of civil service is that it promotes fairness at the hiring stage, but it guarantees nothing, good or bad, about performance.

What it does seem to have guaranteed, at the federal and local level, is structural rigidity. Unlike with patronage, under civil service, written regulations are invariably installed that have as their purpose to define precisely the scope of duties and the boundaries of permissible conduct by the employee. Theoretically, the approach seems a sound one: When everyone is following the same protocols, government will offer its services uniformly—no more favoritism—and effectively, because the provision of services is not dependent on any individual but upon carrying out the letter of the protocols, which, presumably, anyone can do. However, by insisting on conformity, the system discourages independent judgment—exercising it can lead to a bad evaluation—and rarely permits freedom of action in situations that require an imaginative and humane approach to people's problems. While it is manifestly true that no bureaucracy can operate without rules, unthinking rigidity in their application leads people to feel distanced from their government—they don't see it as responsive to their individual needs—and in the worst cases causes them to view it as foe rather than friend. To the extent that such perceptions are held, government cannot be a unifying force in the society and instead moves that society in the direction of entropy.

As it happened, the authors of Philadelphia's Home Rule Charter introduced a salutary degree of suppleness when they got around to addressing the makeup of the city council. They did not do so intentionally. Their concern, at that point, was solely to assure that the council would have a bipartisan component, which had rarely been the case during the seventy-five years of Republican rule. It would, however, be impossible to assure the desired representation if all seats continued to be chosen on a district basis, since the dominant party was likely to win all those elections. The remedy provided by the charter was to divide the council into ten district and seven at-large members, but with each party nominating only five candidates for the at-large berths. That way, the minority party would always have at least two seats in council. While it was clear that those two would be in no position to pass legislation on their own, they presumably would act as watchdogs on the majority, offering a safeguard against the dreaded corruption.

In the years after 1951, the two Republican at-large members on the now Democratic-dominated council rarely did much barking and were never in a position to learn of corrupt activities, since they were excluded from Democratic Party caucuses and other private meetings, where any wrongdoing that was afoot was likely to take place. The at-large system, therefore, did not succeed in carrying out its purpose other than in the purely cosmetic sense of having two live Republicans on hand for council sessions. Moreover, the charter had not given the seven at-large members any specific functions. There seems to have been an assumption they would concern themselves with city-wide affairs, but that duty was not spelled out, nor were the district representatives restricted to district legislation. Because the at-large members, whether Democrats or Republicans, seemed to have nothing in particular to do, a number of good government experts, over the years since the charter's adoption, have urged a return to all-district elections, on the theory that seventeen (or more) district seats would mean that each member, by having to serve fewer people, would be able to be more responsive to constituent needs.

The experts, however, failed to see something that was quite clear to average citizens. For them, whereas in the past they'd had only their district council member to go to for help, now, thanks to the at-large system, they had seven additional resources. The expanded access could be important. The district council member might be lazy, inept, overwhelmed with work, or so certain of re-election, because the district was a safe one, that he or she didn't need to bother to respond when asked for help. Any at-large member, of course, could also meet that description, but since there were so many of them, the odds of finding one or more willing to assist were excellent. The result was that the people of the city gave the at-large members duties the charter hadn't contemplated. As time went on, the assumption left unspoken in the charter about the role of the at-large members was also often implemented. It seemed simply logical to city-wide organizations to go to an at-large member with their problems. These practical employments of the at-large system tell us how ordinary people can make useful to themselves offices that—regardless of why they were created—give them a broadened access to government. The issue is not how often the access is used but that it is available.

Another aspect of the charter, as originally written, provides a pristine example of good government theorizing. It had to do with its budgetary provisions, with two men in charge of establishing the system. One was Lennox Moak, then considered to be the nation's leading expert on municipal finance, and the author of textbooks on the subject that are still in use. The other was Edmund Bacon. His input was required since he was now the executive director of the planning commission, a post he had accepted in 1949, which meant he headed the agency that was authorized to write the capital improvement budget for each year (that is, the public projects that were to be implemented that year and funded for the next five). Under the charter's terms, the annual operating budget had to be in accord with the capital budget, not the capital budget with it. The proviso was a way of stating, in monetary terms, that a city's present and future were inextricably wound together, forcing politicians, who tend to be concerned with today and not tomorrow, to be futurists, to that extent anyway.

The charter further provided that the planning commission's proposals could not be rejected by the mayor, although a memorandum from the mayor, pointing out disagreements, could be attached to the budget when it was submitted to the council. Such disagreements seemed likely to be rare, however, since the planning commission was now to have nine "commissioners," as they were called, consisting of three of the mayor's cabinet officers and six citizens appointed by the mayor.

The planning mechanism that the charter put into place seemed an entirely admirable one, something of a marvel of democratic structuring, and in many ways it was. At the operational level, the director and staff of the planning commission had considerable independence in developing capital improvements, as they should have, both because they were professionals and because they should not have their proposals (which had a life span beyond that of any four-year administration) unduly subjected to political tampering. At the same time, it was proper that the mayor's commissioners, as representatives of the people, should have an oversight function. In this manner, the staff's expertise was acknowledged, but any high-handed inclinations on its part could be thwarted.

Despite all these excellencies, Bacon (who by now was considerably more sophisticated in political matters than when a young planning director in Flint fourteen years earlier) recognized that the mayor's commissioners had some of the characteristics of one of Barney Samuel's blue-ribbon panels. The three cabinet officers had time-consuming concerns, and the six citizens, no matter how well-intentioned, would also be busy with their affairs. Since Bacon favored public representation in principle, he was willing to live with the commissioners, but he was aware that weak commissioners or those concerned with their own agendas presented a danger. Even more worrisome to him was a provision in the first draft of the budget section of the charter dictating that the executive director of the planning commission must report to the developmental director, who in turn reported to the managing director, who reported to the mayor. In this fashion, layers of bureaucracy were being laid down, at any one of which the commission's proposals could be weakened, misinterpreted, or discarded as they went up the line of command. The same system could make it impossible for the executive director to inform the mayor of any problems the commissioners were creating, possibly out of self-interest. Bacon, therefore, recommended language, which was adopted, giving the planning commission's executive director, unlike the head of any other agency, direct access to the mayor.

The reporting language that Bacon succeeded in dismantling in the case of the planning commission illuminates the underlying danger of the managing director's role as policeman to keep the mayor pure of possibly corruptive influence. A mayor who requires that kind of protection probably shouldn't be in office in the first place, and one who is capable finds him- or herself forced behind a door that is opened only as far as the managing director—who is not an elected official—allows it to be open. The mayor, therefore, is effectively cut off from his or her own executive offices, and the likelihood of corruption becomes greater rather than lesser because of the mayor's lack of firsthand knowledge of the goals and motives of city administrators. (The mayor, as a politician, is much more likely to recognize those motives than is the non-political managing director.) In practice, Philadelphia mayors have recognized the difficulty and have not allowed the managing director to be a gatekeeper; the post has become almost entirely administrative. Nevertheless, the statutory role of the managing director illustrates (as does civil service) how an overriding concern to provide honest government can lead to ineffective government, and possibly to corrupt government, too.

The new charter was approved in the same election in which Clark was elected mayor; when he took office in 1952, he didn't disappoint the expectations of the reformers who had supported him. Not only were the Republican rascals thrown out of office, but the Democratic Party hacks, generally recognized as being as bad or worse than the Republicans, were held at bay by the upright Clark. The governmental changes and the many construction projects Clark put into effect (including a new airport) quickly attracted outside attention. A portion, and probably a sizable portion, of the favorable media coverage Philadelphia was now receiving came from liberal commentators, who saw the city's revival as proof that the policies they favored at the federal level (and which they now saw in danger with the passing of the New Deal) could also work in the cities. And no doubt there was some satisfaction on their part that the corrupt machine that had been replaced was Republican. In any event, the image of the best and brightest—largely gentleman reformers sweeping away corruption and contentment in America's most dreary city—made for an attractive story. So did the timing. The reformers had come into power at the outset of the second half of the twentieth century. The Depression was in the past; World War II was in the past. It was a time for new beginnings.

That had been Bacon's view, too. He had awaited with high hope the coming of the reformers to power, and with apparent good reason. His experience in 1951 in helping write the budgetary provisions of the new charter had served to confirm his belief in the integrity, the ability, and the vision of the new leaders, most of whom he knew. To them, he didn't think it would be necessary to have to explain the importance of developing a coherent physical design for the city's future to match that of the governmental changes that were to be inaugurated. Accordingly, two days after Clark took office, Bacon paid him a visit to lay out his plan for Penn Center as the keystone for a center-city developmental continuum. "This is something I've saved for you as a present," he told Clark. "You can espouse it for your administration and for the city."

To Bacon's stunned dismay, Clark dismissed the idea out of hand. Bacon's immediate reaction was that Clark mistrusted him because he was a holdover from the Samuel administration, but that didn't make sense when he thought about it. Clark knew Bacon was a member of the ADA and a longtime ally of Phillips, who was Clark's closest adviser. It was only as he got to know Clark better that he realized how much of a typical upper-class Philadelphia gentleman Clark was: personally cautious, elitist, and conservative, despite his political liberalism. Such a person would not want to be associated with any project that could be accused of being ostentatious, which, Bacon sensed, was Clark's reaction to Penn Center.

Clark, however, may have also had other motivations. He thought of himself as a statesman and not a politician, but he was politician enough to be wary of promoting any renewal plan that didn't have the approval of the business establishment, which Bacon's didn't. Above all, Clark liked people he thought of as "practical." He was much like John F. Kennedy that way. Visionaries like Bacon and Kennedy's brother-in-law Sargent Shriver are unappealing to that mind-set. To it, the best ideas are those, like civil service, that have been tried before and could be tinkered with to improve them, a pussyfooting approach that is the hallmark of political liberalism. For such individuals, ideas that don't have ideological or experiential credentials (which Bacon's lacked) are to be avoided.

Clark's rejection of Bacon's plan, however, had reverberations that go beyond his personal inclinations. In it, we see described an inherent limitation of political reform movements, which makes it difficult for them to instigate ideas that go beyond conventional thinking. In the case of Clark, he had a mandate to reform the government; he would have been considered a failure if he had not done so. Within the reform context, nevertheless, the changes he brought about were not daring ones. There is nothing daring about wanting to create an honest government (when the citizenry is crying for it), nothing daring about embracing routine public improvements like a new airport, nothing daring about installing civil service in place of patronage. The reformist approach, as well exhibited by Clark, therefore, has the same high regard for "realistic" solutions to urban problems as does the machine approach. The solutions of the reformers may be different from their predecessors, but the mainstreaming effect that is created is the same: An idea that is out of the mainstream is considered a threat to its placid continuance until and if it can make its own way, in which event the reformers (like the machine politicians they oppose) will likely embrace it.

As a consequence of this reaction to his unrealistic idea, Bacon found himself in regard to Penn Center and the new reformers in the exact same position he had been a decade earlier with the planning commission and the old corrupt Republican organization. He was not about to be deterred now, however, any more than he and Phillips had been then.

An important first step had been taken even before Clark's inauguration. At that time, James Symes, the president of the Pennsylvania Railroad, announced that he was going to tear down the Chinese Wall and its terminal across from City Hall. Although the replacement 30th Street Station had rendered the terminal superfluous, the Pennsy had delayed demolition since it had no financial motive to go to that kind of expense. Now there was one. The events of the last several years, culminating in the election of Clark, had convinced Symes that some kind of downtown renewal was about to become a reality, which meant the property occupied by the Chinese Wall and the terminal would become prime real estate. Symes spoke of his decision late in January 1952 in a speech at a luncheon held jointly by Phillips's Citizens Council on City Planning and the Chamber of Commerce. (That the council and the chamber were now cooperating with one another was an indication of the extent to which some of the outsiders of 1942 had become the insiders of 1952.)

After Symes revealed to the assemblage that the razing of the wall was to begin immediately, Bacon took over the podium. In what he remembers as a smoke-filled room with not many of the guests, including Clark, paying attention, he unveiled his Penn Center plan by means of a slide presentation. "Our basic proposal," said Bacon, "is that a great shopping concourse be built, one level below the streets and passing under them, open to the sky with shaded walks adjacent, with gardens, trees, and fountains, penetrating through the center of the entire tract, connecting with the subway concourse and flowing directly into the Suburban Station waiting room under Pennsylvania Boulevard. This is essentially a pedestrian super-block, below the street level where it belongs, because most people are going down to the subways and trains anyway, tying together the great modes of transportation and, through underground connections and shuttle lines, tied directly to the parking complex and the super-highway. A bus terminal on the western end, on Eighteenth, completes the transportation picture, and here we have, truly, an entrance to a city. Along each side of the concourse adjacent to Market Street, and Pennsylvania Boulevard, are proposed two levels of shops, with normal frontage on these streets, and with dual access to the concourse as well. Street level sidewalks are extended along the inner sides of these shops, overlooking the concourse, and a system of stairways and escalators carry the people from one level to another. The shop structures are kept low so as to permit sunlight to flood the concourse, and three tall office towers are proposed extending north-south parallel to the numbered streets straddling the concourse. These great towers overlook the garden court, which provides a fine foreground for them, creating an architectural unity that should be impressive indeed."

One person who was taking notice was a leading figure in the city's real estate business. Immediately after the lunch, this man, in great alarm, left for New York to meet with officials of Equitable Life Assurance, who had been thinking of investing in Philadelphia's renewal, as they had, a few years earlier, in Pittsburgh's. The emissary warned Equitable about Bacon's idea. It was crazy, impractical; it wasted space with malls and greenery. For sound advice, Equitable was told, it should look to solid businessmen, like the realtors.

With opposition to Penn Center mounting, Bacon recalled and decided to apply the lesson he had learned during the campaign to create the City Planning Commission. Since there was no way he could take the Penn Center plans to every nook and cranny of the city—he couldn't use the staff of the planning commission since Penn Center wasn't a commission project—he decided to avail himself of the same approach that had proven successful for the Better Philadelphia Exhibition. This time, instead of to Gimbel's, he went to the city's leading department store, John Wanamaker, and persuaded its executives to give him floor space. There, he installed scale models of Penn Center designed for him by a brilliant young architect named Vincent Kling. Soon enough, Bacon began getting phone calls from business executives wanting to know more about his proposal. Few of them had seen the Kling models, but their wives had when they were shopping at Wanamaker's; the women had been impressed, had told their husbands, and in that indirect but effective way (one that Bacon couldn't have guessed would have happened), the collective consciousness he hoped for was aroused. The arrows had begun to move toward the idea.

Other arrows moved toward the idea for another reason. By the time of the Wanamaker display, the demolition of the Chinese Wall had begun. While it still stood, it had been universally recognized as an eyesore, but it was only after it was gone that its negative impact could be fully appreciated. Because of it, the beautiful parkway, the Art Museum, and Fairmount Park beyond could be glimpsed only from a few angles north of City Hall. With the wall gone, a splendid vista was opened that could be readily perceived as part of the downtown continuity and as amenable, as it hadn't been before, to upgraded usage in the form of hotels, private homes, and apartment and office buildings, all abutting the parkway. Replacing the wall with a big department store flanked by a miscellany of office towers going in every direction, as proposed by the Better Philadelphia Exhibition, would, it was now finally apparent, block again all that had been gained. Bacon's design, to the contrary, if it was adopted, would both reinforce the powerful diagonal of the parkway and create its own line of force, with both lines targeted on the City Hall axis. Moreover, Bacon's generous use of malls and green space and a small plaza facing the parkway (see the illustration on page 2), all of which had been derided as despicably visionary and wasteful of packageable space just a few months earlier, was now obviously congruent to and supportive of the suddenly commercially desirable parkway area.

Although Equitable Life Assurance never did get involved in Penn Center, New York real estate developer Robert Dowling, who had also played a major role in the Pittsburgh renaissance, became interested, and he had the ear of Symes and the Pennsylvania Railroad. When the mighty Dowling endorsed Bacon's idea, the remaining opposition to it melted away. Dowling, however, wanted to make Penn Center very profitable. Three high-rise buildings, he decided, weren't enough; a half dozen would be twice as good. He liked the idea of the underground shops, but felt it was nonsense to open them to the sunlight; they should have a concrete roof over them. He also disapproved—which meant the Pennsylvania Railroad, which owned the property disapproved—of wasting portions of the lower level on shrubbery and flowers. An unadorned passageway would do, permitting more space for retail leasing. Other developers entered the scene, each with his own practical ideas, leading eventually to the dreary appearance of the concourse described in the Prologue. The vision had become "realistic."

Even as the ground-level portion of Penn Center was becoming the focus of the central-city redevelopment in the mid-1950s (with Clark basking in the credit for it), not far away a great deal more construction was going forth, and for that Clark's role was pivotal. The reality of honest government he'd brought, coupled with the widespread belief he engendered in the unlimited possibilities of the city, had created a hospitable atmosphere for downtown residential growth, and not just along the parkway. A few blocks south of Penn Center, the Rittenhouse Square area had managed to remain fashionable through the bad times, but the streets around it were long in decline. Old mansions had been cut up into rooming houses, and the smaller dwellings on the side streets had lapsed into slum conditions. All that changed under Clark's impetus, as individual developers renovated house after house. The young urban professionals of the 1950s, growing numbers of whom worked in the new Penn Center office buildings, moved into the refurbished neighborhood, by the dozens, then the hundreds, then the thousands.

Given the new vibrancy of the city, it is probably correct to say that the residential revitalization of the Clark era would have taken place if Penn Center had not been built. Nevertheless, Penn Center represents a suggestive contribution to the making of the American city of today and of the future. In a narrow but not unimportant sense, it illustrated how it was possible to establish an interconnected, multimeans, non-obtrusive transportation network. It offered room for travel by foot, by subway, by bus and train, all in a single complex. By creating an underground system for delivery of merchandise and other supplies to the stores and office buildings, it showed how to avoid cluttering nearby streets with trucks, a design contribution that was to be replicated on a larger scale subsequently in Market East.

However, the great significance of Penn Center lay in its complete rejection of the prevailing notion, fostered by Modernist architects and planners, that only buildings counted and not their relationship to one another. As described in the Prologue, the lines of connection that were established could be extended, which would not have happened if Penn Center had been conceived of as isolated fragments occupying space. In Bacon's plan can be seen in miniature the philosophy of cellular growth that Oglethorpe created in Savannah for an entire city and that the builders of Beijing, over the centuries, had also understood. Ideas that have power re-evince themselves in many powerful ways over long periods of time.

On a completely pragmatic level, Penn Center and the continuum that eventually spread east and west as well as northward to the parkway from it proved to be vastly profitable for the city. Had it not been for the tax revenue generated by the expansion of the continuum, the municipal financial problems, as they were to develop, would have been a great deal worse than they proved to be.

But they were bad enough, and not just for Philadelphia. The era that was about to descend—sooner in some cities, later in others—would make a reform movement like Philadelphia's appear naive in the optimism it provoked, if not a cruel hoax. By the 1960s, urban observers were already predicting the death of the cities, and even optimists were hardly likely to have disagreed with Jeanne Lowe when she warned in the title of her 1967 book that cities were "in a race with time."

The litany of the prospect of urban desiccation has not ceased either. By the 1990s, American cities were being depicted as commercially hollowed out.[5] Their last fruit was about to be scooped from their gourd, their remaining middle-class populations eager to leave them. They were becoming, in effect, concentration camps for the poor, the criminal, and the drug-addicted. Mumford's good city had been replaced, it seemed, by the city without expectation.

If the obituary writers of the city are ignoring everything that doesn't fit their perspective, they are, nevertheless, able to trace accurately a series of events that, during the second half of the twentieth century, take on a grimly deterministic quality in the telling. Theirs are stories of city politicians, ranging from the corrupt to the most zealous of reformers, who rarely comprehended the nature of the tide of troubles that was overcoming them, or else did understand but were incapable of turning it aside. Theirs also are stories of real estate developers and financiers and planners who wreaked havoc on the cities. Theirs are stories of federal programs that, with the best of intentions, helped destroy the urban infrastructure. Theirs are stories of how decisions were made that were designed to vitalize the national economy and in some ways met that goal, but also had unintended and sickening effects on the cities.

Theirs are, that is, stories of entropy. When we sort them out, we find two major themes that, at points, impinge on one another. One theme largely deals with external events. It has to do with suburbanization and with the accompanying highway building that provided new ways into, but also out of, the cities. That lethal linkage is our concern in Chapter Eight. The second theme, that of the fragmented efforts by the cities to save themselves, is the focus of Chapter Nine.

8

The Lethal Linkage

One day in the late 1950s, Richardson Dilworth, Joseph Sill Clark's successor as mayor of Philadelphia, remarked, "The suburbs are becoming a white noose strangling the cities." While his description was an unusually vivid one, he was hardly alone in his perception. Across the country, other mayors were equally aware that large numbers of their tax-productive white populations were moving beyond their borders. The departures were particularly pronounced in the old northern cities. In Brooklyn, for example, during the 1950s, around 500,000 whites left to be replaced by virtually the same number of African-Americans and Puerto Ricans.[1] Among blacks alone, approximately 5 million would trek northward from the time of World War II until about 1970. Although a major factor, Jim Crow laws were never the sole reason for the black exodus from the South. The large majority of the new arrivals in the cities had been sharecroppers, a form of employment that began to decline rapidly with the introduction of the mechanical cotton-picker in the early 1940s.[2] The former sharecroppers came north, at least in part, because they had no place else to go to earn a living.

As important as racism was in prompting the white flight from the cities following World War II, suburban living had long been attractive to city dwellers for other reasons. Probably no one has better stated the underlying psychological principle than did Frederick Law Olmsted in 1868 in his preliminary report to the developers of Riverside in Illinois: ". . . we should recommend the general adoption . . . of gracefully curved lines, generous spaces, and the absence of sharp corners, the idea being to suggest and imply leisure, contemplativeness and happy tranquility."[3]

Olmsted realized that Riverside, and other suburbs for the well-to-do like it, was selling a dream that, as with any dream, might not bear any relationship to day-to-day reality. Not everyone, after all, who looks forward to the contemplative life has the cast of mind to enjoy it when the opportunity arises; tranquility could be disrupted by family or business problems in the suburb as well as in the city; and the husband who had to journey from suburb to his job in the city and back again might discover he had precious little time available for leisure. What is being sold isn't necessarily what is being bought.

Nevertheless, places like Riverside quickly found buyers for the reason given by Mumford: ". . . the early romantic suburb," he notes, "was a middle class effort to find a private solution for the depression and disorder of the befouled metropolis. . . . The instincts that prompted this exodus were valid: caught in the new urban wreckage of the industrially expanding city, the old cry, 'Women and children first,' was a sound one. Life was actually in danger in this new urban milieu . . . and the merest counsel of prudence was to flee, as Lot and his household had fled from the sultry hell of Sodom and Gomorrah."[4]

Although the suburbs of the second half of the nineteenth century carried out their refuge function, they did not provide a sufficient amount of housing for all those who were attracted (and could have afforded) to live in them. The reason rose from the railroads, which were deeply involved in their creation.* The rail station was the hub of the new suburb, and housing rarely radiated far from it, deliberately so: Suburban advertising of the period typically em-

---

* Sometimes literally so. At places, railroad companies, either acting on their own or in a joint venture with real estate developers, laid tracks on the outskirts of cities with the intent of having suburbs built along the right-of-way, thereby creating a new source of revenue from passengers going to and from the city.

phasized that every home was "within easy walking distance" of the rail line, obviating the necessity and inconvenience of relying on horse and carriage to get to and from the station.[5] Because of the easy walking distance requirement, with few exceptions the new suburbs, therefore, were quite small, which would seem to suggest that they would make up for in quantity what they lacked in size, and by the end of the nineteenth century, in fact, there were a goodly number of them. However, the developers recognized another requirement: Their potential customers wanted a sylvan setting, and to maintain it few suburbs were built much closer than three miles from one another. As a result, the suburbs of the late nineteenth and early twentieth centuries made only relatively modest structural and population incursions upon the natural habitat. Large areas of woods and farms remained undisturbed; neither did the railroads themselves destroy the environment in a significant way. All they required was the width of their tracks and a fraction of an acre for a depot.

The need to restrict housing to the station area was removed by the arrival of the automobile. A car could deliver people to and from the transit line* in a fraction of the time the horse required, and could be readily used, as the horse could not, for the journey to the city. The automobile permitted developers to thrust further outward. They bought up the hitherto undisturbed farms and tore down forests, with the amount of habitat destruction limited only by the continuing recognition that buyers wanted a home surrounded by a plot of land of their own.

As the suburban population grew, so did the number of people who preferred to use their cars for all their traveling. The existent roads between the suburbs and the cities, however, were neither numerous enough nor wide enough to meet the new demand. During the 1920s and 1930s, efforts were made to improve the ex-

---

* It wasn't invariably a railroad. Some suburbs, fairly early on, were served by electric trolley or both railroad and trolley; buses began to become common only in the 1930s.

istent connectors, but the emphasis, by and large, was on building interstate toll roads. (The New Deal's National Resources Planning Board was enthusiastic about the interstates as a means of creating jobs and propping up the Depression-hit cement and asphalt industries.) During that era, New York Parks Commissioner Robert Moses was the planner who first grasped the potential of multilane expressways to serve suburbanites, and no one built them with the fervor he did. In 1936 alone, three parkways were opened on Long Island. Almost immediately, they were awash with traffic, without any apparent relief of the load on the older roads, and no one seemed certain where all the new traffic was coming from. In fact, the parkways were creating their own traffic. Each time a new route was announced, developers got to work building new suburbs or expanding old ones; since many of the developers' customers were already in their new homes before the road was completed, their cars were ready to sluice onto it the day the ribbon was cut. Moreover, since the expressways were promoted as easing travel between city and suburbs—a perception that continued to be believed long after it was proven false—their presence encouraged people to move to the suburbs, creating the need for ever more expressways.

Following World War II, Moses unleashed another spate of highway building. Unlike the parkways of the 1930s, the new routes did not stop upon reaching the borders of New York. Instead, the Cross-Bronx and Van Wyck (Queens) expressways sliced through the city itself. Inevitably, both roads were bumper to bumper in traffic within days of their opening. Still another Moses project, the Long Island Expressway, not only failed to relieve traffic congestion but became the most crowded of all. New tunnels and bridges, too, were engulfed by traffic. When, for instance, the Brooklyn-Battery Tunnel was completed in 1950, it was projected to carry 8.4 million cars in its first year. It passed that figure after seven months. By 1952, the tunnel was facing a traffic load three times its engineered capacity. Vehicles were lined up for blocks outside it.[6]

More was to come. Between 1955 and 1965 alone, the public investment in highways in and around New York came to about $2.7 billion. Because of the size of New York and its metropolitan area, the transportation problems and the attempted solution of them had a colossal quality that was never duplicated elsewhere,[7] although Los Angeles came quite close. Meanwhile, new interstates were being built, too, in many instances making it possible for through traffic to bypass cities entirely. Off-ramps, however, were added to provide connections to the metropolitan areas, in some instances via expressways that had their own ramps to accept and eject suburban traffic along their paths. In these ways, the new roads variously ignored the cities, surrounded them, connected them, slashed through them. They destroyed parts of them, too, beyond the direct path of their routes. The devastated appearance of much of today's South Bronx can be traced to the Cross-Bronx Expressway. To make way for it, thousands of homes and places of business were plowed under by bulldozers, destabilizing whole communities. Gone entirely was the pivotal East Tremont sector, which had been a strong, racially integrated neighborhood.[8] In other cities, proposed connectors had a purely lunatic quality. In New Orleans, the Riverfront Expressway was designed to ram its way right through the historic French Quarter. Only outraged protests from citizens prevented it from being built.[9]

We might wonder how the Riverfront Expressway could reach a stage in which it had official backing. The answer is to be found in the cost/benefit system that had been established as the method to make such decisions. Under its terms, the cost of acquiring land and then constructing the proposed highway was factored; next, an analysis was undertaken to determine the amount of time the road would save for the people expected to drive their cars over it, with a dollar figure applied to time at so much an hour. If the time saved in dollars was greater than cost in dollars, the route was approved. As is apparent, this method did not take into account the possibility that the road might have much heavier use than predicted, so that there would be little or no saving in time for drivers;

neither did it take into account that the route might knock down historic monuments or tourist attractions, as in the case of New Orleans; nor was the method concerned about the desecration of the landscape and the souring of soil caused by the highway, which meant crops could never again grow upon it; nor was it concerned that small communities bypassed by some new glorious interstate or suburban connector would lose business or jobs; nor did it matter that cities presumably serviced by the route would see their land value and tax receipts decline as a result (as would have happened in New Orleans and did happen in New York because of the Cross-Bronx Expressway, as well as in other cities where the expressways destroyed viable neighborhoods and spread slums in their wake). A mathematical mantra had been substituted for thinking.

The highway program was one prong of a federal effort to prevent a recurrence of the Depression. The war had created millions of jobs in the defense industry and removed millions of young men from the employment market by putting them in uniform. With the war over, it was assumed (wrongly, as it turned out), that the defense industries would be cutting back exactly at the time all those discharged servicemen would be looking for work that might not be there. Highway planning and building would offer both white-collar and blue-collar job opportunities.

Of greater importance was the GI Bill of Rights. Its immediate purpose was to deflect a large number of veterans from the job lines by making it easy for them to attend college, where presumably they'd learn skills that would make them attractive to employers after they graduated. The GI Bill also helped carry out a long-range prong of the federal program: the fostering of economic stability through the encouragement of suburbanization. Under the GI provisions, backed by a supportive FHA, down payments of as little as 3 percent were offered for buying a new house, compared to 25 percent for existent housing, and with financing at a modest 3–4 percent. Although these regulations applied to new homes everywhere, cities had little land available for such purposes compared to that which could be found in the countryside. Consequently developers, eager to make sales to this new mortgage-favored market, set about expanding old suburbs with tract housing or building entirely new ones (like the Levittowns). The growth meant a need for shopping facilities, bringing about jobs, both temporary and permanent (in the case of the people hired to work in them once they were completed). By the 1960s and earlier in some places, between the new housing and the shopping malls, so little harvestable suburban land remained that most of the new residential construction was in apartment buildings, causing the suburbs to replicate the high-density housing of the cities that had caused so many people to want to flee from them in the first place.

As was intended, suburbanization had a boom effect on automobile sales. City dwellers rarely required more than one car and, depending on the distance to their jobs and public transportation, might not need any; by contrast, suburban families had to have at least two, one for the breadwinner to use for work and the other for the spouse to get around the suddenly vast suburban landscape, where almost nothing was any longer within easy walking distance.

Suburbanization, therefore, met an important national purpose by helping to establish and them maintain a healthy economy. The number of jobs created in the automobile industry alone made the effort worthwhile. In terms of goals met, few social engineering projects ever undertaken by any government have been more successful.

The success, however, brought with it a series of negative ripple effects. Their inception can be found in the application that was made of federal transportation funds. Congress, influenced by the Big Three automakers and their suppliers, like U. S. Steel, put taxpayer money into the automobile-carrying highways to the virtual exclusion of funding for mass transit. For example, during the decade when Moses was spending nearly $3 billion on his expressways, not a penny went to laying new tracks for New York's public transportation system.[10]* Similarly, the 1956 Interstate Highway Bill, which included funding for urban expressways like Moses's, allocated $27 billion for that purpose, but there was no matching bill for public transit at a time when financially troubled railroads were already cutting back on commuter services and bus companies were eliminating unprofitable routes.[11] Altogether, during the quarter century between 1948 and 1973 when the highway mania was at its height, the federal government spent $317 billion for new roads and just $3 billion for mass transportation.[12]

The Long Island Expressway offers a hint of what might have happened if the federal and local dollars had been more evenly divided. It cost $500 million to build, but could have served the same number of commuters for $20 million and at a real savings in time for them had it become a rail line instead of a highway. Or, if it and other expressways like it had only incorporated wide lanes exclusively for buses, the bus also would have provided a faster means of travel than the automobile, even when the time required by passengers to get to and from their pickup points was included. As it was, the buses used the same lanes as the cars, serving to slow both them and the cars.[13]

It remains questionable, however, whether even heavy subsidies of mass transit in the post-war era would have saved the railroad industry. Its main profit base had never been in passenger lines but in freight transportation. The new interstates and expressways for the first time had made long-distance trucking of freight feasible, and railroad revenues from that source rapidly declined. Coupled with the losses on passenger service, railroad bankruptcies followed, like that of the Penn Central (a desperate amalgamation of the 1960s between the Pennsy and the New York Central). As the private entrepreneurs, one after the other, left the scene, the government had no choice but to move in. Of great

* Classism apparently also was a factor. With the exception of the suburban lines, mass transit was increasingly viewed as a vehicle for poor people, who neither deserved nor required having money spent on their needs.

concern were the commuter rail lines; belatedly, government realized they had to be saved; if they were allowed to cease to run, the specter of gridlock loomed. (The mathematics was simple: Suppose we have a railroad car in which forty passengers are seated; it takes up about the same amount of space as two automobiles driving a normal distance apart, each with two passengers. The rail coach, therefore, accommodates a net of thirty-six commuters who otherwise would have to drive their cars or ride buses on roads that were already clogged.) The ironic result was that all the automobile drivers creeping along the expressways were required to pay taxes to guarantee the continuance of the commuter lines they scorned.

As another consequence of the highway boom, suburbs became, to a significant extent, industrialized. Prior to the days of the interstates and the city-suburban expressways, the cities served as the freight terminals of the nation, which meant that manufacturers built their plants in the cities in order to be close to the rail yards for picking up raw materials and delivering finished products. The arrangement, however, had never been a satisfactory one. In big cities, adjacency could be a very broad concept. Manufacturers' trucks were likely to have to traverse considerable distances between plant and terminal, over narrow and crowded streets. That was time-consuming, and time was money. Perhaps even more important, because of the limited amount of land available in a city and the high cost of it, factory owners had no option but to build their plants vertically, which ordinarily is a much less efficient way of manufacturing a product than when the assembly line is on a single floor. In the suburbs, plants more often could be laid out horizontally because of the relatively greater space availability. Only the distance from the rail depots to the suburbs had prevented factory owners from exercising that option.

The intersecting highways and expressways solved their problem. Because of them, trucks could now drop off material and pick up products at the door. Seemingly overnight, industrial parks began to dot (and at places overwhelm) the suburban landscape. The new plants not only took up space themselves but ate up additional chunks of land for employee parking lots. The final stage of the suburbs had been reached: They were now factory towns.

Had there been a plot to destroy the vitality of cities, it is difficult to imagine one more cunning than the non-conspiratorial sequence of events that did take place. The expressways attacked the cities in two ways. First, their presence made it attractive for people to move to the suburbs while continuing to work in the cities; second, other people who might have remained in the cities moved to the suburbs because that was now where their jobs were. As the suburban industrialization progressed, the old, inefficient city factory buildings became untenanted eyesores, attractive only to vandals. The cities' housing stock suffered, too. The homes that working-class people left behind when they departed the cities either remained deserted or were bought by speculators who produced overcrowding by subdividing them into tenements principally for impoverished African-Americans.

The underfunding of the urban mass transit had furthered the inner-city poverty. Because of it, the municipal bus companies were unable to buy the number of vehicles necessary to establish adequate numbers of criss-cross transfer points, which meant that black inner-city residents, who rarely owned or had access to a car, could find it virtually impossible to get to jobs in the suburbs, or, if they could, only after hours of delay. (Most of the time was lost at the transfer points.) The suburban employers, quite apart from racial motivations when it came to blacks, were generally unwilling to hire anyone from the city who was dependent on public transportation. Their experience had taught them that such individuals were likely to remain only until they found work closer to home or else, discouraged by their long commutes, they would quit even if they didn't have another job. Not only that, the bus service could be unreliable in bad weather as well as being slow at any time, which meant the employers couldn't count on the inner-city workers showing up on schedule; they were also often unavailable for extra hours because they could stay only until the last bus left. The picture was a dismal one: that of large numbers of underskilled people who had entered the workforce but weren't able to get or keep the few jobs in the suburbs for which they might have been hired, and at which, when they were hired, they earned low amounts of money (they arrived late or weren't available for overtime).*

But that wasn't all that was happening to cities. At the very time they needed a larger tax base to provide for new dependent population elements, they also found themselves retaining extra-territorial institutional functions that were suddenly becoming costly to them. (An extra-territorial function is one serving both the indigenous population of a locale and those who live beyond its borders.)

Extra-territoriality has been an important force in making cities into cities. In towns and villages that remained towns and villages, by contrast, provision of services remained primarily for the benefit of the inhabitants, and today's suburbs haven't shifted fundamentally from that purpose. It is true that workers who don't live in the suburb receive services—like police protection—during the hours they are there, as do visitors and out-of-town students. However, the scope and availability of other kinds of services point up the distinction between suburbs and the cities around which they cluster. For instance, a suburb may have state or even federal agency offices, but their purpose is to serve the locals; the state and federal offices in the cities handle not only city activities within their purview but those of the entire region. (A federal court in a big city will hear cases from the city and also its suburban regions, and often from several nearby states.) Medical schools are part of the same picture: because, with few exceptions, they are located in cities, so are the big teaching hospitals that take in patients from

* The same set of circumstances held true for factory work in outlying areas within the city limits. Most of these factories, like the suburban ones, once would have been located within walking distance of inner-city residents.

the region. Religious bodies are also likely to have their principal cathedrals and administrative offices, out of which regional ministries emanate, in the city. Museums, concert halls, and theaters are other institutions that are primarily of the city but that serve visitors and audiences from beyond.

The extra-territorial value of cities was recognized by England when it was colonizing America. The Crown encouraged the establishment of cities like Boston, New York, Philadelphia, and Baltimore because it understood, based on its experience at home, that they were regional stabilizing forces. Drawn together in them were the colony's administrative and legislative offices; the city was the hub for cultural activities and the trade center for the colony. The latter activity was of particular importance to England. The depots created in the cities for the arrival and shipment of goods to and from the interior made them sites where customs could be collected with little waste of time and a high percentage of success. If there were no cities, the Crown's agents would have had to make time-consuming and often dangerous journeys to the hinterlands to visit villages and farms where their coming would be heralded and the locals often able to avoid payment.[14]

The extra-territorial function of cities has meant, since the time of the founding of the nation, that sizable portions of their land is not taxable. Federal buildings were exempt under the Constitution, as were state buildings by an extension of the same doctrine. Churches could not be taxed because of the separation clause of the First Amendment. Hospitals could be taxed, but it was in the interest of cities to exempt them, too, since they were caring for the sick, a burden the city would have to take up if the private hospitals weren't on hand. (Many cities built their own municipal hospitals, but their purpose was to serve indigents whom the private "charity" hospitals couldn't or wouldn't accommodate.) Universities and colleges, as well as private secondary schools, were held free from taxation under the same theory. The amount of exempt land varied from city to city, but today it will typically be between 15 percent and 25 percent (not counting the city's own government buildings), or roughly four to five times that exempted in suburbs or small towns. (In them, most of the exempt property, other than that of the municipality itself, is church-owned.)

Extra-territorial land, therefore, represents a loss of income for the cities and also an outlay of revenue to provide these properties with police and fire protection and other vital services. However, until after the midpoint of the twentieth century, that cost was more than compensated for by the desirable population elements that the exempt institutions attracted: professors, lawyers, doctors, civil servants, clergy. Along with business executives, they made up the solid, home-owning middle class that every city needs to fund itself. At the same time, the support personnel that the institutions hired added to the employment base for the city's working class. Even the students helped, and not only because they spent money in the city while in school; those studying for the professions were likely to continue to live where they were educated because of the opportunities offered there following graduation.

Suburbanization changed all that. Lawyers and doctors might still have their offices in the cities, but increasingly they didn't live there, and many of the professors and civil servants followed them out.

When that happened, the shortfall in tax revenue became meaningful, ranging from $30 million to $200 million annually for a city with a million or more people, depending on size and the assessment rate.* The cost of providing services to the extra-territorial institutions fell increasingly heavily upon city residents, who were, on the average, far less able to pay than were those who had departed. The problem displays itself in its most egregious form in the case of the private universities, which use large amounts of land and require considerable city expenditures on their behalf, but which have such high tuition fees that the city

---

* By the mid-1990s, cities in thirty states had challenged exemptions for some non-profit organizations, with mixed results in the courts.

parents who are paying for the services can rarely afford to send their children to them.

At the same time, in part because of the tax shortfall due to extra-territorial functions, these same parents are offered public schools for their children that are inferior to the suburban schools, which, in turn, are superior in part because relatively few suburban tax dollars need be dedicated to extra-territorial functions, thereby freeing up more money for education. As a consequence, parents find the suburbs to be desirable places to have their children educated; as they move to them, they bring to their new community tax revenue that serves to improve their schools further, just as the schools they left behind in the city further decline because of their absence.

As the power base seemed to shift inexorably from cities to suburbs, the cities took on the aspect of having become satellites to their own moons. The transformation was unfortunate for both sides.

Because the cities were desperately competing with the suburbs for jobs and attractive population bases, the suburbs became viewed by the cities as dangerous opponents. Simultaneously, the suburbanites were seeing the cities as alien places, with alien people who had needs irrelevant to their own. Lost sight of, much too often on both sides, was the underlying fact that the cities and their suburbs made up a metropolis in which the city portion continued to have strengths as a cultural, educational, and medical center, and as habitat for large numbers of potentially productive workers. By the early 1970s, a dawning awareness of the relationship evidenced itself in various proposals to establish regional government. No idea could have been more counterproductive. Minorities in the cities perceived regionalization as a scheme to assure continued white domination—all those white suburban voters electing white officials to govern the city—while suburbanites feared regionalism as a scheme to force them to support the same minorities with their taxes. What was required then and now—and what has too often failed to occur—was for the cities, as the largest entity in the metropolitan area, to take up metropolitan leadership by promoting the virtues not only of the city but of the entire region. Cities, that is, need to recognize (and so do suburbs) the mutual benefit that occurs by attracting business and tourists to the totality and not to fragments of it. If that scenario were to be adopted, extra-territoriality would take on a new and enriching dimension for both cities and suburbs.

That present-day cities have not been much able to exert their old regional leadership, and instead have lost a great deal of it, is not entirely their fault. Their task was made much more difficult for them by the compounding of a prescription that, ironically, was intended to restore their health. This elixir was formulated during the same post–World War II years during which the federal government embarked upon its suburbanization remedy.

The Lethal Prescription

By the 1940s, Dr. C. E. A. Winslow of the American Public Health Association was one of the nation's most articulate and influential advocates of slum clearance. "The sense of inferiority," he wrote, "due to living in a substandard home [and neighborhood] is a far more serious menace to the health of our children than all the unsanitary plumbing in the United States."[1]

That a connection existed between ghetto living and the development of mental health problems had long been recognized. In 1890, Jacob Riis described the relationship with eloquence, and even he was not the first to have done so.* Winslow, however, was on to something else. He was saying that the effect of living in a slum was, by itself, sufficient to cause parents to neglect the physical health of their children and, by implication, their own as well. No doubt, Winslow was correct about the neglect, but he is not helpful in ascribing the causation to a "sense of inferiority." Poor people may very well believe they are considered inferior by the more well-to-do, but that doesn't mean they hold that view of themselves. Much more likely to bring about the neglect of health that Winslow described is the sense of futurelessness that multi-

---

*By Riis's time, too, medical science had established that the spread of communicable diseases was directly related to unsanitary conditions that spread epidemics from a city's slums to the rest of the community. In Boston and its suburbs, as just one example, raw sewage had been dumped by contractors into the Charles, Mystic, and Neoponset Rivers, leading in 1889 to the establishment of a Metropolitan Sewage Commission that made disposal a state responsibility.[2]

generational living in inferior conditions instills upon its victims. As such people see life, it is not going to get any better no matter what they do, so that the only rational decision on their part is to concentrate solely on today, not on a tomorrow that may never come or, if it does, will be exactly like yesterday. Immediate gratifications, therefore, not long-range considerations, have a consistent value among people who live in slums that generally isn't to be found among those who have expectations. This is why a welfare mother, on the day the check arrives, will buy junk food, clothing, and toys for her children or take them to a movie, even when she knows that, by so doing, she will not have sufficient money for the rest of the month. With this as the psychological provenance, it is not surprising that concern for one's own long-range health and that of one's children has a low priority. On a more pragmatic level, poor people can also be faced with great difficulty in getting to health care. To reach a clinic, the poor person may have to travel across dangerous territory occupied by juvenile gangs and other predators; young mothers and the elderly are particularly unlikely to be willing to run that gamut until the need for a doctor is critical, by which time the health damage may have been done.

Nevertheless, even though Winslow didn't understand the ramifications of what he was seeing, his understanding that poverty can cause illness—even when the plumbing works—was a valuable one, and it received widespread attention, largely because it bore the imprimatur of the Public Health Association. The obvious next step, to provide health care and to educate the poor about the importance of regular checkups, might not have worked, but it also wasn't attempted in any meaningful manner. Instead, the alternative solution of getting rid of the housing that was causing the illness was adopted by the Public Health Association Committee on the Hygiene of Housing.[3] It produced a handbook entitled *An Appraisal Method for Measuring the Quality of Housing*, in which the committee advocated a technique that became known as Twitchellizing, after Alan Twitchell, its leading proponent. Soon enough, cities across the country set about

Twitchellizing their housing stock. Under the formula, each house on a block got a dwelling score and the block itself an environmental one. House scores included such factors as "deterioration, safety and sanitation . . . [and] degree of room crowding," while the "criteria for poor environmental quality includes land crowding . . . linear incidence of non-residential land use, hazards or nuisances from industry, railroads, street traffic, absence of water or sewer installations in the block, and inadequate basic community facilities such as parks and schools. . . ." The two scores were then added together; if the total was between 150 and 199, the block was considered "sub-standard" [sic], and if over 200, it was "unfit for human habitation."[4]

Since "bad" blocks tended to be in the oldest and poorest neighborhoods, the resulting Twitchell maps showed clustering of "sub-standard" and "unfit" blocks, so that the substandard blocks were inevitably on their way to unfit status and there might be little point in attempting to rehabilitate them. The Twitchell scores were submitted to federal housing agencies, whose bureaucrats used them to determine allocation of funds to local redevelopment authorities for them to acquire the land, clear it of its structures, and presumably eventually build new housing on it.

The great attraction of Twitchellization was its alleged scientific nature. As one city report remarked: "It is widely recognized as a technique which will yield objective and comparable results in any urban community. . . ." This was good because "both environmental and dwelling appraisals are based on measurable facts" and not on individual judgments, which were not to be trusted because they were subjective.[5]

In Twitchellization, therefore, we see thinking analogous to the cost/benefit analyses for highway building that became popular around the same time and for the same "scientific" reason: In both, land was considered to be a blank piece of paper, devoid of human associations and sentiments.

In the case of Twitchellization, the exclusive focus on generating statistically defensible numbers meant that the thinking and the feelings of the people who lived on the bad blocks were to be ignored. As a result, no notice was taken of the significance of "good" houses on "bad" blocks, which strongly indicated the presence of individuals who possessed communal leadership qualities that, if they were nurtured, could turn a "bad" block around. Instead, the homes of these people were to be razed along with everyone else's. Apparently, it also never occurred to the local officials (who saw Twitchellization as a way to get a lot of federal money) that the people they dispersed would remain as poor as they had been, and that their mental health was likely to worsen because, through their removal, they would lose friendships and other community connections. In this fashion, Dr. Winslow's humanitarian goal for them was thwarted by the psychological chaos that the application of his concern produced.

Twitchellization did have its contemporary critics. Among them was Edmund Bacon, who in 1949 wrote: ". . . we should approach the problems of planning for redevelopment, not in terms of individual [block clearance] projects, but in terms of whole neighborhood structure, its people and its institutions."[6] Assessments such as his were widely dismissed, and not only due to their despised subjectivity. They also presented an unwanted challenge to the dominant theme of Twitchellization, that all poor people and their conditions were fundamentally alike. If thinkers like Bacon were correct, the poverty situation was far more complex than the majority wanted to believe.

The same year that Bacon raised his objections, Congress passed a new housing act, the first since 1937. The need for one seemed clear. Studies were by then suggesting that housing in America was in worse shape than it had been at the time of the Depression. The 1950 census figures confirmed the studies: They delineated 5 million dwellings (most in big cities) as beyond salvaging, with an additional 15 million homes requiring major repairs and still another 20 million showing signs of deterioration that could cause them to become substandard, too.[7] Although Twitchell's finer calibrations were to be discarded, the Twitchellized city maps provided the first blueprint for slum clearance under the 1949 Housing Act.

Renovating slums, however, was only one aspect of the new law. It was also designed to provide the means for redevelopment of an entire city. In order to help bring that goal about, Title One of the act granted municipalities the right to take any property under eminent-domain proceedings, slum or not, as long as it had been in the past or (supposedly) would be in the future predominantly residential in character.*[8] "Here," as Robert Caro remarked in *The Power Broker*, "was power [given to cities] new in the annals of democracy."[10]

For redevelopment to succeed, the private sector, it was recognized, would have to be encouraged. An early Title One program in New York near Washington Square illustrates how the system was intended to work.[11] It called for the removal of a largely blighted industrial and commercial sector, which was to be replaced by new businesses and apartment houses. Prior to Title One, a developer would have had to draw up plans and obtain funding at considerable personal cost. Under Title One, those expenses were paid for by a federal loan to the city, contingent upon approval by the appropriate federal agency. In the case of the Washington Square development, once the authorization was obtained, the City of New York bought the earmarked properties for $41 million and sold the land to the developers for $20 million. (Two-thirds of the difference was borne by the federal government and the remainder by the city.) Everyone was expected to be a winner under the system. The owners of the condemned proper-

---

*A characteristic that, as it turned out, could be very loosely interpreted. As one example, New York's Lincoln Center for the Performing Arts qualified for Title One funding on the grounds that apartment houses were to be built adjacent to it.[9]

ties would win because they'd get more for them under city-taking than they could have on the open market. The developers saved outset costs; by paying for land at less than half its value, they could hardly lose, either. Neither could the city. Once the project was completed, it would bring new business and some residents to the area, thereby increasing the city's tax rateables (income based on tax rates) and its general prosperity, which meant the federal and local investment would be paid back many times over.

During the years that followed the enactment of the 1949 act, a number of Title One programs, like the Washington Square area redevelopment, fulfilled the law's goals or, at the least, did no harm. Nevertheless, the billions of dollars in federal money that the act made available encouraged greed and promoted sweeping alterations. As Bacon observed in 1972, all too often ". . . valuable sections of cities representing significant periods of development and sensitive and beautiful texturing of the city's surface were swept away, making a tear in the city's fabric, and a gap in the evidence of the flow of history. Historically valuable buildings, such as the very great Metropolitan Building in Minneapolis, were destroyed in the name of improvement, the continuity of Larimer Street in Denver, even the feeling of association within a place was obliterated, as expressed by a bellboy in Boston—'They have taken away Scollay Square.' And these are only a few of a very much larger catalogue."[12]

As all this was going on, the cities (as most wanted to do, but also acting under the mandate of the housing act) were engaged in slum clearance. Their duties were not limited, as before, to tearing down old houses and replacing them with new. Rather, the authors of the 1949 act had finally recognized that poverty-level tenants and home-owners evicted for redevelopment purposes would rarely be able to afford to live in the replacement housing, and even those who could had to live somewhere during the interim while the construction was going on. Until then, no one had much seemed to care where. Title One sought to solve the needs of the evicted by requiring that municipalities take on the responsibility of resettling them in "decent, safe, and sanitary housing within their means." The relocation of these people and the cost of moving them could also be carried out by the project developer, under city supervision.[13]

In some cities, the relocation protocols were carried out effectively and honorably, but horror stories soon abounded. One of the most publicized and thoroughly documented involved Manhattantown, on New York's Upper West Side.[14] Begun in the early 1950s, the Manhattantown plan called for the demolition of six blocks of tenements and replacement of them by apartment houses, apparently intended for middle-class occupants. The existent tenants were served eviction notices and told to report to the on-site relocation office. Once they arrived, they received no counseling, no list of vacancies, no information on finding an apartment, despite the fact that the developers had been given a $1 million credit off the $4.5 million sale price, in return for which they guaranteed to level the property and take care of the moving costs. Frustrated tenants who turned to the city's Bureau of Real Estate, which was supposed to make sure the developer carried out the relocation, rarely received help from that quarter either. In the end, more than four of every five tenants received no assistance from any source, nor were their moving expenses paid.[15] Meanwhile, the City of New York, under the direction of Moses, by then chairman of the Mayor's Committee on Slum Clearance, was publishing statistics that untruthfully stated that the vast majority of tenants dispossessed by projects like Manhattantown were being accommodated by public housing.[16]

Whether or not Moses personally ordered the cooking of the statistics isn't clear, but he was informed enough to know that they had to be false, and he showed no compunction about using them. His rationale seems to have been that city planning was a form of political combat in which any tool, including lying, was appropriate as long as it helped carry out his purpose, which was to dictate single-handedly the physical development of the city.

Independently wealthy, Robert Moses had begun his career in the 1920s by making himself useful to powerful state politicians. From them, he sought and received appointments to various planning posts. At one point, he held eight offices simultaneously, ranging from New York State Parks Commissioner—the only job for which he accepted a salary—to directorships of the toll-collecting bridges in New York City.[17] In aggregate, the positions he held gave him virtual unilateral control over how millions, sometimes hundreds of millions, of dollars were spent annually. For that reason, contractors and developers, like those behind the Manhattantown project, sought to gain his favor, and politicians feared to cross his path lest job-producing projects in their districts not get built because of his wrath. From the mid-1930s until the end of his career, which stretched into the 1970s, he had opponents, but few challenged his authority successfully, and many were bruised or destroyed, as Rexford Tugwell was, as a result of the fight. Moses was helped by widespread public admiration of him, prompted by the media, which rarely challenged his assessment of himself as a dedicated and selfless public servant whose only goal was to make his city a better place to live. His power, however, from the early days onward, ultimately was based not on image but on his control of how money was to be spent.

By contrast, planners like Bacon have as their only coin the power of their ideas, which means their proposals are tested and sometimes reformulated in a democratic process as they seek to gain support for them. Such planners challenge with ideas and are challenged in return by the response to them. Moses, the autocrat as planner, had no cause to constantly challenge himself, as Bacon did. As a result, his ideas became sterile. They were carried out repetitiously—one overcrowded highway much like the other, one disastrous slum clearance like its predecessors—with little or no questioning on his part (or allowed by others) of what the experience of each could teach. Because he didn't listen to people, because he didn't have to listen to them, human consequences became of scant consideration to him, and apparently were of no importance at all if the humans were black.

Moses's deeply ingrained racism first publicly manifested itself in the 1930s. By then, he had already built for New York State a number of parks. He had assured they would be havens for middle-class (that is, white) people by banning use of public transportation as a means of reaching them. He followed that same policy in New York City, using WPA dollars to build parks that were on the affluent outskirts of the city where the poor could not get at them.[18] (Ironically, one of them was named for the slum reformer Jacob Riis.) Moses claimed that financial strictures forbade the building of parks in Harlem. To be viable, he said, such an enclave had to have at least three acres, or 130,680 square feet, which, at the going price of $30 per square foot, would have brought the cost to $4 million for acquisition alone. His premise, as his critics pointed out, was nonsensical. Vest-pocket parks, the size of a single building lot or even smaller, could readily and economically be built, planted with trees and grass, and provided with benches.[19] If Harlem continued to be neglected, the result, Moses's opponents said, would be havoc in the future. Moses won, and the opponents were proven right.

What Moses didn't understand, or did understand but didn't care about, was that whenever government provides amenities to the affluent portion of its population as he did and not to its poor in some equitable fashion, a powerful message is sent to those who are neglected that the government holds them to be of low value. On the contrary, if the poor are provided with something they don't need in the bread-and-butter sense, like a park, the signal is one that encourages a sense in them that they are viewed as worthwhile. When poor people feel valued by their government, they may still lash out at the conditions in which they live, but their rancor is more likely to be containable both by themselves and the agents of government. A park is by no means the only way in which value messages can be transmitted. We will return to that subject in Chapters Eleven and Twelve, but here is one example: When police departments don't consider inner cities as hostile territory to be conquered, but rather establish in each district a community outreach program, the interchanges that necessarily result eventually have the same containing effect. They do nothing to solve poverty, but they make violent resolutions to a situation much less likely, on both sides.

Moses's failure to build parks in Harlem, however, cannot be considered a positive breach of duty on his part. His blatant and illegal disregard of the needs of the people dislodged by projects like Manhattantown was. That kind of breach is noticed by its victims, as the absence of a park might not be, and remembered by them and by their children. The black street protests that became prevalent in New York during the decade following the Manhattantown "relocations" were fueled in part by a perception of a callous and bigoted city government, of which Moses was the perfect representative. Few figures in the history of cities have been more influential progenitors of chaos than Robert Moses was.

We don't know the extent to which New York disobeyed the federal relocation law; however, we do know that Moses's vaunted "vast" majority who were allegedly transferred to public housing refers only to those whose movements could be traced. Other city figures, which seem more accurate than those put out by Moses, indicate there was no record whatsoever of as many as a third of those forced out of their homes, and that estimate (based on what happened in other cities) may well be on the low side. It seems likely that many of the enforced wanderers eventually arrived in Harlem, to conditions worse than those they had endured in the tenements that had been condemned. Others, possibly a larger number, didn't go so far. In the case of Manhattantown, prior to its authorization as a Title One project, streets surrounding the site were occupied by four-story brownstones that typically accommodated one family to a floor. Within months after Manhattantown got under way, two and sometimes three dispossessed families were illegally being rented space on each floor.[20] Crowded as they were into rapidly decaying buildings—eight to twelve families using facilities intended for four was alone enough to guarantee that result—the new brownstone residents even so could consider themselves lucky. During the first two years of snail-paced demolition, tenants remained in 280 of the 338 buildings that had made up the complex.[21] They had been served eviction notices as required by law, but the owners wanted to move as few tenants out as possible, in order to continue getting income from them. As one building was torn down, the tenants who hadn't yet found other quarters would be moved to another building with each move at an increased rent.[22]

The checkerboarding was, of course, entirely against the law, but, because the developers were wired to Moses and other New York politicians, they were able to proceed with impunity.[23] The living conditions afforded were dreadful. "[Of the tenements] still standing," said a report of the Women's City Club, "broken windows [were] gaping sightlessly at the sky, basement doors yawning uncovered on the sidewalk; and surrounding them were acres strewn with brick and mortar and rubble where wreckers and bulldozers have been at work."[24] Inside, Caro noted, were "unlit flights of stairs that had steps missing." For the tenants, it was pointless to complain; no repairs were about to be done to buildings scheduled for demolishment. They had no heat, no hot water.[25]

Judging by the slowness at which the work progressed, it seems evident that the developers had no intention of completing the project in the "reasonable time" that Title One called for, since the longer they delayed, the more money they made from their captive population. The same motivation would explain why they made no effort to find "decent, safe and sanitary" housing for the residents elsewhere: To do so would take money out of their own pockets. After two years, not a single brick had been laid for a new building.[26]

The Manhattantown developers had invested $1.1 million,

most of it borrowed, for land valued at $15 million;[27] from the rents they collected and the fees they paid themselves for services they didn't provide, they allegedly skimmed off more than $300,000 in profits. (That's in 1952 dollars.) They also didn't pay taxes, with the arrearages eventually reaching $600,000. Ultimately the developers were themselves evicted, but instead of indictments, they were handed golden parachutes in a buyout of more than $500,000 and "consultant" fees in excess of $300,000.[28] (The project was finally built under the name of West Park.)

The Manhattantown scandal reached the attention of Congress and became part of the background of evidence that inspired the Housing Act of 1954.*[29] Although the Title One provision remained in effect, the new law broke sharply with the philosophy of the 1949 and 1937 laws by emphasizing rehabilitation of existent housing and neighborhoods. To encourage such efforts, loans by banks to low-income sectors were to be guaranteed by the federal government. The 1954 Act also took cognizance of the bad judgment, the helter-skelter construction, and the inhumane treatment of the poor that had become the hallmarks of redevelopment, and sought to stem these ill effects by requiring that each city develop a "workable" program before it got any money. The criteria that had to be met to make a program eligible included a specific system for relocating dispossessed tenants, a code to assure minimal standards for all housing, and citizen participation in the renewal effort. It all sounded quite good, but there were problems. The workable program regulations were easy to get around, as New York Mayor Robert Wagner showed when, as part of his city's effort, he listed dozens of groups as "interested" in his renewal plans, but didn't mention that every one of them was in opposition.[31] But probably the worst obstructions occurred at the federal level. The new rules were complex even by bureaucratic standards, which helped make the projected programs extremely

---

*A committee appointed by President Eisenhower declared that cities had a need for "urban renewal," apparently the first usage of that term.[30]

expensive to administer and implement. The result was that by the mid-1960s, although more than 800 cities had "workable" renewal programs underway, few were ever completed.[32]

Of the projects that did get started, 56 percent of the total value of the new construction (by the early 1960s) was in private homes. Just 6 percent of the money went to publicly subsidized housing, the remainder to commercial and governmental building, with much of that amount devoted to rehabilitation of downtown business districts.[33]

Despite the theoretically improved regulations, the problems of the dispossessed tenants remained severe. In a continuation of the old theme, more than 90 percent of the replacement apartment housing went at rentals the former tenants could not afford. By 1965, the situations faced by evicted families may even have worsened. The sociologist Herbert J. Gans summarized what most often occurred: "Local renewal agencies were supposed to relocate the dispossessed tenants in 'standard' housing within their means before demolition began, but such vacant housing [was] scarce in most cities, and altogether unavailable in some. And since the agencies were under strong pressure to clear the land and get renewal projects going [a lesson learned from Manhattantown and similar debacles], the relocation of the tenants was impatiently, if not ruthlessly, handled. . . . [A] 1961 study of renewal projects in 41 cities showed that 60% of the dispossessed tenants were merely relocated in other slums; and in big cities the proportion [could go] over 70%."[34]

The truth was even worse. The study to which Gans refers seriously understated the failure rate. To begin with, it did not take into account the "disappeared" tenants who had left and found places on their own before or after they were evicted. Considering their financial means, almost all of them, like the Manhattantown migrants, would have ended up in conditions at least as bad and probably worse than those they left behind them. The study also made the questionable assumption that all public housing (the most likely destination for evictees under city relocation programs) was "standard" and not slum itself. But, even assuming that public housing was always superior to the houses that had been condemned, the families sent there might not be able to stay. As soon as their incomes rose above the rent ceiling imposed by the local authority, they'd be evicted,[35] and (since their income was "high" only in a public housing sense) they would have no choice but to move back into the slums. Further tending to make the relocation statistics look better than they were was the carrying out of the Twitchell proposition that all dwellings in a "bad" area must be razed. As an example, when Boston's largely Italian West End was torn down because it was declared a slum, 41 percent of its residents, even so, lived in standard housing, and presumably could afford to move to other standard housing; yet they and families like them elsewhere would appear in the government studies as part of the 30 percent to 40 percent of "slum" families that had been relocated successfully.[36] (The only reason the West End was condemned was to make way for luxury housing, a not-uncommon occurrence under Title One.)

Very little money, in any event, was spent to relocate anyone: just half of 1 percent of all urban renewal funds available between 1949 and 1964.[37] Almost exactly two-thirds of those dislodged were African-Americans, and nearly 100 percent of them ended up in other slums or in public housing. Urbanologist Charles Abrams's aphorism "Urban renewal is Negro removal" became widely quoted.[38]

Urban renewal could also be used to enforce segregation where it hadn't existed before.[39] Although integrated housing had always been rare in the United States, it had existed in substandard neighborhoods, principally in southern cities. Few, if any, of these communities remained after renewal had its way. They were either gone entirely, replaced by commercial or governmental buildings, or else the homes built on the old sites were so expensive that they practically assured a new all-white ownership.

Perhaps the most destructive consequence that urban renewal

had upon the cities, however, was the population pop-outs that, in the 1950s and 1960s, occurred on a large scale. The pop-out phenomenon has most frequently been described in terms of whites heading for the suburbs in flight from blacks, indicating a purely racist motivation that, as we saw in Chapter Eight, wasn't always present. Neither were the pop-outs invariably a matter of whites fleeing blacks; blacks fled blacks, too.

To illustrate the process in its simplest form, assume an inner-city neighborhood in which Blocks A, B, and C adjoin one another. The deterioration is at its worst in Block A, where almost all the houses are unfit for human habitation by Twitchell standards. Their tenants are the poorest of the black poor, have little education, and are mired in functionlessness. Heroin addiction, introduced to the inner cities by the Mafia,[40] is prevalent, and so is crime. The Block B people are nearly as poor as those on Block A, their housing conditions almost as bad and the drug culture nearly as prevalent, but they recognize they are marginally better off than they would be if they lived on Block A. It is only when we get to Block C that we find any properties that are owned by the inhabitants. Although they are still quite poor and have meager job skills, fewer of them are on welfare; the Block C people are more likely to be victims of crime than perpetrators of it.

Deeming Block A to be beyond repair, the city decides to raze it. Immediately, the Manhattantown effect sets in. The Block A tenants, because they are so poor, have very narrow transportation corridors, and so most of them move no farther than to Block B. The Block B landlords subdivide their properties to get rentals from the newcomers. Seeing what is happening and not wanting to be neighbors with the Block A people, the Block B people head for Block C. The Block C people see the Block B people as being just as undesirable as the Block B people did those from Block A, and so they move out, too.

At this point, we have to add three more blocks to our picture, Blocks D, E, and F. The Block C people move to D, which is also black but lower middle class, with a much higher percentage of home ownership. The C people aren't welcomed by the D people, who worry they are the advance guard for the even more undesirable A and B people. So the Block D people move to E, which is white working class and where they aren't welcome. The whites of E move to F, which is also white but a step up economically and where they are considered trash, causing the F whites to head to affordable suburbs. Eventually, the blacks who started on Block D may also move to the suburbs to avoid lower-class blacks and whites; once they get there, the in-place whites may again flee from them. As an end result, the pop-outs have caused the city to lose substantial portions not only of its stable white population but of its stable black population, too.

While the pop-outs often generally followed this scenario, there were variations. Uncertainty alone was the instigator in many cities around the country. People of a neighborhood would see the wreckers arrive and set about tearing down a nearby block; immediately rumors would spread that their street was next. The city might deny such intent and often did, but in the past it had lied about its demolition plans (or seemed to because it hadn't yet decided what they were), and so there was no reason for the residents to think they weren't threatened. Their concerns were likely to be fed by land speculators who used or created the rumors as scare tactics to allow them to buy up properties at panic prices. The newly deserted houses would be boarded up as the speculators waited for the market to hit bottom; alternatively, they hoped the depopulation of the neighborhood would mean that their land would be condemned and they'd make a profit by selling it to the city under eminent domain. However, if the city, for one reason or another, never did tear down a certain block, the boarded-up houses on it continued to remain in place for years, spreading blight as the remaining folks got out and their former homes were boarded up as well.

As part of this degenerative process, bankers red-lined entire sectors of the inner cities as unacceptably high-risk, even though many individual streets contained housing that was up to standard. The red-lining made it nearly impossible for prospective home buyers to obtain mortgages in the quarantined zones, and neither could existent home-owners or local retailers obtain loans to refurbish their properties. In this way, red-lining (which continues in many cities) far worsened the conditions that had been in existence before it was imposed. Little was done about it, however. Because the bankers were often major political contributors or sources to whom the mayor went to finance municipal projects, they were rarely called to task for the havoc they were creating (on top of the havoc that the mayor's urban renewal program was causing).

As we look back over the period that roughly began with the Housing Act of 1949 and culminated with Lyndon Johnson's War on Poverty, a rather consistent pattern emerges. We see the federal government making large amounts of money available to cities, which, time and again, causes their leaders to think in terms of large-scale projects upon which politically influential developers can make large amounts of money and which will make large numbers of jobs available to construction workers, thereby satisfying the union orbiters. In such a milieu, populated by such games-players, thinking small is out of favor, even when small-scale thinking might produce the greatest long-range benefit.

Scattered-site housing provides an example of this thesis. It literally scatters subsidized housing for low-income families so that they aren't segregated in the worst neighborhoods. In this approach, an existent community isn't threatened by a mass arrival of poverty families, and the appearance of the community is improved because the subsidized houses, which had been in a state of decay, are rehabilitated before the new tenants move in. By its nature, therefore, the scattered-site approach was supportive of individual needs and community values. However, by its nature, too, it would not generate the kind of profits as macro-renewal did and hence was unpopular with developers, which explains why when planners like Bacon proposed scattered-site housing in the 1950s, it was almost invariably rejected.

A paradox suggests itself: When cities don't have enough money available to them, their housing stock will deteriorate for that reason, but when they have too much money available too quickly, in their eagerness to spend it (and enrich their influential orbiters), the leaders make decisions that worsen housing conditions for great numbers of their people and enter upon construction binges that (as Bacon observed in his 1972 article) destroy sites of historical and aesthetic value.

The capacity that cities showed to create chaos in their slums during the urban renewal years and thereby (due to the resultant population pop-outs) to broaden the harm they were causing, further exhibited itself in the transformations that took place in public housing.

For close to the first twenty years of its history, public housing principally consisted of one- and two-story garden apartments that might or might not be interspersed around low-rise tenements. But by the 1950s a new and lethal convergence of circumstances was at work. The arrival of poverty-level blacks from the South to the northern cities continued at flood proportions, people who, like their predecessors, required low-rent shelter. However, the concomitantly occurring slum clearance had made less housing available than ever before at rates these families and individuals could afford. This was why, as Gans reported, cities were having trouble finding even indecent, unsanitary, and unsafe housing for their black poor. To meet the crisis, the only feasible solution was to build more public housing.

There was never any question where it would be placed. It would be in black neighborhoods and preferably in the heart of them, because city officials believed that a public housing project that had even an adjacency to a white neighborhood could prompt rioting by the whites and assure further white pop-outs to the suburbs. The decision-making, rather, centered on which inner-city location would be chosen and on the architectural form the new construction would take. The many desolate patches of cleared land suggested ample room, in most cities, for more housing of the garden-apartment variety. However, the expectation of the cities had always been that this land would be upgraded by commercial or (less often) residential development. As we have seen, those goals were sometimes met, but the private sector, as a whole, remained leery of investing in the inner cities despite the cheapness of the land and the possibility of subsidies. To them, it made more sense to buy elsewhere in the cities or in the suburbs, where the acquisition costs were greater but the likelihood of making a profit was also markedly greater. As a result, much of the cleared land remained cleared, which is why so many playgrounds and schools were eventually built on it: There was nothing else to do with the space. Even so, hope springs eternal, and cities were reluctant to dedicate significant portions of the razed sectors to public housing, since its presence would further discourage investors. Timing was a factor, too. When a sector was condemned, there was an immediate need to house its population elsewhere. With these considerations in mind, garden-type apartments, it seemed clear, took up too much of the space available. The answer was to build upward, not outward.

Practicality was not the only reason the high-rises seemed a good idea. A major push for building them came from the liberal orbiters.[41] They were horrified by the ghastly conditions of life in the ghettos, and humane considerations, if nothing else, demanded that these victims of society should be transferred to modern, comparatively roomy quarters, well above the dangerous streets. High-rises also fit within the liberal planning orthodoxy that had been inspired by Le Corbusier's "radiant city" of lofty apartment buildings set off by green plazas. Here, it seemed, was an opportunity to turn the "radiant city" into a reality, not for the benefit of the rich but for the poor; nothing could have been more appealing to the liberal mind.

The high-rise solution was welcomed in city after city. In 1957, for instance, Chicago's public housing authority opened the Henry Horner Homes, which consisted of seven buildings of seven floors each and two of fifteen. The following year, the next project opened, on an even larger scale. It had two buildings of ten stories and six of seventeen. In 1962 came the largest public housing project in the world, the Robert Taylor Homes, which had twenty-eight identical sixteen-story buildings capable of housing 40,000 people, the population of a small city.[42] The Pruitt-Igoe Homes in St. Louis were similar, and in New York, high-rises went up by the dozen, averaging fourteen floors each.

The high-rises turned out to be one of the worst housing disasters in American history. Within less than a decade from the time the first one went up, it was apparent they were inveterate breeding grounds for crime and vandalism. An early report came from Harrison Salisbury of the *New York Times*; in 1958, newly returned from an assignment in the Soviet Union, he wrote of the $20 million Fort Greene project in Brooklyn, which (prior to the Taylor Homes) was the nation's largest, with 17,000 residents: "I saw shoddy housing in Moscow [with] elevators that don't work and plumbing that stinks," Salisbury wrote, "[b]ut until I visited Fort Greene, I had never imagined that I could find the equivalent of Moscow's newly built slums in the United States. But I have made that unfortunate discovery at Fort Greene and other places. The same shoddy shiftlessness, the broken windows, the missing lightbulbs, the plaster cracking from the walls, the pilfered hardware, the cold, drafty corridors, the doors on sagging hinges, the acid smell of sweat and cabbage, the ragged children, the plaintive women, the playgrounds that are seas of muddy clay, the bruised and battered trees, the ragged clumps of grass, the planned absence of art, beauty or taste, the gigantic masses of brick, of concrete, of asphalt, the inhuman genius with which our know-how has been permitted to create human cesspools worse than those of yesterday.... Fort Greene and projects like it [also] spawn teenage gangs. They incubate crime. They are fiendishly contrived institutions for the debasing of family and community life to the lowest possible mean. They are worse than anything George Orwell ever conceived."[43]

Elsewhere, the same story was to be told. The twin Schuylkill Falls high-rises in Philadelphia became so crime-ridden they had to be closed within a few years of their opening. The $36 million Pruitt-Igoe Homes in St. Louis, also built on the *Radiant City* model in 1954, consisted of thirty-three identical eleven-story buildings; its barren open plazas were quickly laden with cans and broken glass, and became the scene of gang warfare. The Pruitt-Igoe situation, vividly described by Lee Rainwater in *Behind Ghetto Walls: Black Families in a Federal Slum,* became so out of control that the project was eventually dynamited and bulldozed.[44] The Taylor Homes, which may have been worse, remained standing and occupied.

So visible and universal were the conditions created by the high-rises that the Housing Act of 1968 forbade building any more of them for families with children unless the secretary of Housing and Urban Development agreed there was no practical alternative.[45]

An explanation for the juvenile gangs that sprang up around the high-rises came from Hugh Johnson of the New York Youth Board: "Wherever," he said, "you have great population mobility and disrupted population areas"—the high-rises enforced mobility on a wholesale scale and disrupted life in the neighborhoods around them—"gangs spring up to replace the broken stability of the group. Wherever the pattern of life breaks down, kids form gangs to give themselves a feeling of protection and stability."[46]

Undoubtedly, too, as many observers pointed out, the bureaucracy placed in charge of the high-rises was often inattentive to tenants' needs, and rarely bothered to enter an apartment until a disturbance broke out that couldn't be ignored. A circular effect could also be seen. As the number of necessary repairs mounted, the municipalities, often because they lacked sufficient funds or personnel, fell ever further behind on the work. When that happened, the tenants assumed the government didn't care how they lived, so that they lost any interest they had in keeping up their homes, leading to the need for still more repairs, fewer and fewer of which got done. Deterioration caused deterioration.

Culture shock also played a role. The former sharecroppers who made up a significant portion of the population of the high-rises had had little experience in urban living before they came north. As Nicholas Lemann points out in *The Promised Land*,[47] for most of them their homes had been shacks on the property of the plantation owner whose fields they worked. Conditions on them differed from slave days only in that the workers were free to move from one plantation to another, which they did frequently in the rarely realized hope that the new master would not cheat them, as the previous one had, of their contracted share of the proceeds of the crop they'd harvested. The roving from one plantation to another caused their culture to become a rootless one. In it, the concept of family was loose; marriages occurred but rarely were permanent since there was no place for them to be permanent. Children were ill-educated even by meager southern standards for blacks, most of them ending up in the fields with only a few years of classroom learning behind them.

Richard Wright described the essence of the plight of the northward-heading migrants: "Perhaps never in history has a more utterly unprepared folk wanted to go to the city. . . . We, who were landless upon the land; we, who had barely managed to live in family groups; we, who needed the ritual and guidance of institutions to hold our atomized lives together in lines of purpose; we, who had our personalities blasted with two hundred years of slavery . . ."[48] And Wright wrote these words in 1941, referring to the generation of blacks who began arriving in the big cities of the North prior to World War II. The sharecroppers of the post-war years who followed them were even less sophisticated in city ways than were their predecessors, so that to them Wright's vivid lament can be even more accurately applied.

This is not to say the sharecroppers were entirely without supports when they reached the northern cities.[49] They often had relatives or friends already living there, and they would temporarily move in with them or close to them. From the kin and friendship circles came leads for jobs and practical tips about handling the welfare bureaucracy. A young mother, for instance, was taught how to get on Aid to Families with Dependent Children and how to keep the checks coming by making sure no employed man or indication of one could be found in the apartment when the welfare worker arrived. Other kinds of networks were also formed. Mothers looked after each other's kids; folks drank and played cards together. When someone won on the numbers—policy games were omnipresent in the slums—they partied together, and the religious among them formed churches in deserted storefronts. Their communities became more well-formed, less insular, more heterogeneous, but also more dangerous because crime was more prevalent, than had been true of the floating society of the plantations.

In the high-rises (which many were eager to enter for the same reason the white liberals thought they would be desirable for them), the country people found themselves, in Bacon's words, "packed into a vertical filing case," floor after floor pressing downward and upward on one another. The environment was entirely foreign not only to that from which they came but also to the slum community that had been their most immediate previous home. Supervision of children, difficult enough in a four-story walkup, became practically impossible for mothers who might live on the tenth floor of a building in which the only ready access to the Le Corbusier plazas below was an elevator that often didn't work and, when it did, was dangerous because of the mugger who might be lurking there.

The guidance from institutions, which Wright saw as necessary, was in short supply, too, and when it took place it was fortuitous, most likely taking the form of a social worker who happened to care or a concerned Visiting Nurse. It was never systemic.

Because of the depressing environment and the pressure of the various authority figures upon them, the high-rise tenants became increasingly dependent, and from that dependence (following the classical psychological pattern) resentment grew. From resentment came aggression that, lacking any other outlet, took the form of destruction of the territory that seemed to threaten them from all sides. Alcoholism (that good friend of a sense of futurelessness) became rampant, and so soon did its cousin, drugs. Meanwhile, the children raged on the plazas below, and they grew up (if they weren't murdered) to become the parents of the next generation, and on and on.

It is no happenstance that the garden apartments that preceded the high-rises—a few of which continued to be built afterward—proved somewhat less deleterious to tenants and the city of which they were a part than were the high-rises. Garden apartments certainly were not good places to live. All the pressures of the crime-breeding ghettos could be found in them and on the mean streets around them, just as in the high-rises, and the same was true to a lesser extent of scattered-site housing, to which a number of cities finally began to turn in the 1960s when the evidence of the high-rises could no longer be ignored. Nevertheless, the alternatives to the high-rises had in common that they were on the ground, which meant they offered a familiar way of living for people who came from a rural life. In them, contact with neighbors could readily take place out of doors and wasn't dependent on the vagaries and dangers of elevator travel. A sense of community could be achieved in such circumstances, and the supervision of children was more feasible, since the smaller ones anyway could be kept in sight. Perhaps most important, garden and scattered-site housing meant one had a home of one's own, a sense of personal space that could never be achieved in the high-rises. One, that is, had a piece of the land, not a piece of the hallway.

It is hard to define the value that living on the land has for people in any statistically measurable way. The response will vary in the intensity and the form it takes from individual to individual. However, beyond doubt, whether we are rich or poor, the higher we live above the ground, the more separated we are from the events of the world below us. The fire truck speeding by might be glimpsed from our twentieth-floor aerie, but we can't run to the door and open it to see what is going on. We look down on trees; they aren't on our eye level, part of our immediate, touchable universe. In the high-rise apartment, the only things that grow are in pots, but they aren't of the earth as are the flowers of the backyard. We may be safer far above the earth—unless we are living in a public housing high-rise—but the safety is monochromal, non-eclectic; it lacks the varied urgency of the streets and their ever-shifting reality. The world we see from above may be pretty, but like a picture postcard it is only a representation of life.

When we are well-to-do and live in high-rises, we have educational and experiential resources that minimize the effect of the divorcement from the land. Because of our circumstances, we also have available to us wide transportation corridors that can take us far from our usual habitat each day. But the sharecroppers from the South, who knew land and little else when they were led into the high-rises, had none of these resources. That so many of them responded in violence or despair to the enclosed world into which they had been thrust (with the best intentions of the thrusters) is not surprising. What is remarkable is how many of them diligently and even passionately strove to create viable communities in these Golgothas; people such as they exemplify the human spirit at its questing best. If the high-rises are to remain, it is such people, not the bureaucrats, who should become their administrators.

Model Cities, the next major effort to solve the inner-city housing problem, was inaugurated in 1966 as a component of Lyndon Johnson's War on Poverty. The Neighborhood Development Programs enacted by the subsequent 1968 Housing Act and the community block grants of the 1970s were variations of the Model Cities philosophy, which itself had its origins in the unworkable "workable" programs demanded by the 1954 Housing Act.[50]

In an immediate sense, however, Model Cities can be seen as a reaction to the controversial community action programs that had been launched in 1965 by the Office of Economic Opportunity (OEO), headed by Sargent Shriver, the late President Kennedy's brother-in-law.[51] The idea behind the community action effort was to seek out individuals and organizations in big city ghettos and give them money to try to improve the lives of the people they represented or claimed to represent. The scheme immediately backfired politically as mayors heaped blame on Johnson for turning over millions of dollars to black radicals who seemed mainly intent on mounting street demonstrations against them. Johnson, who seems to have suspected that the real radicals were to be found in the OEO, was sympathetic to the mayors and also concerned about the price he might have to pay at their hands, if he didn't do something, when he ran for reelection in 1968. He was, therefore, eager to dump or downplay community action, but he also neither wanted to desert nor appear to be deserting the civil rights movement.

Model Cities served Johnson's purpose as a replacement. Although it contained a panoply of medical and various social programs, the emphasis was to be on construction, not confrontation, as was made clear by placing Model Cities under the auspices of the Office of Housing and Urban Development (HUD). Model Cities funding went through HUD to the cities to administer, not to the beneficiaries, which satisfied the mayors' demands. There were limitations, however, on how the money could be spent. Title One–style slum clearance was not to be permitted. In its place, neighborhood associations were to be created, with salaried positions available for local leaders; these groups would work with planners and architects to design and carry out physical rehabilitation of their communities.[52]

The initial response at the city governmental level was positive, and not only because white mayors rather than black activists controlled the money. There was also the hope that if the slums could be made habitable, the most significant cause for the urban riots of the period would be removed. An accompanying expectation, at least in some quarters, was that Model Cities would encourage middle-class black families to remain in the newly re-furbished inner cities rather than move into white areas and prompt more population pop-outs.

Almost from the outset, Model Cities encountered problems. The original plan (connoted by the word "model") was to establish pioneering programs in a handful of cities and learn from their experiences before applying the concept more widely. However, because the federal money was available and because of the need to respond to black demands (or, perhaps more accurately, seem to respond), nearly every city wanted to come aboard immediately, and politically it was difficult to deny their demands. As a result, sufficient time wasn't taken to work out a viable structure for Model Cities—Americans are a very impatient people, it seems—and failure stories quickly began to outnumber those of success. In city after city, evidence emerged that the Model Cities jobs were handed out not on the basis of an individual's commitment to the goals of the program but rather based on political connections. Self-styled black leaders who yesterday had lived in poverty, today were wearing expensive clothes and riding in limousines. The white media was affronted by their new affluence, and so was the white middle class to which it catered.

Within the inner cities themselves, however, those who managed to get on the Model Cities gravy train were rarely treated to the same opprobrium. As one black woman activist who didn't have political connections said of one who did: "Good for her. I admire her." Her reaction to the lucky woman suggests the underlying cynicism, born of long experience, that constantly hampered Model Cities in achieving credibility in the eyes of poor people. Prior to it, inner-city blacks had all kinds of programs foisted on them, each of which allegedly was designed to help them, and none had. So why should Model Cities be any different? From that perspective, those who did latch onto good salaries, who could afford the limousines and the fur coats, were seen by their fellow blacks not as exploiting them but as successfully manipulating the white man's system. The underlying wish behind that view was also articulated by the woman activist when she said of the politically connected woman: "That's one lady who's gotten out of here."[53] The goal, as she saw it, was not to build a better ghetto but to put enough money together to leave it, and she was hardly alone in that thinking. Programmatically, Model Cities ignored this understandable human ambition.

Model Cities—and the community block grant and revenue-sharing programs that followed in the 1970s—was also like any large-scale enterprise in which human beings become involved at various levels. Goals, which seemed clear at the outset (in the case of Model Cities to improve the targeted neighborhoods), become clouded as they engender individual agendas and develop cross-purposes. Not only do clashes occur among individuals, but each individual may have his or her own ambivalent responses. Thus the community activist who opposed Model Cities because she saw it only as producing "gilded ghettos," as a saying of the period put it, freely admitted that, if she couldn't find a way to get out herself, she'd rather have a gilded ghetto than the existent one. For that reason, she'd be willing to participate in the program, but her disappointments from previous government programs weakened her expectations and therefore her willingness to give her heart to the new effort.

Even the community control proffered by the Model Cities legislation had an ambiguous character. It clearly marked an advance over the days of urban renewal when decision making was entirely in government hands, which had meant that protests, at the most, could undo one decision but not prevent the next one. In Model Cities and its successors to the present day, community people were given a broader role to play but still were required to work within an administrative structure that wasn't designed by them, and in which the financing and therefore the right to hold back the financing was determined by government. That might be the best or only way to proceed, but it is not community control, which is what Model Cities was promoted as offering.

At the very least, however, Model Cities also represented a

remarkable departure from the callous days of destroying neighborhoods to make way for town houses, expressways, or commercial development. Racist planners like New York's Moses had
gone out of fashion, and so as a consequence had many of the
worst evils they had perpetrated.

Model Cities, which was brought to an end by Nixon following his reelection in 1972,[54] has been used by conservative thinkers
to demonstrate that liberal social planning does not work. We
can't, it seems, solve the problems of the slums by throwing money
and programs at them. The proof is in the apparent conclusion:
Life in the inner cities has, if anything, deteriorated since the War
on Poverty was inaugurated, with Model Cities as its disgraceful
centerpiece.

The critique itself is open to criticism. It is not even factually
accurate. As a matter of history, liberals aren't the only ones who
throw around money in that allegedly profligate manner. It was
under not liberal Democrats but a conservative Republican,
Nixon, that the community block-grant programs came into existence. It was under Nixon also that sizable increases in welfare
payments were authorized, the food stamp program was expanded,
and SSI, which provided Social Security payments to the disabled,
became law.[55] The critique also fails to mention that certain of the
programs introduced during Johnson's watch indicate that liberal
social planning does work. The Job Corps has had its ups and
downs, but on balance its impact has been more positive than
not,[56] while the early-education program Head Start is widely considered to be a success.

Finally, the critique doesn't recognize that the War on Poverty
did bring about an end to a great deal of poverty. Doors of opportunity were opened and millions of black Americans walked
through them, obtaining middle-class incomes in government positions created, directly and indirectly, by the multipronged Johnson initiatives. Many of these individuals, however, found new
careers as overseers of other blacks who remained on welfare and

who continued to require a variety of social and (all too often) penal services. In that way, the very failure of the Johnson effort to end systemic poverty had made individual success possible. The newly upwardly mobile blacks also found themselves in a position, as they hadn't been before the War on Poverty, to offer the opportunity for college education to their children, who gained the qualifications that made it likely they would succeed economically, too.

The perilous situation that cities were facing by the end of the 1970s began to appreciably worsen in 1981 with the coming of the Reagan administration. Billions of dollars in financial supports were withdrawn. In total, between 1980 and 1991 the federal portion of the city budget declined from 17.7 percent to 6.4 percent.[57] Programs for the poor were a particular target, including school lunch programs, the curtailment of Head Start funding, and the venomous Reaganite attack on SSI, the most humane of the Nixon protocols.

In 1992, Presidential candidate Bill Clinton promised a more humane approach to city problems, but in office he has had only indifferent success in carrying out that goal. On the low-cost housing front, the Clinton administration's proposed Housing and Community Development Act of 1994 called for issuance of vouchers to inner-city minorities to be used to obtain homes in upscale city and suburban locales. The plan was not an original one, or even one associated with Clinton's Democratic Party. The same idea, in only a slightly different dress, had surfaced a quarter-century earlier in the Nixon administration, where its advocate was Nixon's HUD secretary, George Romney. His advocacy cost him his job. The whirlwind of criticism he garnered was identical to that which doomed regionalism as an approach to mutual city and suburban problems. Middle-class whites didn't want to share their streets with poverty-level minorities, and black politicians didn't want to lose their voter base in the city districts they represented. Henry Cisneros, Clinton's HUD secretary, believed such opposition would not break out again, but it seems doubtful if he will ever find out if he was right or wrong. At the publication deadline for this book, the 1994 act seemed unlikely to pass the Republican-controlled Congress in any form. HUD, nevertheless, made use of its administrative authority to institute a limited voucher pilot program in which eligible families could move only to "reserved" buildings, that is, in locations that would not threaten the middle class. Turning next to the horrific and destabilizing effects of high-rise projects like the Robert Taylor Homes in Chicago, in 1995 HUD ordered the demolition of five of these projects (but not the Taylor Homes).[58] The intent was, as far as possible, to move the tenants to scattered-site and low-rise garden-type apartments, a victory (if a meager one) for those who had long cried in the wilderness for just such an approach.

The policies of neglect, if not downright antagonism, toward cities that were the hallmarks of the Reagan and Bush administrations and of Republicans in Congress continuing into the Clinton administration have been attributed to the unwillingness of city voters—and most notably the minorities among them—to vote for Republican candidates. That and even less worthy motives, prompted by bigotry, undoubtedly are at work. However, there is also an underlying view, by no means unique to Republican (or indeed some Democratic) politicians, of an inexorable progress toward a new metropolitanism, in which cities become increasingly irrelevant economically. As one author put it,[59] the commercial vitality of the nation was now to be found at those large complexes of industry and office buildings located just outside the borders of the city. Others felt the path went even farther out, and that the existent suburbs themselves would become suburban not to their city but to exurban sites, where the new centers of commerce would be found, buttressed by fax machines and telecommunication devices that would allow them to carry out their functions in a mechanistically sophisticated and isolated splendor.

If that was to be the future, the big cities themselves were hardly blameless. As we have seen, during the urban renewal era, with few exceptions they carelessly and greedily ploughed up their innards, and encouraged the flight of their residents in the process. They were left with a vast poverty population that they lacked the funds to help even before the federal supports were withdrawn.

When all these portents and mistakes are taken into consideration, we might decide that the great old American cities have become like the beggars on their own streets, out of pocket and without prospects. Nevertheless, we also find—hardly uniformly, nearly entirely absent in some cities, more frequently present in others—the continuing presence of a vigorous opposition to entropy. The opponents, just as they always have, insist that the viability of a city can be retained when it has a consistent vision of its capacities. Such a city, because it comprehends them, will be able to exploit its inherent strengths. It will set into motion programs that make its vital center, its polis, aesthetically and economically attractive to outsiders (so that they will want to move there as individuals and businesses). For that to occur, leadership is needed that understands that a city's land is not a blank piece of paper on which anyone can write whatever they please, but rather a series of connections, just as a stream in the wilderness is connected to the environment through which it flows.

10

The Architecture of Connection

The basic principle of harmonious connection in urban design was described by Eliel Saarinen this way: "Were a great number of the most beautiful and famous buildings in architectural history all re-erected to form a single street, this street should be the most beautiful in the world, were beauty merely a matter of beautiful buildings. But such would most certainly not be the case, for the street would appear as a heterogeneous medley of disrelated edifices. The effect would be similar to that produced if a number of the most eminent musicians all played of the finest music at the same time—but each in a different key and melody. There would be no music, but much noise."[1]

Noise without music was the frequent result of the wholesale land clearance of downtowns permitted and encouraged by Title One of the 1949 Housing Act. When the wrecking balls had finally done all their work, the typical site had become barren of historic character, and all familiar connections were gone. In this emptied arena, no intellectual basis existed for harmonious composition. It followed that the now-meaningless land would be sold off to almost anyone for any purpose.

This is not to say that buildings should be saved solely because they are old and familiar. A city's physical plant needs changes as the needs of the citizens, of commerce, of government, change. The goal, rather, is to recognize existent environmental strengths and to preserve or transform them in ways that cause new elements to have an enhancing and not a disassociative effect.

At the heart of such thinking is an ambient connector theme.

An example of its transformative power can be seen in the development of Philadelphia's Society Hill and adjoining Independence Hall area. By the 1950s, the neighborhood had become down-at-the-heels, with slum dwellings mingled with deserted factories. Much of the housing, however, was from the colonial period and could be rehabilitated if there was an impetus to restore its former glory. During a walking tour of Society Hill, Bacon conceived of constructing a series of verdant walkways to be cut through the middle of blocks. Each would offer a unique view and in their totality a panorama of the nearby historical monuments and buildings. In this manner, every movement of the eye within the walkways provided connections with the nation's past in a setting that was visually pleasing and relaxing itself. The little parks were built, causing investors to become interested in restoring the surrounding houses. Society Hill was on its way to becoming one of the most beautiful downtown areas of any city in the world.

As the Society Hill experience suggests, the wise course to follow for the revitalization of a blighted area is to establish the connectors before the rehabilitation begins.* If they have their own sequential integrity, the connectors will give direction to the restoration by means of their energetic thrusting through space. The likelihood of disassociated development thereby decreases, and the prospect that blight will never again visit the area increases.

As desirable as they are, connectors need not (and sometimes cannot) be in place before construction begins. As Bacon has pointed out, the new buildings themselves can serve as connectors as long as it is understood that no building ends at its own lot line but that each is part of a total symbiotic relationship of mass within space. When that occurs, because the structures aren't in an archi-

---

*This may also be the only time it can be done. The blight has lowered real estate values and caused property abandonment, so that the municipality may be willing to dedicate portions of the unused land for connector purposes; once the swing is upward, free space will be perceived as a waste, both by the city, which wants to maximize its tax revenue by intensive use of it, and by developers, who want to turn the maximum profit from packaging the land.

tectural quarrel with one another, as happens in miscellaneous development, it becomes possible to comprehend (as with Penn Center) how their concepts can be extended in new and complementary sequences.

Bacon's dictum had an early application in Savannah. There, as was described in Chapter Two, before the first house was built Oglethorpe established a connector system when he set aside varying-sized packets of land for public enjoyment, all in a rhythmic progression. The continuing power of Oglethorpe's design can be seen in Forsyth Park, built in 1851, more than a century after he founded the city. Considerably larger than any of Oglethorpe's spaces, it appears to have always been planned to be where it is, due to the way the smaller squares lead toward and away from it, like separate but integrated movements of a symphony. (See Diagram 10 on pages 32–33.)

Penn's plan for Philadelphia was much less imaginative than Oglethorpe's for Savannah in its use of open spaces. Penn provided for just four parks of the same size, equidistant from one another and from Center Square. He therefore imposed a rigid design rather than the free-flowing variations that Oglethorpe's plan permitted. Nearly 300 years passed before Bacon's little parks in Society Hill broke the mold. They are not equidistant from one another and they vary considerably in size and shape, yet they are also sufficiently alike that they achieved the same rhythmic continuity for their corner of Philadelphia that Oglethorpe had achieved for Savannah. In each instance, just as in a finely crafted piece of music, the effect is organic; each cell or note inextricably relates to those that precede or follow from it. We move toward coherence rather than drift into entropy.

A number of American cities have attempted to develop meaningful connector systems as the keystone of their efforts to renew their downtowns. Other cities have rejected the concept, in whole or in part, and for still others (like New York, after the Tugwell plan was rejected in 1940) there is little or no evidence that such thinking crossed the mind of anyone in authority. It is to the consequences of these decisions that we turn next. For exemplars, ten cities of various sizes are considered: Baltimore, Detroit, Los Angeles (the largest), Milwaukee, Minneapolis, Philadelphia, Phoenix, Pittsburgh, St. Paul (the smallest), and San Antonio.

Of them, the first in the post–World War II era to make a substantive effort to initiate a large-scale renewal was Pittsburgh. For more than a century prior to that time, the city had virtually ignored any considerations that didn't have to do with accommodating its steel mills. Smoke filled the air, and clouds hung over the city, dark and heavy with pollution. As unattractive to visitors as it was to residents, Pittsburgh had become to the United States what Birmingham was to England: the excrescence of industrialism at its worst.

For the same reason that it was a terrible place to live, a handful of Pittsburghers had become extraordinarily wealthy, and none more so than the Mellons. They controlled the city, financially and politically. They had plundered it, and eventually they saved it.

The author of the rescue was Richard King Mellon, who understood that it was necessary for Pittsburgh to reverse its national image in order to attract new business and thereby add to his bank's profits. To reach that goal, an obvious step was to make the city reasonably livable, which meant solving the pollution problem. Beyond that, Mellon concluded that a bold architectural statement was called for to depict a newly vigorous city reaching out for white-collar industries to enrich its traditional blue-collar base.

While the war continued, such planning had to be held in abeyance; the exclusive focus was on turning out armaments, a task for which the Pittsburgh mills were admirably suited. Within three months of Japan's surrender, however, on November 14, 1945, Mellon, wearing his mantle as president of the Regional Planning Commission, urged immediate and unified action to build a $6 million park where the Monongahela and Allegheny Rivers joined to form the Ohio. The "Point," as it was called, was by then an eyesore even by Pittsburgh standards. But the choice was an inspired one. Mellon and his advisers had rediscovered the city's focus right where it had begun 200 years earlier as Fort Duquesne, built by the French to protect themselves from the British.[2]

Placed in charge of the rejuvenation was a brilliant young man named Jack Robin. Brought on board, too, was the New York developer Robert Dowling, and along with him as an investor, Equitable Life Assurance. The Mellon-appointed mayor, David Lawrence, served as courtier to maneuver the program through the political process.

The result was today's Golden Triangle. There rose the Equitable skyscrapers; there were planted lovely parks surrounding the world's largest fountain; there in part was reconstructed the fort. Although the office towers are hardly architectural landmarks and the design was not without its excesses, as an entity it was of sufficient power that it thrust outward, connecting to the old downtown nearby and fostering its rehabilitation.* Out of the process came new jobs so that when, years later, the steel business that had created the city fell on hard times, Pittsburgh was able to survive that loss. By then, environmental controls also had been enacted. The air was clean, and one's hands and clothes did not get dirty as one walked down the streets. No longer was it necessary to turn on the streetlights at noon because of the smog.

Mellon was not the only wealthy man to try to revitalize his city. In 1971, Henry Ford II embarked on a like venture in Detroit. Ford's version of Mellon's Golden Triangle was Renaissance Center. Situated well off from the downtown, Renaissance Center, completed in 1977, consisted of a luxury hotel, four office towers, and circular-internal levels of upscale retail shops. The complex, viewed from the outside, has a self-contained, fortress-

---

*That was not the intention. The Golden Triangle was conceived as a single grand project in land packaging, not as part of a holistic design for the revitalization of the central city.

Pittsburgh's Golden Triangle, where the three rivers meet, 1992.

like appearance. The center draws customers toward it but simultaneously away from the downtown district that Ford wanted to see prosper. Not surprisingly, soon after Renaissance Center opened, Detroit's great Hudson's Department Store, the last bastion of its central energy, closed its doors.

By itself, Renaissance Center did not doom Detroit's downtown. Other factors were very much involved, including the city's widespread poverty, the white flight to the suburbs, and the crime rate, frequently the highest in the country. Nevertheless, had Ford and his architect built toward Hudson's rather than away from it, Detroit's problems in reclaiming its urban core would have been less monumental than they turned out to be.

In Baltimore, we see both the Detroit and the Pittsburgh models at work. Baltimore's Charles Center is akin to Renaissance Center in Detroit. Built circularly, it too turned away from the retail stores of the central business district, denigrating them and

Detroit's Renaissance Center. Note how the four buildings to the right turn in on themselves and away from the downtown area to the left.

causing many to close. Baltimore's Inner Harbor development, on the contrary, replicates philosophically if not physically the result of the Pittsburgh effort. As with the Golden Triangle, the Inner Harbor displays strong sequential relationships in a setting that is even more dramatic and much more variegated than Pittsburgh's. Throughout the Inner Harbor, the spirit is lively and generous. Each element of the development seems to welcome the next; marketplaces with boutiques have a festival-like atmosphere, mingling with an aquarium and a world trade center, all focusing on the bay, which is filled with boats and ships and a sense of American history. Immensely successful commercially, Inner Harbor represents the fruition of planning by a business and political leadership that had the ability to perceive and the daring to carry out a coherent vision to serve the future of the city.

On the commercial side, a goodly measure of the credit for Inner Harbor belongs to developer James Rouse, in whose earlier Quincy Market in Boston can be seen the prototype for the Baltimore concept. First famed for his suburban shopping malls and

Harborplace with shops in Baltimore's Inner Harbor.

the creation of the town of Columbia in Maryland, Rouse had also been fascinated by central-city renewal. In the late 1950s, he made a speech on that subject to the American Institute of Planners in which he addressed the view, as popularly held then as it has continued to be, that people simply don't want to go into the downtowns to shop. Instead, the retail trend was unalterably away from the polis and toward the suburbs and malls like those Rouse was building there. Rouse told his audience that such thinking was nonsense. Make the downtowns fun for people to visit, he said, and they will come; you won't be able to keep them out. Don't do that and no matter what else you try, he warned, your prophecy of decay will be a self-fulfilling one. With the exception of Bacon and a few others, the planners on hand to hear Rouse were unanimous in their rejection of his message.

Bacon believes the majority felt threatened by Rouse's words. By then, planners, taken as a profession, considered themselves possessed of a special and complex knowledge that only they were capable of interpreting and administering. They had developed

liturgies of cost-benefit analyses and similar arcane economic sci-
entisms to establish their expertise, and since politicians couldn't
understand what the planners were talking about, they tended to
accept the planners' pronouncements, lest they appear to be igno-
rant themselves. The planners' positions in government, therefore,
were unassailable, their careers assured. Rouse's simple notion of
fun represented a danger to their domain, for if he was right, then
their calibrations were irrelevant and the orthodoxies of their
priestcraft open to question.

Rouse's career, in any event, points up how the fortuitous arrival of an imaginative entrepreneur can have a positive impact on
a city's renewal prospects. However, the capacity of such a person
to bring about change is dependent ultimately on the quality of
the local leadership that the entrepreneur encounters. For this reason, Rouse, despite his genius for creating fun, has had little if any
positive effect on Phoenix, another city into which he went adven-
turing. Perhaps because of its sudden, rapid growth, Phoenix gives
the impression of running away from itself. When the original
downtown became congested with traffic, the solution was to
build another one several miles farther out; when the same thing
happened to it, a third downtown came along, a process that theoretically can be repeated as long as space exists for expansion. The
fragmenting expansion suggests that the government has no idea
of the city as an entity, and sees no purpose for it, save possibly to
serve the needs of the land packagers. Consequently the connections of space and mass that had made Phoenix (despite the heat)
an attractive place to live have gradually become eroded. In that
kind of structural wilderness, a developer like Rouse can do nothing more than create another fragment, since there was no focus
(as there was in Baltimore's harbor) around which to build.

Los Angeles presents in extreme the sprawling rootlessness
that Phoenix seems to be striving for. Of it, more truthfully than of
Oakland, Gertrude Stein could have said: "There's no there
there." The absence of identity no doubt has its origins in Los Angeles's history of restless annexation of disparate communities.

Nevertheless, the human disassociations that are the hallmark of Los Angeles primarily arose from planning decisions. As mentioned in Chapter Eight, the highway mania hit the city hard. Its once-excellent mass transportation system was deconstructed* and replaced by freeways that have caused the city's notorious pollution and traffic congestion. They have also isolated vast numbers of people from their environment and from each other. For car-equipped Los Angelenos, the daily journey typically is from the garage at home to the one in the building in which they work. Their city becomes an object that they see only fleetingly, from behind glass, so that it has a perpetual second-hand quality for them. Almost entirely lacking in Los Angeles is the vitality of the piazza, that place of bustle and commerce and human interconnection. For the most part, Los Angeles sidewalks in the principal retail and business districts, and nearly universally in the residential areas, give a deserted feeling; an almost ominous absence of participation can be felt, as if it were a city being viewed by vast hordes of secretive people who never make a public appearance. Only the underclass is constantly visible, and it, like the earthquake faults that underlie the city, makes its presence felt in unpredictable outbursts of destruction. The effect ultimately is dispiriting, dangerous, and entropic.

The view from the inside of a moving automobile, while it may be the most dramatically evident in Los Angeles, has increasingly become the perspective from which people see the world around them. Building designers have catered to that perspective. As design critic Thomas Hine has dryly observed, "Recent commercial architecture strives for bigger, less subtle, effects that can be appreciated while exceeding the speed limit" on expressways.³ The result is a plethora of office towers that, to the pedestrians

*By the 1990s, a major effort was finally underway to improve public carrier transit, accompanied by staggering cost overruns, flooding, and other engineering disasters. The new subway system concourses are replete with ornamentation that is singularly rococo and may, therefore, appeal to southern California taste.

Commerce Square, Philadelphia, a joint venture of Maguire Thomas Partners and IBM Corporation; I.M. Pei and Partners, Architects; Hanna-Olin Ltd., Landscape Architects.

In *The City as Sequence*, Bacon wrote: "The invitation [in almost all office towers] is to enter into the private interior of the building. . . . In Commerce Square, the invitation is open to everyone to enter into the special garden space . . . [where] the monumental gateway establishes a subtle transition from the more public space of the sidewalk to the more private, yet in no way exclusive space of the courtyard. The enclosed garden it contains is entirely different from the usual public space smeared around the edges of skyscrapers, often worthless or worse. It stands in violent contrast to the spiked wrought-iron picket fence so often and so disastrously used, with its message of hostility and exclusion." In an interview with Bacon, Harry Cobb, of I. M. Pei & Partners, the architect of Commerce Square explained, "It was my intention at the street level that the space be the figure and, up in the skyline, the building would be the figure. The transition from the skyline to the street is the whole intention of the work. What I wanted to prove is that you can build two million feet of office space in a way that would produce a figurative space at the street level in which the building becomes the residual element of the composition. The building serves the space [by so doing] rather than dominating the space." Cobb's design proves that it is possible to create a building that adds to the drama of a city's skyline and yet, as Bacon points out, provides a green and restful welcome to the pedestrian, who is aware of the high building but is not visually or psychologically dominated by it as is true with the more conventional skyscraper.

standing in front of them, are obtrusive and overbearing fragmenters of the city landscape. (Only great architecture will serve both the pedestrian and the motorist. See also facing page.)

A quite remarkable example of sequential renewal was initiated in Milwaukee in the 1970s. As with Detroit, by then the Milwaukee polis was in a severe and apparently chronic state of decline. The retail community, however, was not about to give up and formed a redevelopment corporation to do broad-scale planning. Named to direct the project in 1977 was Stephen F. Dragos, whose role was comparable to that of Jack Robin in Pittsburgh.

Milwaukee's main downtown shopping street was The Grand Avenue. Along it, within three and a half blocks of one another, were two department stores, Gimbel's (later bought by Marshall Field) and the Boston. Between them was the Plankinton building, which dated from the early 1900s and had consisted of a two-story arcade with skylights and ancillary office space. Over the years, the arcade upper level was demolished and replaced by more offices; the attractive skylighting was lost in the process.

Employing Edmund Bacon as a consultant, Dragos and the Milwaukee Redevelopment Corporation agreed it would be a good idea to connect the three buildings by means of a series of upper-level walkways, with the Plankinton restored to its former appearance. Rouse was brought in as a joint partner to revitalize the retail offerings. Diagrams 12–15 depict what occurred, step by step. In Diagram 13, Gimbel's is on the left, the Boston is on the right, and the Plankinton is the blank area. In Diagram 14, we see the buildings connected as they were by 1982. Had nothing more happened, the project would have been a success within its own configuration, but the remainder of the downtown would not have been assisted.

However, as Jon Wellhoefer, Dragos's successor, has described it: "The energy created by The Grand Avenue development sent out lines of force that led to new mixed and residential zoning throughout the entire downtown area."[4] Wellhoefer's description is

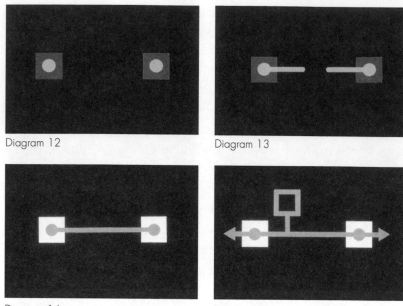

Diagram 12

Diagram 13

Diagram 14

Diagram 15

depicted in Diagram 15, where we see how the first act of connection caused new sequences to suggest themselves. This is what happens when the renewal path takes the form of a vector: It allows direction to flow outward, having the opposite effect to that of the enclosing circle, as occurred with Detroit's Renaissance Center.

In the case of Milwaukee, the expanded walkways eventually crossed the Milwaukee River, pressing onward to create interconnections among office buildings, stores, museums, the convention center, and hotels. Between 1977 and 1982, the initial period of the development, the project encouraged $1 billion in investments, and in total has added more than 15,000 new jobs to the city. Visitors came from afar, bypassing suburban shopping malls along the way because they wanted to see and enjoy the continuum that Milwaukee was now offering.*

*Milwaukee has continued to suffer from severe sociological and financial problems, as have virtually all other American cities. The Grand Avenue achievement helped, but the thinking that went into it needs to be matched by other creative ideas for the city's future.

A similar, only slightly less ambitious, connector system was developed in downtown Minneapolis. There the process began with a small group of retail store owners who saw that an advantage might be gained by connecting the blocks on which their businesses stood. They did so, as in Milwaukee, by constructing covered skybridges that allowed pedestrians to move rapidly and safely above the traffic from one establishment to the next, and warmly, too, a considerable benefit in Minneapolis's cold winters. The result is schematically depicted in Diagrams 16–19. Diagram 16 depicts the first stage. In the Diagrams 17 and 18, we see that, although the skybridges were serving their purpose admirably, it is apparent they still remained fragmented. However, as Diagram 19 shows, when the IDS Center (named for Investors Diversified Services) was completed, with its dramatic Crystal Court, all the existent skywalks were connected to it. At that moment, they became like so many arteries finally finding a heart.

By then, Minneapolis government leaders had recognized the value of the skybridges; as shown in the final diagram, they extended them into new developments and injected them into old ones, permitting the rehabilitation of numerous loft buildings of historic importance.

In Minneapolis's smaller sister city, St. Paul, we find an example, even more impressive than in Pittsburgh, of how a single person can turn a city around. Unlike King Mellon with his millions and his access to the first line of the nation's funding sources, St. Paul's George Latimer had only his office of mayor going for him. When Latimer was elected to his first term in 1976, he inherited a city of considerable beauty. The cathedral and the state capitol topping St. Paul's hills had long given architecturally satisfying exclamation points to the grammar of its connectedness, and a number of buildings of great, if deteriorated, charm from the Victorian era also remained standing. But St. Paul seemed to be in a condition of precipitate and permanent decline. The downtown stores were losing sales volume each year, and the important nearby Lowertown area had become a slum. Forecasters of the

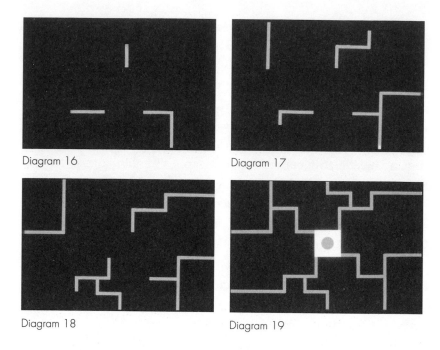

Diagram 16

Diagram 17

Diagram 18

Diagram 19

death of cities were likely to include St. Paul when they wanted to prove that urban malaise wasn't confined to major metropolises.

Soon after taking office, Latimer focused his attention on the central business district, aware that if it couldn't be salvaged, no linchpin for renewal would exist. He also recognized that the city's tax base was insufficient to make even a start. At that time, the federal government had begun issuing Urban Development Action Grants, and Latimer obtained one of the first for St. Paul. Simultaneously he engaged the services of a private developer to act, in effect, as the city's partner in revitalization.

The results were dramatic. The Victorian structures were restored to assure that the city's linkages to its past would not be lost. A solar hotel was built, as were two high-rise office buildings, a three-level enclosed shopping mall, and a new glass-enclosed park with a wonderful old carousel that featured hand-carved horses. Also revitalized in the heart of the downtown was Rice Park, the focal point for St. Paul's Landmark Center, which had been scheduled for demolishment but was saved when Latimer obtained a federal grant to fund its restoration as a cultural center with a new theater. Throughout the downtown, an enclosed skywalk system was developed that allows pedestrians to travel anywhere in the center of St. Paul without having to go outdoors.

Latimer next turned his attention to Lowertown. For its renewal, he and his deputy mayor came up with a plan for a private development bank that would be capitalized with foundation grants. Within ten years, the bank had obtained approximately $350 million from investors, a return on its original capital of about forty to one. Property taxes from Lowertown in the same period increased five-fold, and along the way warehouses were refurbished and transformed to become private residences.

But perhaps the most remarkable leadership quality that Latimer displayed was the way he managed to engage the people of St. Paul in saving their own city. As David Osborne, co-author of the book *Reinventing Government*, put it: "[Latimer] used voluntary organizations to operate recycling programs, to perform energy audits, and even to manage a park. . . . He used millions of dollars worth of volunteers' time in the city's parks, recreation centers, libraries and health centers."[5] By the time Latimer left the mayoralty in 1990, he had also kept St. Paul's budget growth below the rate of inflation and had reduced the city's debt.

The importance of the individual in revitalizing a city can be further seen in the history of San Antonio's Riverwalk. Its story begins in the early years of the twentieth century, by which time the San Antonio River had become a municipal disgrace afloat with garbage and trash, as well as a potential danger from flooding. When in 1913, it twice burst over its banks, a commission was formed to decide what to do about the river. Even as commissions go, this one was slow afoot and did not make its report until six years later, at which time it proposed that the river be paved over at various junctures, including at its horseshoe bend, which is now the heart of the Riverwalk. The

The restored Rice Park in St. Paul.

idea of transforming the river into a largely underground stream gained new support in 1921, when a major flood put downtown streets under nine feet of water; fifty people died, and property damage reached $50 million. The business community urged immediate adoption of the 1919 plan, but opposition quickly arose from a group of women who formed the San Antonio Conservation Society. Their president, Emily Edwards, wrote and produced a puppet play entitled *The Goose That Laid the Golden Egg*, which depicted what she saw to be the consequences of the obliteration of the city's greatest natural resource. Through the play and other means, she and her friends succeeded in arousing the public consciousness, and the plans to cover the river were placed in abeyance. The conservationists, however, offered no new ideas about how to make the river more attractive or safe, and had there been another flood, the discarded plan would have almost certainly been enforced and today's Riverwalk would be a parking lot.

The necessary vision for the future came from a San Antonio landscape architect named Robert Hugman. Inspired by a visit in 1927 to New Orleans, where he had observed the restoration of the French Quarter, in 1929 Hugman began talking to San Antonio officials, to citizen groups, to anyone he could collar, about his dream for a "quaint, old cobblestoned street rambling lazily along the river. A street with old world appeal. Small shops, a studio apartment . . . a cafe, cabaret and dance club . . . [and floating on the river] gaily covered boats fashioned after the gondolas of Venice. . . ." Think, he said, of a "ride down the river on a balmy night, fanned by a gentle breeze carrying the delightful aroma of honeysuckle and sweet olive, old-fashioned street lamps casting fantastic shadows on the surface of the water, strains of soft music in the air. . . ." Hugman's romantic imagery captured the public imagination, and his brilliant solution to the flooding problem, by means of a channel bypass and floodgates, made his idea an eminently practical one, too.

Contemporary view of San Antonio's Riverwalk shows how faithfully Hugman's 1929 vision was carried out.

Even so, ten years passed before the availability of WPA funds made construction possible. When the Riverwalk was completed in 1941, Hugman could look out to see the boats gliding by, see the ever-changing vistas of graceful streets and pedestrian bridges, observe the old stone masonry admitting varying patterns of light and shadow on high curved walls, see the sun spotting down through the trees by day, witness the festival appearance of the colorful lighting by night. On viewing all this in 1941, Hugman might have paused to reflect, as Bacon did in 1990 when walking through Market East: "All this was once a figment of my imagination."

But in the Philadelphia of the mid-1950s, today's Market East did not exist, even as a figment. Although by then Bacon's Penn Center conception was beginning to energize the western spoke of the axis created by City Hall, Market Street east of City Hall was showing signs of decline, and that was bad news for the city.* Located along that spoke were the city's principal department stores: John Wanamaker just across from City Hall and, clustered five and six blocks farther east, Gimbel's, Snellenberg's, Strawbridge & Clothier, and Lit Brothers. By the 1950s, these major players in maintaining the city's retail viability were finding themselves encroached upon by schlock outlets and the city's first porno movie house; hovering around them were loft buildings, matched in their dreariness only by the soot-covered bricks of the Reading Railroad Terminal. The milieu had become one that—at a time when suburban shopping malls were already subtracting business from the downtown—seemed to guarantee a further and

*The north–south spokes, at that time, required little or no rehabilitative attention. Broad Street, as it emerged north of City Hall, was dull visually but economically stable. Broad Street immediately south of City Hall was more interesting architecturally and—in conjunction with City Hall—bespoke the meaning of the polis. Along these blocks were to be found office buildings, banks, cultural centers (a theater, the Academy of Music), a university of the arts, and the historically important Bellevue-Stratford Hotel.

perhaps devastating decline in traffic for the department stores, and for retail outlets on Chestnut Street, just a block to the south.

Viewing the situation with due alarm was the vice-chairman of the planning commission, who in 1957 declared, "Market Street [East] is becoming a row of empty warehouses," which was an exercise in hyperbole but economically not far off the mark. His pronouncement was taken seriously; the next day it was repeated in one-inch headlines by the Philadelphia *Inquirer*. We might think, considering all the urban renewal money that was then available, that upon hearing the grim news from the vice-chairman, the leadership of the business community would immediately band together or, at the least, invite in James Rouse to see what he could do.*

But such thinking was not to be found among Philadelphia's retailers, the realtors, and the financial community that backed them. To this leadership, the vice-chairman was not making a prediction but stating an irrevocable fact. It is far from clear, for that matter, that all elements of that leadership were unhappy about the decline; it augured for rapid turnover in properties, loans, and mortgages, which could be profitable for realtors and bankers.

The aura of pessimism, to the extent it was sincere, was furthered by a visual component. The newly vibrant appearance of the western spoke of the axis, initiated by Penn Center, emphasized the grimy depressed appearance of the eastern spoke. City Hall itself added to the contrast. Viewed from the west, it now offered a dramatic anchor for all the new construction, but from the east it had a blocking effect. It was as if Market East was an unloved offspring whose mean parent, City Hall, wouldn't even let it look at the wonderful new clothes and toys it had bought for the favored Market West child.

*They were well aware of Rouse. Bacon had proposed he be named to manage the shops that were planned for the Penn Center concourse. The Pennsylvania Railroad, which owned the property, rejected Rouse. The failure of the concourse shopping section sprang from that decision.

Perhaps the answer was to tear down City Hall, Bacon thought, in that way removing the barrier that separated the two portions of Market Street, just as earlier the Chinese Wall had been a barrier that had kept hidden the splendors of the Benjamin Franklin Parkway. "It was one of the worst ideas I ever had," Bacon later said, but it was probably a necessary one since it forced him to recall his original insight of Penn Center as a line of force targeting on City Hall. In a moment he recalls as one of extraordinary clarity of vision, he realized that the line didn't have to stop at City Hall, bouncing back off it in westward directions, but could also be perceived as proceeding through City Hall like a laser beam. In that event, Market West and East weren't separate spokes but a continuum of immense possibilities, in which City Hall had never been an interruption nor a barrier but was the central focusing sequence, just as William Penn had visualized the site to be. (See Diagram 4 on page 230.)

With that perception established in his mind, Bacon had no doubt what he must do next: offset the verbal empty warehouse image, issued by the planning commission vice-chairman, with a visual image of his own.* He did so by making drawings of Market East as a congruent extension of Market West. His Market East plan, which subsequently took the form of three-dimensional models, depicted a multilevel complex of gardens, courts, shops, walkways, and office towers, extending from City Hall to the department stores farthest east. A reproduction of Bacon's design was published in the *Inquirer* a few weeks after the vice-chairman's prediction. It posited, as Bacon had hoped, a counter-view of the future, but it was one that looked to be fearsomely expensive to achieve.

That was the beginning of the struggle. A few weeks after Ba-

*Nearly forty years later, in 1995, Bacon employed the same strategy, this time to combat an insipid and timid plan put forth by the National Park Service for renovation of Independence Hall Mall, in which the Liberty Bell is housed. With the assistance of other architects, Bacon presented a model that offered a continuum of sensory experiences with a historic context for adult

con's drawing appeared, the city's business establishment, up in arms, sent an emissary to meet with him in the city planning commission office to advise him that the city's leaders had lost confidence in his sanity. He did not, it seemed, understand the value of a dollar. A committee, he was told, had been formed to hold him in check. Based on his experience with Penn Center, Bacon had expected the opposition. "If they'd agreed immediately," he later remarked, "I would have decided my idea was a bad one." He was especially pleased by the formation of the sanity committee, since it gave him a way to maintain communication with those who had the financial capacity to turn his vision into reality.

The vision also proved to have popular appeal, which was furthered when the *Inquirer* published a seventeen-page magazine supplement featuring the Market East of the future. Meanwhile, the business coalition, after many discussions with Bacon, worked with an architectural firm to come up with a more "sensible" plan than his. That meant there was now recognition that a plan of some kind was needed. In these ways, the arrows began to move toward the idea.

As Bacon's model of coherence shows (see Diagram 7 on page 18), however, the process toward acceptance can be a lengthy one, and so it proved for Market East. Although the basic idea was accepted as a goal for the central city by Mayor Dilworth and each of his successors, political opposition continued, sometimes on the perceived merit of the plan, sometimes on details of it, sometimes simply because the opponents were against anything the mayor favored. Similar concerns continued to emanate from portions of

---

visitors and—an age group that has always been important to Bacon, going back to the Better Philadelphia Exhibition—their children. For them, there would be an old-fashioned carousel, an "enchanted village," and fountains in which they could play, giving them not only an enjoyable but also a visceral participation in their nation's heritage. As he did in 1957 for Market East and ten years earlier with Penn Center, his goal was "to put ideas out and let them germinate," in the expectation the arrows would move toward his "figment of imagination" and give it reality.

the business community. Financing remained an issue, too; there were those who argued that the money needed to complete the project could be better used for other municipal purposes, and still others resolutely held to the notion that the commercial track of the city was inevitably westward and that Market East for that reason, no matter what was attempted to be accomplished there, was doomed to failure.

Bacon sought to deal with these concerns. Portions of his 1961 Comprehensive Plan for the City of Philadelphia dealt with the development of the central city, as did, more specifically, diagrams he issued in 1963 and 1967. In each of these efforts, he sought to counter the common way of thinking of renewal as separate projects that had no relationship to one another. Even Penn Center had been considered by real estate developers and politicians as nothing more than an exercise in land packaging, albeit an unusually commercially viable one. Now the 1961 plan and its successors were showing the entire area holistically, with Market East no longer a lonely fragment fit for desertion, but rather at the very heart of the new ambience. As the illustration on page 227 shows, the plan depicted existent and future transportation routes that would feed travelers into the central city speedily and conveniently.

Nevertheless, during this period nothing was built, and as a result the deterioration of the business district continued. As all this was going on, one architect after another came on board, contributed design ideas for Market East, and bowed out. Each change brought about its own disputes, but with them also came new thinking and a deepening commitment to Bacon's original and airy multilevel concept.

A step forward occurred in 1969 when agreement was reached to join the hitherto separate Penn Central and Reading* suburban

*In 1971, the Reading followed the Penn Central into bankruptcy. By the time Market East was completed, all commuter trains were part of the regional mass transit system.

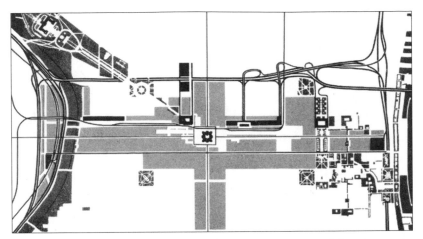

The Philadelphia central-city continuum as proposed by Bacon in 1963. The Market East sector is depicted in white to the right of Center Square.

lines underground at about 10th Street. Around this time, construction also began on a new high-rise office tower, One Reading Center, the first to be built on Market East in nearly fifty years, a strong indication of aroused developer faith in the area. The evolving design for the total revitalization of Market East reached its final form when drawings by John Bower were accepted.[6] There was a kind of symbolic completion in that: Bower had been associated with Vincent Kling, the architect who'd worked with Bacon on Penn Center.

After that, the pieces of the puzzle began to fall into place. Rouse was brought in as tenant in charge of the multiform shopping complex that became known as Gallery One. It opened on August 11, 1977, exactly twenty years after Bacon's drawings had appeared in the *Inquirer*. In 1983, the adjoining Gallery Two was completed, extending the mall to 11th Street and thereby to the below-ground passageways to Penn Center. The following year the commuter rail tunnel opened. The dramatic eastern signature at 7th Street became possible when the Mellon

Bank, which had bought the Lit Brothers building, saved it from the wrecker's ball at the behest of Bacon and others. By then plans were underway to construct the new convention center just north of the Reading Terminal; it opened in 1993, as did an adjoining hotel.

Even a coherent design like Market East that radically alters the existent architectural landscape opens the possibility that it will violate people's vocabulary of their city. When that happens, the reference points they had are gone, and along with them the emotional associations that were part of their lives. The sense of deprivation can be keen, as it was in Boston when Scollay Square was taken away. That danger was avoided in Market East. The most evocative of the landmarks, City Hall, was left unscathed, as was the Lit Brothers ornamental facade, both significant nouns in the city's locational grammar. The late decision to retain the Reading Railroad Terminal building (even though it no longer served its transportation purpose once the underground commuter link was completed) also proved a wise one. Once cleansed of its generations of dirt and with its facade restored, it revealed itself to be a handsome building. More important, its juxtaposition to the new One Reading Center office tower provided a desirable historic continuity, adding character to the total continuum in a variegated associative rather than disassociative way.

The redesigns of central cities that have proven successful differ markedly from places like Detroit's isolationist Renaissance Center and most suburban shopping malls in that they do not cater solely to a middle- and upper-income clientele. They are in the city and of the city and thereby partake of its economic and ethnic diversity, yet, unlike so many other forbidding places in cities, they have a welcoming quality. In the case of Philadelphia, although crime is by no means absent along Market East, the frequency has sharply declined since the project was completed. No doubt the brightness and the very size of the crowds has had a deterrent effect, but also reflected is the enjoyment that Market East offers, which thereby lessens the likelihood of antisocial activity. The town fair is one of our oldest and simplest ideas about happy congregation, and (as Rouse recognized) it remains one of the most valid.

In Market East, we also see once again the lasting power of a valid idea. Bacon's original conception for Penn Center, although denigrated in many ways by the developers who took it over, had such force that thirty years after it was the figment of his imagination, it came to fruition—almost exactly as he had first envisioned it—in Market East.

To establish a continuum as its core act of rejuvenation, a city need not have an initiating design focus of the kind that Philadelphia, Savannah, and Washington, D.C., enjoy. In Milwaukee, for example, the Plankinton building and the two department stores appeared (and had been long assumed) to be entirely discrete entities, and they remained that way until the moment of creative vision that identified them as sequences to one another, not as separations. The physical act of joining them by the skywalks followed. Once that was done, a new force was created that thrust outward in vectors, creating their own sequences. The effect was as if Milwaukee had inserted an entirely new nervous system into an old body.

The great strength of the continuum philosophically is that it doesn't carry within it its own limitations, as a circular plan does. The continuum may eventually be stopped by geographic or political boundaries, but that is all. The Market East continuum in Philadelphia is necessarily halted when it reaches the Delaware River, which marks the eastern boundary of the city; however, when we follow its path westward, we see it easily arches the Schuylkill River (since Philadelphia continues west of it) where it comes upon the 30th Street Railroad Station. As Diagrams 20 and 21 make apparent, at that point its energy expands rather than diminishes when the future of the site is considered. The 30th Street Station holds a key centralizing position on the Northeast Railroad Corridor (Boston and New York to the north of it, Baltimore and

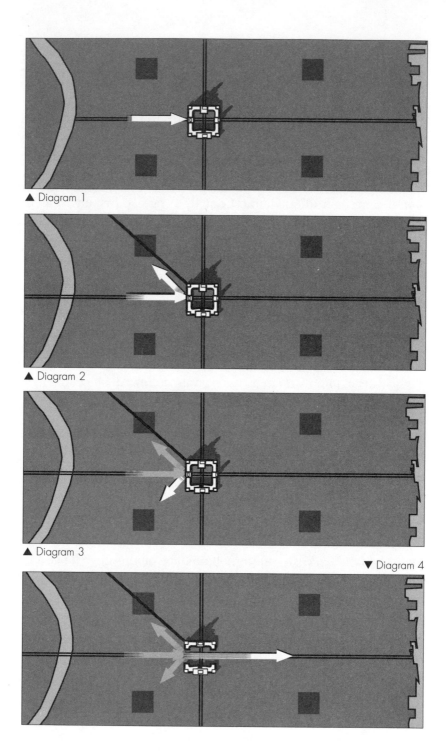

▲ Diagram 1

▲ Diagram 2

▲ Diagram 3

▼ Diagram 4

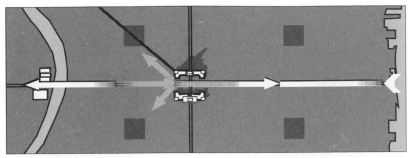

▲ Diagram 20

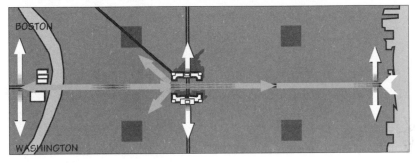

▲ Diagram 21

Washington to the south), the importance of which for freight and passenger travel will continue to grow in order to meet the need to conserve the world's rapidly dwindling oil supply.*

As the six diagrams of the Market Street continuum show, an idea for the future is always an idea for the future as it pulsates over time and space.

The outward-thrusting city renewal that creates sequential connections (as in Milwaukee and Philadelphia) and the inward-turning ones (like those of Charles Center in Baltimore and Re-

*Rail travel need not be dependent on petroleum. It can operate through magnetic levitation, in which cars ride on cushions of air; it also can be extremely speedy (rates of 250 to 275 miles per hour feasible), and also quite efficient in energy usage (about 7 percent of the rate of consumption on standard tracks). High-speed models that move over conventional tracks, while less efficient environmentally, are also feasible and may be favored, at least in the immediate future.

River Scenario for development west of Center City, Philadelphia, showing twin towers with connecting suspension bridge, steps leading to restaurant barge on river. (H. Leonard Fruchter, developer; Bernard Himel, AIA, architect)

naissance Center in Detroit) have their analogies in and are expressive of human psychology. In all of us, inward and outward thrusts are present. Our private thoughts, when our minds are working at their sharpest, allow us to synthesize our experiences and draw conclusions about the nature of our world, the people within it, and the society of which we are a part. This inward mode of realization is, however, like the inward mode of a Renaissance Center, essentially circular in that it is self-referential and complete in itself. It can give us moments of heightened awareness that make life worth living, but intellectually it is sterile, since our conjectures, if we do not act upon them in some manner, remain only that.

Action can be taken in many forms, including private ones

(such as writing out our ideas or making drawings of them), but that which we find most often satisfying is the congregational. By telling people our ideas, the feedback we receive can cause us to further ponder and reshape our thinking. Indeed, the very act of verbalizing allows our formulations to become more crisp and definitive than when they were articulated only in the shorthanding language of our private ruminations. The possibility to affect changes begins with this vectoring movement: out from inside ourselves, toward other people, and the thrust of their ideas back at us.

Some of our social institutions are structured to inhibit any form of outward questing. In a police department, for example, the patrol officer or detective reports to the sergeant, the sergeant to the lieutenant, the lieutenant to the captain, the captain to the inspector, the inspector to the chief, and then orders come down from chief to inspector to captain to lieutenant to sergeant to detective and patrol officer.

The amount of information the system contains, therefore, is rich vertically but sparse horizontally. In one city, a police captain in charge of investigating adult and juvenile drug gangs broke free of the vertical pattern. Careful not to let his superiors know what he was doing, he instituted regular roundtable discussions of all the cases on which his detectives were working.[7] "One squad, let's say," he explained, "is working on a case in which the suspect is a man who wears a green hat, and another squad is looking for a suspect who drives a yellow car. Under ordinary police protocol, the green hat detectives would have no knowledge of the yellow car case, save by happenstance, like talking around the water cooler. Using the roundtable, however, a green hat detective might say, 'Hey, I have a snitch who mentioned a guy who drives a yellow car,' a piece of information to which he'd paid no attention until then because he knew nothing about the yellow car case. Next thing you know, we'd have an arrest. Happened all the time." That which had been self-contained had been broken by the outward thrust of energy. One cell of information ("the man in the green hat") had been joined to the next cell ("the suspect in the yellow car"), and the resultant sequence caused the action (the arrest) that would not have taken place had the fragments not been connected to make a whole.

The absence of the captain's roundtable can also be found, all too often, in the way our universities purvey information. The students of structural architecture, for example, are kept separate from the landscape architects, and both from the urbanologists; all three are isolated from those who are majoring in city planning. Each discipline is likely to hold the other in contempt. Because of the self-centered and self-indulgent specialization, the "green-hat" and "yellow-car" information that should be exchanged is not.

When students such as these are let loose upon the public to ply their trades, the lot-line philosophy they have imbued, in which nothing beyond the perimeters of their specialization is of interest to them, causes them to lose sight of any congregational purpose. The architects among them, because they haven't been taught to consider space as a continuum in which people exist and have needs and responses, see land only as a place to situate a design. As a result, they may be on their way to making a fortune, but they are also creating an unsatisfactory city for its people. Similarly, much of the teaching of city planning is based on the premise that establishment of trends through computer modeling will predict by itself (as cost/benefit analyses were supposed to do for highways) which program should be imposed upon people. In this construct, the danger is that the sophisticated technology of statistical manipulation will lead the planner (and urban theorists are prey to the same conceit) to see people functioning only as units. Ignored is that which is not quantifiable but which is what is important about people: their emotions, their feelings, their thinking, their loyalties, their will to accomplish, their sense of relationship to other people and places. Planning, that is, fails to serve its purpose when it is considered as a science but can succeed as an art form, for it is only then that the impetus is away from objective quantification and toward appreciation of the importance of the subjective nuances of the human experience.

11

Dimension and Direction

When Lewis Mumford wrote that "the final test [of an economic system] lies in its ultimate products—the sort of men and women it nurtures and the order and beauty and sanity of their communities," he was also laying down the guideline by which leadership is to be measured. The true leader is the one who, as in Bacon's model of coherence, has the capacity to understand and the willingness to attempt to draw the arrows of public spirit toward Mumford's multifaceted but holistic ideal of the good society.

In our cities, such persons have emerged in many ways and with varying credentials. They can be artists, authors, journalists, or business executives; they could be planners, like Bacon, or community activisits with no portfolio other than that which contains the vigor of their ideas. They may, at times, as Bacon's career shows, work within the government and at other times lay pressure on it from without. Within a city, however, we have only one person at a time to whom leadership has been granted as a matter of electoral right, and that is the mayor.

In the careers of two big city mayors who were contemporaries, we find acted out, not perfectly but still illuminatingly, the differences between elected leaders who do and do not offer to nourish the best aspirations of their people. The first was, in his time, one of the most powerful politicians in America, Richard J. Daley of Chicago.

Time can be a harsh master. In a single instant, a person's apparent nature can be capsulized, summarized, and engraved, so that when people think about that person, the image of the crucial moment is the one that will first occur to them. For tens of millions of Americans who were alive then or who only later knew of that moment by seeing a recording of it, Richard Daley's defining instant occurred on Wednesday evening, August 28, 1968, in the Chicago Amphitheatre, where the Democratic Party had met to select its candidate for president.[1]

Senator Abraham Ribicoff of Connecticut was on the podium to place the name of George McGovern into nomination. On the previous Sunday night, approximately 1,000 protestors against the Vietnam War were holed up in Lincoln Park when they were attacked by the police, allegedly for breaking a curfew. The cops swept through the area, clubbing into submission anyone who came in their path, including seven newspaper reporters. Daley, who was by then in his fourth term as mayor of Chicago, supported the attacks on the reporters the next day by declaring: "They think because they're working for a newspaper that they can do anything, they can violate any law, they can take any action because they are newsmen." So encouraged, on Monday the police violence broke out again, this time in Grant Park, which was much nearer the downtown area along Michigan Avenue, as well as in Lincoln Park, where police were heard to be shouting, "Kill, kill, kill." Reporter Mike Royko recalled the scene: "Clergymen trying to calm the situation were beaten. Some people were tossed into the park's lagoon, including a man who was going home on a bike. Police beat people many blocks from the park, invaded a couple of homes, sprayed Mace in the shocked faces of residents who leaned out of their windows to look. . . ."

On Tuesday the Chicago newspapers again protested the violence against their reporters. (They seemed less concerned with the fate of the protestors and bystanders.) That evening the officially condoned thuggery entered the Amphitheatre itself, where a television interviewer was punched in the stomach by a security guard.

On Wednesday evening, the battle of Michigan Avenue took

place in front of the Hilton Hotel. Once more, anyone who came in the way of the cops was likely to be clubbed; others were chased into the hotel lobby, and still others pushed through windows. While this was going on outside the convention hall, inside it the chairman of the Colorado delegation had addressed the podium to inquire: "Is there any rule under which Mayor Daley can be compelled to suspend the police-state terror being perpetrated at this minute on kids in front of the Conrad Hilton?" Led by Daley's son, Richard M. (who succeeded his father as mayor in 1987), members of the Chicago delegation shouted insults at the Coloradan.

As Senator Ribicoff came to the rostrum, he said, "If we had McGovern, we wouldn't have the Gestapo in the streets of Chicago." At that, members of the Illinois delegation leaped to their feet, gesturing, making thumbs-down motions. In response, Ribicoff declared: "How hard it is to accept the truth, how hard it is."

The cameras focused on Daley. He was also on his feet, waving his arms, as he shouted at Ribicoff. Visually, the moment could not have been worse for him. The elegant-looking Ribicoff appeared calm, a man who obviously had the right to be where he was, while the pudgy and balding Daley had the aspect of a man completely out of control, red-faced, screaming, malevolent. His conduct suggested that this indeed was the kind of man who would order police attacks on anyone who tried to thwart him. The image was fixed.

Daley was a hot-tempered man whose ego did not readily countenance opposition. Nor was the bloodshed outside the Democratic National Convention the only time he had given his imprimatur to violence. Just a few months earlier, a riot broke out on Roosevelt Boulevard in Chicago's inner city, following the announcement of Martin Luther King's assassination.[2] Daley, who had observed the disturbance from a helicopter, ordered the police chief to "shoot to kill any arsonist or anyone with a Molotov cocktail in his hand because they're potential murderers, and to issue a police order to shoot to maim or cripple anyone looting any stores in our city," unless they were children (they were to be Maced).[3] The following December, Fred Hampton, Illinois chairman of the Black Panther Party, and his associate Mark Clark were murdered by Chicago police. Daley didn't order these killings, but they were a product of the lawless use of law he had encouraged.

That was one measure of the kind of mayor Daley was. There were others.

Richard J. Daley[4] was born in 1902 in the Bridgeport section of Chicago's South Side, less than a block from where he would live as mayor. He was an only child, his father a sheet-metal worker. Educated by the Christian brothers, Daley as a teenager joined the Hamburg Social and Athletic Club, a gang of street toughs who were involved (it's unclear if Daley was) in Chicago's race war of 1919, which left fifteen whites and twenty-three blacks dead.

As had been true of the volunteer fire brigades of the nineteenth century, the Hamburgs became involved in local politics. The members provided election-day muscle for the precinct captain, and some eventually rose through the ranks to hold elective office themselves. One Hamburger became a city councilman, another a congressman, but none was as successful as Daley, who had become president of the Hamburgs while he was still in his early twenties. Years later, when he was mayor, he appointed many of his old pals and their sons to posts in his administration.

From the time he took his first low-level patronage job, which emanated from his Hamburg association, save for one brief interlude Daley stayed on the public payroll for the remainder of his life, a span of more than fifty years. In 1935, he won a seat in the state legislature as a write-in candidate when the incumbent died a few days before the election, and remained there until 1946, when he suffered his only defeat at the polls as a candidate for Cook County sheriff. Along the way he had gotten his law degree but never practiced, other than for handing out his card to lobbyists and others who wanted to do business with the state. The legal work that resulted was handled by Daley's partner.

By then, Daley's reputation among his cohorts was as someone who never engaged in graft and never reported anyone who did. In the seamy world of Chicago politics, the latter was a useful quality for an underling to possess, but not by itself a ticket to advancement. For that to begin to happen, one first had to become a ward leader, a title that brought with it admission to membership in the powerful Cook County Democratic Committee, which consisted of the fifty Chicago ward leaders and a representative from each of the thirty suburban communities within the county. Daley became a ward leader in 1947 and, because of the huge majorities he rang up for party candidates, quickly gained entrance to the inner ruling circle. Once there, he was also freed of any remaining financial problems as a veritable flood of city legal work found its way to his law firm.

Daley's next political job was in the administration of reform governor Adlai Stevenson. The association with Stevenson gave Daley a good government aura and favorable notice in the press. Even so, he resigned that slot in 1950 to become clerk of Cook County, an elected position that became open to him when the incumbent died. In 1953, he sought the chairmanship of the Cook County Democratic Committee and won when his opponent died. (The mortality tables always seemed to work to Daley's benefit.) Two years later, he was elected mayor. It was widely assumed he'd resign as party chairman; he didn't.

He had good reason not to. He knew the caliber of the men he was dealing with on the committee, in large part because he was like them himself. He realized, therefore, that even if he appointed a loyalist, that person might develop ambitions to become mayor himself (as Daley had from that same base). Alternatively, the chairman might not be ambitious himself, but could fall under the sway of Daley's opponents. Either way, the danger was that the committee might deny him renomination as mayor. That's why his predecessor was no longer in office, and he was.

By serving as mayor and chairman, Daley didn't necessarily avoid being unseated from one job or both, but he had significantly lessened the chances. Patronage was the key. The mayor had some jobs to hand out, the chairman others. As mayor and chairman, both reins were in his hands. Ward leaders became entirely dependent upon him and his good will. To keep the patronage jobs the ward already received (which often included the ward leader's) and to get new ones, the captains, far from thinking of rebellion, would bend every effort to see that the faithful got out on election day and supported the one and only author of their good fortune. Because of all the rivalries and jealousies within the organization, many of which impinged directly or indirectly on the duties of the mayor, one had to be a master political mechanic to carry out the dual functions. Daley was a master mechanic.

By keeping both jobs, he also removed ambiguity from the process of favor seeking by those who were outside the party structure but who wanted city contracts. Previously the Cook County Democratic Committee, by retaining the veto over the mayor's continuance in office, had to be considered by such supplicants, but now, since the mayor was the committee, separate approaches weren't needed. It was still a good idea for the supplicants to deal first with their local leader, and contributions would be offered to that person, since that was the way things had always been done, but the local leader no longer made the decision; only Daley did and everyone knew that.

Political power is like money put out to earn interest; the more of it there is to be invested, the higher the rate of return. Daley serves as proof of that theorem. The longer he held the governmental and the political office, the more Chicagoans recognized and acknowledged his power; the very belief in it caused it to grow. Had Daley been a crook, that wouldn't have occurred, not in the long run anyway. News of his nefariousness would have gotten out, and he might have gotten rich but been held in contempt long before he was ever indicted. However, because he was incorruptible, the only feasible way to succeed with him was to please him, to let him know what a great leader he was; the sycophancy not only served to build his ego and increase his confidence in his singular ability to be always right, but the very repetition of the praise furthered the perception of his absolute control. Frank Hague of Jersey City boasted, "I am the law." Richard Daley could say, without boasting, "I am the city."

It was a city that soon bore his mark physically, too. His expressways, in number and size, rivaled those of Robert Moses in New York.[5] Particularly impressive or dispiriting, depending on one's point of view, was the swath cut by the Dan Ryan, named after a Southside Democratic politician, which at its widest point was twelve lanes. Another expressway, shooting through the slums, carries one of the few Republican names visible in Chicago: the Eisenhower. Also made possible by Daley was the Circle Campus of the University of Illinois, with its acres of concrete edifices; it replaced an old and viable Italian neighborhood whose residents had been promised by Daley that they would not be disturbed. The Civic Center, a tower of steel and glass with a fountain and a Picasso metalwork sculpture nearly fifty feet high was Daley's, and so was the Convention Center, which Royko described as "squatting like a gray sow along the blue waters of Lake Michigan."[6] There, too, thanks to Daley, Lake Shore Drive became the site of one of the nation's most successful programs to keep rich people from fleeing the city.

And then there were the skyscrapers. The John Hancock, second in height only to New York's Empire State Building, was pushed into being by Daley over the protests of those who feared it would cause traffic congestion on Michigan Avenue and encourage copycat towers in its wake.[7] Both things happened, but the skyscrapers brought new companies and jobs to Chicago. The resurgence of the downtown business district, made possible by bond issues for public projects like the expressways (all of which led into it), left little money for rehabilitating housing for the poor. But even that lack was to be remedied, in a fashion, by still another skyscraping monument to Daley, his public housing projects.

Daley's downtown accomplishments were recognized by the

Republican business establishment. Its principal outlet, the Chicago *Tribune*, had labeled Daley as the worst kind of machine politician when he refused to give up his chairmanship of the Cook County Democratic Committee, but, well before his first term as mayor was over, the tone had turned admiring. "Boss Daley" was now "Dick the Builder."

By the time that term was over, the 1950s were ending, too, and during the decade that followed, just as in the two preceding ones, the city's black population continued to grow.* As long as blacks remained loyal to the Democrats and Daley, the black vote simply swelled the size of the election-day victory.

At no time did Daley display interest in improving white and black relations. Overt manifestations of racial hatred had to be guarded against since Daley didn't want rioting and destruction of property, but beyond that the status quo presented him with no philosophical or moral problems. Neither did he find it useful to seek to improve the living conditions for the underclass, whether black or white; that might result in a reduction of tensions but would also weaken his machine's hold on such people since they would no longer be as dependent on the party and its favors as they presently were. Daley's approach, rather, was the purely managerial one of catering to white biases while simultaneously controlling black aspirations.

Daley took a number of steps to placate white fears. One particularly notorious instance occurred when the route of the Dan Ryan expressway was deliberately shifted so that it could act as a barrier to prevent blacks who lived on one side of it from spilling over to white neighborhoods on the other side.[9] Daley also always

---

*By about 300,000, bringing the blacks to nearly one-third of the total. During the 1970s, the black percentage also increased, not because of continuing migration to the city, but through a combination of an increase in the black birth rate and a loss of white population. By the end of the 1970s, four years after Daley's death, the white presence had dropped from about 63 percent to 46 percent, with African-Americans counting for another 40 percent and the remainder largely Hispanic.[8]

opposed scattered-site housing since, under federal funding regulations, such programs could not be implemented if they followed existent segregation patterns. An unofficial rule (and for that reason one not easily challengeable in court) was that no public housing was to be built in any ward without its leader's approval; in effect, that meant projects for blacks would go up only in black neighborhoods. The same policy was carried out in public housing for the aged, because of the fear that if such a facility was opened in a white area, it would be impossible, under federal statute, to keep out elderly black tenants.[10]

Despite the blatancy of his racist policies, Daley for a long time had little difficulty holding the black vote in line. Ironically, one of the methods used had first been applied upon white immigrants from Europe in the late nineteenth century. Under this system, in black districts across Daley's Chicago, voters not known to be loyalists would find themselves accompanied inside the booth by poll workers who either made sure they pulled the party lever or did that job for them.[11] The voters rarely objected; they were aware that if they did, they could lose their welfare checks or be kicked out of their subsidized apartments. A variation, which was more frequently employed, had the same effect: Voters weren't accompanied into the booth but were told that if they didn't follow orders, the precinct captain would find out and the same punishment follow. As is apparent, this technique will work only when the targeted population doesn't understand the limits of governmental power or is unwilling to test them. As time went on and Chicago's black voters, thanks to the civil rights movement, became politically sophisticated, the terrorization techniques were no longer effective, and ultimately in Daley's last election in 1975, the majority of the city's African-American voters rejected him.[12]

Daley, however, had never entirely relied on intimidation to have his way with the black electorate. He also bought their loyalty. The federal government's multiple antipoverty programs provided him with his purchase order. Since these initiatives were principally directed at helping blacks and were situated in black neighborhoods, even antagonistic whites couldn't object if blacks were given many of the resultant jobs. Those who obtained these patronage appointments—and they got them by the thousands—always knew why they had gotten them and how they could lose them, and they became and remained to the end a significant voter bloc for Daley.*

Symbolism was also used. Daley created the Chicago Commission on Urban Opportunity, through which the various poverty programs were administered and which opened branch offices in the inner city, giving the impression that it was the city of Chicago (hence, Daley) that was responsible for the help that was now being offered, and not the federal government, which in fact funded the programs.[13]

As a manipulator of people, which is the secret to controlling them, Daley was at his considerable best in dealing with Martin Luther King.[14] Unlike officials in southern cities who initially tried to refuse to have anything to do with King's demands, only later to have to capitulate to them to some degree, Daley appeared to welcome King's visit to Chicago, which came about shortly after a riot on Chicago's West Side in July 1965. He telegraphed King offering to meet with him, and when King refused, dispatched his Commission of Human Relations director to greet King at the airport. After King opened his formal campaign in Chicago the following January, Daley moved to upstage him by announcing his own program of slum clearance. While Daley watched, over the next six months King's effort faltered. Then, in July 1966, under pressure from the more militant elements of the civil rights effort, King came up with a list of demands that he proposed to nail to the door of City Hall, in keeping with the action of his namesake in Wittenberg in 1517. Daley recognized the danger and again offered to sit down with King. This time King agreed, only to have

*Estimates vary depending on the politician making them, but each patronage job can roughly be equated to ten to fifteen votes (the job-holder, the job-holder's family, and neighbors and friends whom the job-holder can influence).

Daley reject every one of the demands (which never got posted anywhere). Daley sat back to wait some more.

The thwarted King and his lieutenants hit upon a new tactic. They would carry out a series of marches through white neighborhoods to protest segregation. On August 5, in Marquette Park, King was hit by a rock. The effect was to recapture lagging local and national media attention, setting up the classic battle of good (desegregation) against evil (violent white racism) that had served King well in his southern exploits. "People woke up and literally poured into the movement," one of his white advisers recalled.

In response, on August 17, Daley agreed to hold what he called a "summit," with the civil rights leaders on one side of the table, the politicians and city's businessmen on the other. After the meeting ended with no agreement, Daley tightened the screws on King by issuing an injunction against further marches in Chicago. King responded by promising a protest in Cook County's all-white Cicero if a second summit did not produce meaningful concessions by his opponents.

It seemed to. When King promised to stop marching, Daley agreed to sign a new open-housing plan for the city. Soon after, King left Chicago, having gotten the victory he badly needed. But Daley, just as King's critics believed, hadn't really made a concession. The open-housing program was always intended by him to be a will-o'-the-wisp: It gave the civil rights advocates something to chase, busy work that kept them out of harm's way.* The only visible reminder of the agreement between Daley and King is the Leadership Council for Metropolitan Communities, which runs a program to place black families in integrated neighborhoods, not in Chicago but its suburbs. That may be a worthwhile project, but it hardly addressed the goals that Dr. King spent his career and lost his life espousing.

---

*Much more successful was Jesse Jackson's separate Operation Breadbasket, which focused not on Daley but on boycotts of businesses that had substantial numbers of black customers but few if any black employees.

Although Daley's ultimate image is fixed in the national memory by the television cameras at the Democratic Convention of 1968, his defeat of King may be the best measure of the man. At no time during the course of the various negotiations does any indication surface that Daley understood what King was driving at. Daley may have—he was by no means stupid—but, if so, King's platform for social justice was completely irrelevant to Daley's purpose, which was to retain control of his city. King, therefore, was simply one more problem to be solved, and that and only that is what Daley set out to do in his dealings with King. (King, in that sense, would have been much better off if Daley had been an ideologue; King would then have been back on the familiar turf of the racist opponents in the south, to whom he knew how to respond.)

Daley's approach to King was not substantively different from that he took when it came to expressways and renewal of the central business district. In both those instances, the task was to find ways to create construction jobs and bring in business, and his solutions did exactly what they were supposed to do, just as the task with King was to solve the black threat, which, to Daley's satisfaction (King was gone), is exactly what happened, too.

When Daley's monumental ego and his wrathfulness against anyone who did not agree with him is laid to one side, he can be seen as the paragon of the problem-solver as mayor. His career, however, is nearly unblemished by any indication that he saw himself and Chicagoans engaged in a mutual enterprise that would make their city a good place to live for themselves and their heirs.

In 1955, the same year Daley first won election as mayor in Chicago, Richardson Dilworth achieved the same post in Philadelphia.[15] Both men were then in their fifties, both Democrats, both lawyers, both with a combative nature—Joseph Clark once described Dilworth as "D'Artagnan in a double-breasted suit"—but otherwise the contrast between them was sharp: in their backgrounds, in the paths they took to their political triumph, and in their philosophies of urban government.

Unlike the working-class Daley, Dilworth was born to privilege. His mother came from a wealthy family, and his father was a successful businessman who owned a plant in Pittsburgh that manufactured railroad spikes and tie plates.[16] Despite their affluence, the Dilworths were not, however, of the same social standing—there are all kinds of gradations in these matters—as the Philadelphia Clarks, and in later years, Dilworth would take a dim view of his adopted city's patrician class: "The rich," he remarked, "seem to want the city to be a compound where the poor will be clean, orderly, and well-policed, and will provide fine airports and subways. And they expect all this to be paid for by the same people they would hire as household servants."[17]

Dilworth's outspokenness was one of his most consistent characteristics; another was his courage. Soon after the United States entered World War I, Dilworth, then a nineteen-year-old student at Yale, enlisted in the Marines. He fought at Soissons and at Belleau Wood. There, while under German bombardment, he climbed out of his trench into no-man's-land to free a wounded soldier from the barbed wire in which he was enmeshed and carried the man on his back to safety. Nearly a quarter-century later when World War II broke out, the forty-three-year-old Dilworth, despite his age, managed to talk his way back into the Marines, served in the South Pacific, reached the rank of major, and earned the Silver Star for "gallantry and intrepidity in action."

Dilworth displayed courage of a different kind in 1953. At that time, Senator Joseph McCarthy of Wisconsin was at the height of his power, and virtually no politicians were willing to criticize him lest they be labeled, as so many others had been, as communists or fellow travelers. However, Dilworth, who had gained a national reputation as a liberal reformer, was not deterred.[18] In a speech, he described McCarthy as "more dangerous than a thousand Alger Hisses." McCarthy immediately dared Dilworth to repeat his accusations on national television with McCarthy present. Dilworth happily agreed, and in the debate that ensued he added that, while criminals get punished, "demagogues [like you] remain too long above and beyond the processes of the law."

Dilworth had moved to Philadelphia in 1926—apparently because that was his wife's home—but he was spending most of his weekends on Long Island partying with his rich friends in Great Gatsby–like surroundings. He had, however, by then also developed an interest in politics, his inspiration Woodrow Wilson.[19] His first political venture came in alliance with Clark, who was three years his junior. They established a reform group they called The Warriors,[20] and in the early 1930s they made a run for office, but both were soundly defeated in the primary and that, for a while, was the end of that.

In the mid-1930s, Dilworth, divorced and remarried, was hired to represent Moe Annenberg's Triangle Publications in a dispute involving news dealers. When Dilworth won the case, an impressed Annenberg engaged Dilworth's firm as general counsel for Triangle, which owned the *Daily Racing Form* and the *Philadelphia Inquirer*. The relationship continued after Dilworth became mayor, despite the distaste that Annenberg's son Walter, who was by then in charge, felt toward Democrats and their pernicious liberalism. As Dilworth once recalled: "I could always tell how I stood with the *Inquirer* just by seeing which picture of me they used. They had two of them. In one, I looked like Rasputin the Mad Monk, and that was for when I was in their bad books. If they used the smiling, full-faced picture, then I knew they approved of me. That day, anyway. It was really convenient. Saved time from reading the stories, doncha know?"

Dilworth took the path that led him to becoming mayor out of a moment that occurred in the winter of 1945. Just back from the war, he was standing by himself on the sands of Palm Beach in Florida. "I realized," he told a reporter a number of years later, "I was facing a decision of what to do with the rest of my life. I was either going to devote it to drinking and running around [as I had], or else I was going to do something worthwhile."[21]

By then, the social drinking of his youth had turned into alcoholism, and he entered a hospital for treatment of it. He always
credited the therapy he received there for his recovery, but it may
be that the sheer joy he found in politics and public service was
the real cause of his cure. In any event, his health restored, in
1947 he presented himself to the Democrats as their candidate for
mayor and carried out the rip-roaring if losing campaign described
in Chapter Seven. Two years later, he was elected city treasurer
and in 1952, with the reform movement he had helped create now
at full steam, he became the city's district attorney, taking office
the same day that Clark did as mayor.

At the time, the DA's office consisted of fewer than thirty prosecutors, most of them part-time hacks. Dilworth weeded out the
lazy and inept, even as he aggressively recruited the young, bright,
and capable from the nation's top law schools. Among the objects
of his search were black attorneys. Eventually nearly a quarter of
his staff would be African-Americans, including A. Leon Higgin-
botham, who went on to become a historian and the president
judge of the U.S. Third Circuit Court of Appeals. Until then, the
few blacks on the DA's staff had been relegated humiliatingly to
trying summary offenses in the city's Magistrate Court. Dilworth
was having none of that and assigned them to Common Pleas,
where felony cases were heard. The usual practice was to rotate
prosecutors every few weeks, but when the president judge ordered Dilworth to "get your nigger out of my courtroom," Dilworth responded by keeping that attorney, also later a judge, on
the scene for six months. Reluctantly, the president judge finally
admitted "the boy" did know his law.

Dilworth did not limit his recruitment attention to blacks.
Soon after he took over, he called in his first assistant, Michael
Von Moschzisker, and asked him to undertake a search of the law
schools for female graduates who might be interested in joining
his staff. At that time, women prosecutors were unheard of in any
district attorney's office, in part because few law school classes had
more than one female student, and mostly because it would never

occur to any DA in those prefeminist days to even think of hiring a woman for other than a secretarial position. Von Moschzisker asked Dilworth about his reasoning. Dilworth replied: "It seems to me that one of the duties of government is to encourage the ambitions of all its people. Women are half that population, and we do very little to encourage them. Well, in this office, that's what we are going to do. I don't mean just for the women we hire as prosecutors, but for other women who will see them as role models and will be stirred to continue their educations by their example, so they can hold positions of importance, too, just like men."*[22]

Dilworth's sense of equity did not extend only to blacks and women. When he appointed Samuel Dash, later chief counsel of the Watergate Committee, as the chief of his appeals unit, he explained: "Our duty is to prosecute vigorously on behalf of the people those we think have committed crimes against them, but we are also here to uphold the Constitution of the United States. That means, Sam, when you are going over a case and discover we have violated someone's civil rights, you are to call that situation to the attention of the court, and not wait for the defendant's lawyer to do so. He might not." The same philosophy prevailed in the trials themselves. Contrary to the goals of most district attorney offices, then and since, getting guilty verdicts was not the measure by which a prosecutor advanced. Charles Weiner, one of Dilworth's trial assistants who also became a federal court judge, recalled: "He wasn't just interested in a batting average. He wanted to make sure that justice was done."[24]

In 1955, Clark announced he was not going to run for a second term as mayor, his eyes instead on the United States Senate, where he won a seat the following year. Clark's decision opened the way for Dilworth, who had never been trusted by the Americans for Democratic Action (ADA) reformers who surrounded

*Of the first two women Dilworth hired, one later became a judge and the second a leading criminal defense attorney. A third woman, who soon followed the first two, also went on to become a judge, as well as an author.[23]

Clark. Dilworth didn't listen to their advice as if it were Holy Writ, and he particularly didn't get along with the liberal be-sainted Walter Phillips, whom Dilworth considered to be an insufferable upper-class prig. Dilworth, however, had started the reform movement with his run for mayor in 1947, and the ADA, which had supported him in previous campaigns, was hardly in a position to openly oppose him once he got the nomination. Opposition from the right came in the form of the Veterans of Foreign Wars.[25] They were particularly distressed by the liberal politics of one of Dilworth's running mates, Henry Sawyer (no relation to Robert Sawyer, whose 1948 revelations had sounded the death knell for the Republicans). A candidate for city council, Sawyer was one of the few ADA leaders who was close to Dilworth. True to his style, Dilworth denounced the VFW's point man to his face as a "little tinhorn Hitler," and told him, "I don't need your vote or the VFW's either." He didn't. He won by a large majority, and so did Sawyer.

Dilworth immediately came under attack from the liberal camp when he announced his support for so-called "charter ripper" amendments favored by Democratic Party politicians. With Phillips playing a leading role, a campaign was mounted that led to the defeat of the amendments. The first one, which was much the less controversial, would have allowed office-holders to run for another position without resigning the one they held. The second, however, seemed to strike right at the heart of the 1951 charter by transferring back to patronage a number of civil-service jobs.

In backing the amendments, Dilworth was, to some extent, bowing to the new political reality. Clark and his allies had been brilliant in restoring integrity to city government, but they never succeeded, and often didn't seem interested, in developing support among Democratic Party regulars. Perhaps the reformers didn't perceive the party to be a threat, but more likely they simply found the thought of dealing with professional politicians unpleasant and beneath them. In any case, they seemed unaware that through their 1951 victory at the polls, they might have created a monster. But they had.

Almost overnight, the Democrats had become the city's majority party, and a hungry one. Ever since the Civil War, it had been the Republicans who threw Democrats an occasional bone from their patronage feast, and now the resurgent Democratic bosses wanted to turn that around. The new chairman, Congressman William Green, Jr., although himself a liberal, was also an old-fashioned power broker who disdained the reformers as a bunch of amateur do-gooders who would have no lasting powers, and by 1955 he had whipped together an organization that might have been able to deny Dilworth the mayoralty if he didn't give in to its demands.

However, it is also true that Dilworth had no reservations in meeting those demands. He believed that if reform was to continue, the legitimate needs of the organization had to be met, which included giving it some jobs, or else it would have no reason to support good government. Neither did he see party politics as the unmitigated evil that the ADA-reformers did. To him, parties performed a valuable function, beginning at the committee-person level, where they provided ordinary people a direct and continuing access to government. That the politicians sometimes exploited those same people was not, as he saw it, any different from rich people exploiting the poor to pay for their comforts. When such exploitation occurred, whoever was the author, one called attention to it and tried to stop it, as he had repeatedly. What wasn't to be done was to throw away an entire system just because it had weaknesses. Rather, systems were to be discarded only when they were inherently oppressive, which political parties were not.

Dilworth, therefore, had a set of reasons to support the charter patronage amendment, and they may represent his entire thinking. However, public figures, no more than anyone else, don't always respond to situations and people in purely rational ways. All three of the mayors covered in this chapter—Clark, Daley, and

Dilworth—had strong objective leadership qualities, yet in each of them a consistent attitude is displayed toward his fellow human beings that is quite distinguishable from the other two. Clark's salient characteristic was his disdain; it meant, in leadership terms, that he kept organization politicians from influencing his administration, but his disdain also meant he inadvertently allowed them to generate strength. Daley was a man whose consuming need was to control other people, so that his relationships with them were satisfactory to him only when he made them fear him or when they stroked him. The analogy between Daley as mayor and Moses as city planner is a striking one: Out of the same need to control, both men rejected and may have feared the challenges that occur when ideas are freely exchanged. For his part, Clark was willing to discuss issues, but generally only with those he considered his social equals. Dilworth, to the contrary, was like Bacon in his understanding of the importance of the broad-based colloquy, and his democratic receptivity may very well have sprung from the sheer delight he took in people in all their varieties, which very much included politicians. Dilworth had studied them, had combated them, and understood them well and sympathetically. He recognized (as Clark clearly didn't and Daley probably didn't) that politicians' demands to have jobs to hand out not only was related to establishing for themselves a cadre of supporters, but also had to do with their sense of self-worth: Becoming dispensers of patronage made them feel benevolent and therefore good about themselves. Dilworth's intuitive response to the politicians' needs is akin to his understanding of the need for women to have their aspirations recognized and met, too.

Dilworth's regard for politicians did not extend to running in a pack with them, any more than it did running against them. He had no interest in becoming party dictator, as Daley did: That would make the party's priorities his, which he thought to be wrong since the party was only a segment of the city. Dilworth's approach to political relationships is probably best illustrated by his dealings with city council. There, the contrast between him and the aloof Clark and the bulldozing Daley is quite sharply drawn. The council prospectively was not going to be a body likely to be cooperative with him. It was neither cowed, as Daley's were, nor led by an ally, as Clark's had been. The seventeen men who had been elected to serve on it were, save for Sawyer and one or two others, hacks who owed their seats not to Clark or Dilworth but to party chairman Green. Dilworth could have readily taken council on, exposing its ineptness, and no doubt gained favorable headlines for himself by so doing. But that is not the choice he made. Instead, he held regular lunch meetings with the councilmen, to which he'd also invite various department heads, explaining he wanted to share the problems the city was having and get their input about his ideas. During these get-togethers, he made it apparent to the councilmen that he assumed they were solely interested, just as he was, in what was good for the city. By treating ward heelers as statesmen, very often that was the way they responded, and Dilworth had little difficulty getting his programs passed. It was, as Sawyer described it, one of those beautifully simple ideas that no previous mayor had thought to try.

In 1959, Dilworth was easily reelected to his second term as mayor. Three years later, he won the Democratic nomination for governor and resigned as mayor to take on the campaign. He lost. In 1967, at the age of sixty-nine, he entered his last service to the city as president of the Philadelphia Board of Education, an unpaid position. As mayor, he felt, he had too much ignored the problems of the public schools, and he set about making amends with his usual zest and combativeness. As Peter Binzen pointed out in his study of Dilworth: "The early achievements of Dilworth's board were staggering. In one year, it established 100 kindergartens and 100 school libraries, set up seven experimental 'magnet' schools, hired 3,000 new teachers, doubled spending for books, launched a school building program. . . . Philadelphia became the most exciting city in the nation for educational improvement."[26] In 1972, he resigned the presidency; two years later, he died.

Dilworth's place in the history of cities is not to be found in a listing of his specific accomplishments. It's not that they weren't numerous. As mayor, he pushed Bacon's Penn Center to completion with an enthusiasm Clark had never shown; he completed the removal of the city's wholesale food market from the dirty, rat-infested Dock Street to a modern distribution facility on the city's outskirts; he was, next only to Bacon, responsible for the Society Hill renaissance, which he personally promoted by building a house there, an act that did much to encourage individual buyers and real estate developers. He coalesced the city and suburban mass transit lines into one of the best regional systems in the nation.

He also made mistakes. He was right about his failure to understand that the public school system was declining, and he authorized, against Bacon's recommendation, the building of the destructive high-rise public housing projects. Neither was he able, more than any other mayor of his time, to come to grips with the problems presented by the arrival of large numbers of poverty-class blacks from the South to his city.

But even when we set aside the failures and consider only the positive physical changes he brought about in his city while mayor, we still have to rank Dilworth behind both Daley and Clark. For the most part, the major programs Dilworth carried out were initiated during Clark's administration, and neither did Dilworth engage in the massive commercial building projects that Daley did, which helped solidify Chicago's tax base. In the accounting sense of accomplishment, Dilworth rates only as a good mayor, not a great one.

His significance as an urban leader emanates rather from his philosophy of the purpose of government as an instrument of public ethics. From that philosophy sprang his insistence, as district attorney, that Dash report any violations of a defendant's rights to the court. In making his demand, Dilworth's interest wasn't so much in the defendant, who was probably guilty anyway; rather, it extended from his belief that any conspiracy on the part of government to hide the truth, in this instance from a judge, is a conspiracy against society itself. As Dilworth understood, once the agents of government decide whose rights they will protect and whose not, no one is safe from wrongful government intrusion, not even those who are favored today, since the pattern has now been established by which they can become victims tomorrow.

Dilworth was hardly the first person to grasp that principle, although many who have done so quite nicely managed to ignore it once they were in positions of power themselves. A more nearly unique expression of Dilworth's philosophy of government is to be seen in sending Von Moschzisker off to look for young female attorneys to become prosecutors. Implicit in that act was his awareness that it is not sufficient for government to pass laws that guarantee various civil rights; it must also act as exemplar. To Dilworth, it was that simple: We'll show women achieving, and that way more women will want to achieve, which is a good thing for the society—after all, as he pointed out to Von Moschzisker, we'll be helping half our population do better—and therefore a good thing for government to do. When government performs as facilitator of human aspirations, its act has far greater value, he believed, than can be found in building all the skyscrapers in every city in the world.

From that view of facilitation stems the corollary that was fundamental to Dilworth's definition of "good" government. It would be nice, he thought, if good government also meant honest government, but achieving that state was a less important goal to reach than that government be on the side of the people who elect it. For, as he saw it, when a government is not on the side of its people, or is perceived by them as not being on their side, then public trust in it is not possible, and without trust comes the same kind of divorcement as when buildings fragment the landscape rather than make of it an amenable whole. Without trust, no charter of governance, no matter how finely worded, no matter how great the integrity of its minions, is meaningful because the possibility of union between the governors and the governed is lost.

As applied to city government, Dilworth's corollary means that government must both avoid oppressive acts itself and protect people from oppression at the hands of others. It is fairly easy to accomplish the basics of the first requisite: Under it, a mayor doesn't give orders to the police to murder looters, to Mace children, or club demonstrators into submission, as Daley did. Carrying out the second requirement, however, can be extraordinarily difficult, as becomes apparent when we consider how government in a city is but one force among many. Crime and drugs are potent oppressors, and city governments have shown, at most, only a sporadic capacity to control them. Banks and other financing institutions can be as powerful, sometimes more powerful, than the city itself, and in their search for profits they can act oppressively against portions of the public, as when entire neighborhoods are red-lined, so that mortgages and reconstruction loans are no longer available to them. City unions, which can be a veritable engine of political support for a mayor, may, however, demand in return contracts that, if they are granted, can be harmful to the public in the burdensome taxes they require in order to be funded. And no force can be more devastating in its effect upon a city than the federal (or state) government by enacting policies that reduce or withdraw the financial supports needed to allow the city to educate its children properly or care for its needy.

Thus, regardless of how brilliant in leadership, regardless of how deep in commitment to ethical principles he or she may be, no mayor can hope to succeed always against the many interests that roam across the city's terrain and impinge upon its purposes. However, the mayor can act as a countervailing force, refusing to allow herself or her administration to be numbered among the conspirators against the citizens. When this dictum holds sway, we begin to find the true meaning of "good" government. It recognizes that unfairnesses will occur and that it can be the author of some of them and not prevent others, but its direction is always toward protection and responsiveness, not toward neglect and exploitation. The good government is neither mean-spirited nor merely mechanistic. It knows toward whom its primal duties lie, and it doesn't only try to act in their behalf but is in communication with them.

For a mayor, few duties are as important, and none more important, than seeing to it that the street of conversation remains unblocked. A mayor must move among the people, sit down and talk to them. The format need not be and often should not be the discussion of some immediate problem, but rather talk between the mayor and the people of how they'd like their city to be five or ten years in the future. In that way, the mayor and the citizens both are able to think in terms of long-range goals, which (as a not inconsiderable side benefit) may also give them the perspective that allows them to see an approach to a current dilemma that wouldn't otherwise have been evident. (Only when the desirable future is known will a way be found to reach it.)

Mayors have many avenues of communication open to them, including the generally unsatisfactorily distancing one of television, but whatever method they employ, the goal of communication in a good government is to encourage people to participate in their city. It is only when they are constantly informed about what the administration wants to do and why that the collective consciousness described by Bacon is awakened. When that happens, the people see hope for their city and become willing to participate in bringing the hope to reality. The large number of volunteers who came forward in St. Paul, under Latimer's leadership, were a result of tapping the energy of hope.

The dialogue between government and the people, however, must not be limited to the adults among them. Children, from very early ages, should be participants, too. This is why the role given to children in the Better Philadelphia Exhibition was of such great importance. Encouraged to come up with ideas about how to change their block, their neighborhood, their entire city, they learned to think in terms of the future. For the children of the inner city, no kind of learning could be more valuable as a means of opposing the signals of entropy that are, otherwise, their daily fare and that make them socially negligent as they approach adult life.

In leadership, love also counts. In Daley's career, love for Chicago is not evident, save possibly in the sense that he loved himself, for he saw Chicago as an extension of himself. Clark understood the nature of the city, but his comprehension was one of intellect and ideology. With him, there was no love either, no exuberant vision of the good city, and that's what Dilworth had. His passion was Philadelphia. The people understood that, and that's why, over and over again, they forgave him for his many wild statements, his emotional outbursts. Even when they were most angry at him, they never mistrusted him. His quarrels with them and theirs with him were lovers' quarrels. They understood that he was exactly what he appeared to be, simple and almost childlike in his intensity, a man who thought his city was a splendid place to live. In his best years, he communicated that love, and a generation of Philadelphians walked along with him in the green city of his mind, and found it to be a good place, too.

In 1988, shortly after revelations about his personal life caused Senator Gary Hart of Colorado to remove himself from the presidential race, he was asked to give his opinion about the candidates who had survived him. Hart said he thought they were all "estimable" individuals but ones who lacked "dimension."

Hart's comment contains the nugget definition of political leadership. Just as is true of presidential candidates, mayors who lack dimension may be "estimable," but somehow they are never able to put together any conception that a city has a purpose and its people a purpose within it. Dilworth's passionate vision of Philadelphia, as a congress of people of great expectations whose government had a duty to fulfill those ambitions, was one of dimension. On the national level, Franklin D. Roosevelt had the same quality. His critics have pointed out that many of his programs were failures, and it is true they didn't end the Depression prior to the intervention of the World War II. But what Roosevelt did do, at a time when Americans had lost faith in themselves and the ability of their institutions to protect them, was to provide the protections and provide the hope. He was able to make people believe that, by joining hands with him, great goals could yet be achieved. He gave spirit where there had been none and a zest for experimentation; in these ways, he added dimension to the definition of human possibilities.

Dimension in political leadership is analogous to the role the vector plays in city planning. In both, we see lines of force of indefinite length emitted from the focal point. They give direction. With Daley, we find a focal point but no vectors. He created an imposing structure, and the ideas and plans he carried out could be impressive (when they weren't frightening), but he had no more interest in creating a continuity of community than did Renaissance Center in Detroit. He and it had no relationship to aspiration that was not self-contained.

In cities, as Bacon once wrote, we shouldn't look for victories but for vectors. Victories are too easily misunderstood, too tentative, too much prey to the changes wrought by the next round of events, so that they can take on the appearance of defeat because they didn't prove permanent. The vectors, however, can be permanent. They are constantly pushing us toward the future, where we can reclaim old gains and make new ones. Neither do we need many exceptional political leaders to move us toward that future, any more than we need a whole plethora of designers like Bacon to give us structural ideas of continuity. Exceptional leaders, it is true, are rare, and we should welcome them (when we can recognize them) should they turn up. What is not rare are good people, those who have the will and the capacity to understand the vectors that others have created, and who can learn from them and constantly reapply them.

The final importance of a Dilworth, therefore, lies not in the minutiae of the events of his time nor of the events that followed, but in the enriched dimension of the direction for cities that he pronounced.

12

The Continuum Expanded

In performing her duties, a mayor must deal with forces beyond the city's borders. Among such matters, she has to lobby for federal and state funds, convince the bond market that the city is on a reasonably sound financial footing, find ways to encourage tourism, attract new businesses. But the likelihood is—and this will certainly be true if the city is a very large one—the most persistent and vexing dilemma she will face will be an internal one. A number of phrases have been used to name it, such as: "the problems of the inner city," "the drug culture," and "crime on the streets." Some of these phrases are more inflammatory than they are helpful, but the problems they describe all have a single root: poverty.

When speculating about the future of poverty in American cities, statistical projections from the Bureau of Census suggest that by no later than the end of the first quarter of the twenty-first century (but probably much sooner), the population of our major urban centers will have become markedly different from that of the last decade of the twentieth century.[1] The white percentage of the total, it is believed, will continue on a downward track, although the actual numbers will decline at a slower pace than in earlier years. The black presence will likely continue to increase but not nearly as rapidly as in the past,* and as with whites, the percentage presence will drop. Hispanics and, to a lesser extent,

* Or, other census figures suggest, it may decrease: Between 1980 and 1990, the black presence in the suburbs rose from 26 percent to 32 percent of the whole, and almost all these black families moved to the suburbs from their adjacent cities.[2]

Asians will increase, both in numbers and percentages. They will also make up the youngest element, which means a heavy portion of their Social Security taxes will go to help support not their own elderly but the growing number of elderly blacks and whites. That burden could cause resentment on the part of Hispanics and Asians if they have reason to continue to see themselves as victims of white and black discrimination.

The eventual demographic alterations may be less dramatic than envisioned. If life in the cities improves, fewer whites and blacks will leave; Hispanic birth rates may not be as high as projected, and so on. Nevertheless, we already have evidence from cities like New York, Miami, Los Angeles, and Chicago that the growing number of Hispanics and Asians in the inner cities has led to interethnic animosities, adding to the traditional ones between whites and blacks. Asians setting up retail shops in poverty-level black neighborhoods have been harassed, and acts of violence against them have grown, as exemplified by the 1992 riots in Los Angeles. More troublesome, because of the prospective magnitude of the problem, is the tension between low-income African-Americans and Hispanics, which in cities like Los Angeles has displayed itself most visibly as warfare between juvenile gangs. At the volatile heart of the matter, however, is the competition for the ever-shrinking numbers of low- and semi-skilled jobs available. When we add to that configuration the continued and increasing desperation of economically displaced white working-class members, we have the basis for protracted inner-city tumult of a multifaceted nature that cities previously have not had to face.

In an economic competition between Hispanics and African-Americans, the African-Americans seem temporarily better positioned to be the winners. In 1993, the last year for which statistics were available at the time of the writing of this book, only about 60 percent of Hispanics over the age of eighteen were high school graduates, compared to 75 percent of the blacks (and 83 percent of the whites),[3] which—to the extent a high school diploma means anything—indicates better opportunities for the blacks.* Nevertheless, the situation faced by the poverty-level African-Americans is for them particularly difficult and dispiriting. In the past, blacks were the victims of discrimination from the whites coming down from the top onto them; now they still have the white problem, but added to it is the threat perceived from the Hispanics and Asians moving up from the bottom toward them.

The ferment at the lower end of the economic scale is matched by another at the upper end. There, in most major American cities, we see that an alliance has developed or is in the process of formation between blacks and whites. They have good reason to make common cause. Taken separately, neither group has the numbers or the influence to dominate city decision making, but together they do. At the same time, because they are successful participants in the city economically and politically, they have a shared interest in assuring tranquility in the inner cities, lest upheavals there threaten their positions.

At present, the most visible and frequent form the coalition takes is that of black mayors and other upper-level city officials who, along with input from high-level black advisers, receive counsel and financial support from the corporate and banking communities, which remain overwhelmingly white at the executive tiers. Just as the rising interethnic tensions at the lower levels of the city give cause for alarm, the new black-white coalescence (which will later be joined by affluent Hispanics and Asians) might be considered a cause for optimism. The longer it persists— and it has every reason to persist, out of self-interest—the participants are in a position where they can develop poverty policies that weren't even thinkable as long as the relationship was distant and was marked by competing agendas (black militants versus

* While these figures are probably basically correct, some Hispanics also consider themselves to be black, and it is not clear how the Census Bureau designates these individuals in its educational attainment statistics.

white establishment) and by suspicion and ignorance of each other's view of reality.

Nevertheless, the upper-level ferment carries with it warning signs of its own. A possibility exists that black members of the coalition will believe (and that the white members, out of deference, will agree with them) that they have a special knowledge of the yearnings and frustrations of the poor, and that therefore only they can make meaningful proposals. Quite apart from the fact that growing numbers of the poor aren't black, this is at best a doubtful supposition to make even when applied only to blacks. History is redolent with examples of people who rose from poverty to wealth and influence and became far worse exploiters of the poor than the well-born ever dreamed of being. But even if history doesn't repeat itself, and granting for the moment that the ideas proposed by the black-white coalition have merit, they are virtually certain to prove ineffective if they are imposed upon the supposed beneficiaries, which is how elites tend to act, not necessarily as individuals but associatively. What is required, rather, is a laying out of plans succinctly in as universal a manner as possible in order to spark widespread debate among the beneficiaries and between them and the benefactors. Only in that way will public consciousness be raised, eventually leading to assent and knowledgeable cooperation by all parties.

While a certain amount of lip service has been given to this holistic approach in the past, it has rarely been tried in any serious manner. The constant hindrance has been the underlying assumption by the successful that they know what is best for the unsuccessful. Coupled with that belief is the perception by the benefactors that the poor are stupid. Not only do their failures seem to prove that, but so does their comparative inarticulateness in pressing their arguments. (Lack of vocabulary is frequently mistaken for lack of intelligence.) Things are, therefore, done for them and not with them.

Should that become the synopsis, we will see a reiteration of a pattern of scattershot palliatives. "Worst" areas will be targeted for social services and increased police protection; those deemed to be facing conditions of non-imminent crisis will be largely ignored, and still other neighborhoods that appear to have reached a degree of stability will be neglected entirely. As new "worst" areas evince themselves, which will happen because of the neglect, attention will be shifted from the previous "worst" areas, where only the most egregious symptoms have been contained. If the disaffected (in one area or another) riot, they will likely get infusions of federal and local funds to rebuild their neighborhoods and encourage new business starts,* so that they look better, but with the conditions that prompted the turbulence unchanged. Even in the absence of rioting, the palliative of removing the worst houses on the worst blocks almost certainly will be invoked, and little beyond that. Drug dens will be razed or more likely boarded up, either way spreading the blighted appearance of the streets on which they appear. The goal, that is, will be to try to contain chaos in a chaotic way.

Finding a cohesive approach to the problems presented by poverty has long proven to be a daunting task. One reason is that poverty's manifestations are complex, with the same ill effect at times having separate causes. For example, no one seems to doubt that inner-city schools as a whole provide a quality of education that is inferior to middle-class schools; as a result, too many chil-

---

* Perhaps in the form of enterprise zones. By the early 1990s, this version of supply-side economics had been adopted in thirty-seven states and the District of Columbia, with federal legislation also proposed. Enterprise zones are based on the belief that businesses will be encouraged to move to depressed areas by granting them tax incentives, and thereby increasing employment among the residents. The record of enterprise zones, however, has been fairly dismal. Almost all of them have added jobs to their target areas, but the employees have very often come with the companies and the number of locals hired has been disappointing. Where significant numbers of local residents have gotten jobs from the new inner-city companies, some evidence suggests that the employers have been motivated by the prospect of cheap labor and not by the tax incentives (which, however, they are happy to accept since they were offered).[4]

dren, already handicapped by the daily environment outside the inner-city school, aren't challenged in the classroom and see no point in learning; if they don't drop out, they drift through their educations, reaching adulthood lacking the skills they need to compete in the outside world. No doubt this grim scenario plays itself out repeatedly because of an inferior educational environment, yet we also have evidence indicating that a substantial number of these children fail not because of poor teaching but because of health problems. Inner-city children are much more likely than middle-class children to have uncorrected hearing and vision problems. (When a child can't hear what the teacher is saying or see clearly the words on the blackboard, frustration will result from that reason alone.) Perhaps even more devastatingly, inner-city children are particularly likely to be the victims of lead poisoning, most often due to lead paint in their homes. Studies have shown that these afflicted youngsters have their cognitive abilities reduced, tend to become hyperactive, are unable to concentrate in the classroom, and may be prone to antisocial behavior beginning at an early age and continuing into adulthood. (The delinquency is caused not by the lead intoxication but by the failure patterns it engenders.)

The complexity of the poverty problem is further illustrated by the relationship between inner-city life and narcotics. The connection appears to be an inexorable one: The onerous conditions of inner-city life cause its victims to seek solace in drugs, which in turn causes them to commit crimes to obtain the narcotics to which they have become addicted. There is no doubt that this happens, and it presents a grievous situation calling out for a cure; however, statistical analyses published in 1992 by the U.S. Department of Justice and the National Institute on Drug Abuse point out that African-Americans, who make up the largest portion of the inner-city population, are only about two-thirds as likely to use drugs as their percentage in the total population.[5] Another 1992 government study supported these findings; it discovered that white male high school seniors used cocaine twice as often as did black male seniors. Although neither black nor white drug use was classified by income level in any of these investigations, they suggest that, contrary to popular belief, the causal connection between poverty and drug use is a tenuous one. Evidence associating poverty with drug sales (which may be accompanied by acts of violence) is more convincing, but not entirely so. Blacks are arrested for narcotics offenses at five times the rate for whites, which may mean a much higher incidence of drug transactions in the inner city. However, it could also mean that police are more prone to arrest blacks than whites for the same illegal activity. Police authorities don't dispute the discrepancy between black and white arrests, but argue that racism isn't involved; rather, they point out, drug transactions in white neighborhoods tend to take place in private, but are conducted in the open in inner-city areas, where officers therefore have a greater opportunity to make arrests.[6] Whether racism or convenience or some combination of both is involved, we can infer that the great causal connection between poverty and drug-related crime does not relate so much to either possession or sales as it does to frequency of arrest, leading to significant numbers of African-Americans and Hispanics having criminal records that they would not have if they were white and that diminish their opportunities for finding employment.

The substantial majority of people who live in poverty, however, never commit crimes. The poor, for that matter, can be properly described as remarkably law-abiding when we consider the temptations toward antisocial behavior that they regularly confront and that middle-class people don't. With poverty, as with other matters, what we see depends on what we look at. We can, that is, see the inner cities as places riddled by crime, where we find the manifold deplorable results of a multi-generational sense of future-lessness, and we would not be wrong in reaching that assessment; but neither would we be wrong to see the inner cities as places where large numbers of positive individuals and positive institutions (civic and religious) exist and persist. A weakness, it can be argued, of the liberal analysis of the inner cities lies in its emphasis on trying to understand the causes of crime and other forms of social dysfunction (when, in fact, these causes are obvious and require little study); and the weakness of both the liberal and conservative analyses is that too little attention is paid to the causes of crimelessness and non-dysfunction among these same people.

Regardless of the perspective on poverty that is adopted, the poor and those who try to help them usually agree that the recipe for change must contain at least two ingredients. One is jobs that pay wages that are above the subsistence level and that are likely to be permanent. The second is livable housing. To some extent, the housing goal will be met by reaching the job goal, since the fewer the people at or below subsistence income levels (cash plus food stamps), the more people who don't have to remain in substandard homes, as they can now afford something better. However, not all poor people by any means are susceptible to the employment solution; they may be ill or aged, or women with small children or other domestic responsibilities. Moreover, an exclusive focus on finding permanent employment at a decent wage ignores the deleterious effects that slum life can have on the motivation to find work of any kind.

The relationship between work and poverty has undergone a revolutionary change over the past century. When Jacob Riis published *How the Other Half Lives* in 1890, very few city dwellers believed they would go through life with no expectation of permanent employment. Poverty, rather, rose from the low wages that working-class jobs paid. The union movement proved that wage-based poverty could be eradicated, but not poverty itself. Unions, that is, could negotiate contracts that meant workers would earn enough money to live on, but they could not guarantee that the jobs themselves would be there. At greatest risk were unskilled and semi-skilled occupations, and their numbers, during the course of the twentieth century, have declined precipitously, primarily due to automation and sweatshop competition from abroad. Out of this decline in blue-collar work, we have created an apparently permanent body of people in the cities, largely African-American and Hispanic, who are fortunate to find temporary employment at minimum wages. Their poverty is conditional and, because it is not wage-based, they cannot organize themselves, as the poor of Riis's day did, against a definable enemy. The conditional poor, instead, are left only with an amorphous "them"—the white man, cops, big business, politicians, government, society as a whole—which means their anger and frustration, lacking a specific external object, becomes internalized. When it explodes, it is likely to take the form of destruction of their own neighborhoods through rioting and looting, since their streets are the only visible symbol they have of the power of "them." The difficulty such people have of knowing how to react against "them" is further complicated by the fact that it is "them" who, through granting welfare payments, separate the unemployed poor from starvation. Benevolence of that kind, which offers no future, crushes the spirit, just as having an identifiable foe to confront energizes it.

For conditional poverty to be relieved, and along with it the pervasive and alienating perception of "them" to become less prevalent, it seems axiomatic to say that ways must be found to make the private sector sufficiently healthy economically so that it can make jobs available in the numbers that are needed. Achieving such a goal is in business's interest since a very large workforce that earns substantial amounts of money becomes able to buy products in a quantity that a low-wage, large workforce cannot. However, because the marketplace in which entrepreneurs operate is driven by capitalist values, provision of jobs has never been more than a side effect of the activity. Thus, when the holders of capital are successful in their profit-making ventures, the amount of employment should increase and poverty should diminish, unless the profits result from corporate amalgamation, introduction of automation, or the replacement of native with foreign labor. In those events, employment decreases and poverty increases.

This constant fluctuation of purpose within the marketplace means that employers have no consistent interest in recruiting and training entry-level workers. The interest will be great at times, nonexistent at others. Job training can be stimulated through employer tax credits, as endorsed by the Clinton administration; however, those most likely to be benefited will be individuals who already have skills that employers require to increase productivity. This is not to say that even very low-skilled people may not, in any kind of economic climate, be able to obtain and keep jobs through which, by gaining seniority, they eventually can earn a good income. But if they are laid off, perhaps because the employer went out of business, such persons may quickly reach a state of desperation, since all the years that they put into the job, and that allowed them to gain seniority, have made them older workers who are at a disadvantage when they now have to try to compete with the younger and stronger.

In none of its peregrinations is the marketplace ever entirely closed to individual advancement, because the American system at its core is a meritocracy in which trans-class migrations, unlike in an autocracy, are not only permitted but welcome: Capital is always on the lookout for talent. Consequently, in good times and bad, we have Horatio Alger stories of youth from the most reduced circumstances who, through a combination of luck and pluck and brains, reach positions of great affluence. But their achievements are less heartening than they might appear at first glance. All they really prove is that exceptional people can do exceptional things. By holding such persons out as exemplars, as is sometimes done, to the vast majority who have been unable to overcome barriers, who at best have never done more than eke out a living under capitalism, we are teaching them that they are double failures: first, by lacking the qualifications that employers want, and second, by failing to duplicate the progress the exceptions have made. Far from encouraging ambition, that kind of lesson discourages it. Role models are significant, but they are best introduced to children to serve as a vision of the future and how it can be obtained.

A traditional tool used by minorities to effect upward mobility in the marketplace is civil rights legislation and litigation that seeks to enforce fair employment practices. The resultant laws may remove bars to class advancement, may even establish hiring quotas,* but since the market continues to be based on merit, only the best competitors in the class are likely to become winners in any permanent and meaningful way. Civil rights protections are important in developing a more equitable climate for minorities, but they are not designed nor have they functioned to relieve the poverty of the less-able competitors.

Therefore, what we see in the private sector is a quite large engine of employment that operates under governmental constraints and initiatives (such as tax credits), and that has a profit interest in full employment, but with contrary motivations that historically have been so numerous and shifting that we have never been able to rely upon it as a continuing initiator of longer-term employment of the very poor. That being the case, the alternative becomes government both as employer of last (and sometimes first) resort and as feeder of trained (and therefore prospectively valuable) workers into the private sector.

As described in Chapter Nine, Lyndon Johnson's War on Poverty offered that dual track, and eventually moved millions of the target population out of the ghetto and into middle-class life. Here, in a quantitative sense, was the truly heartening story. Men and women who previously had had no success, who typically had very little education, whose possibilities for advancement had been held back by bias, showed that, when given opportunity, they had capacities that others (and perhaps not even they) believed they possessed. The statistics tell the story: Between 1970 and

* Which, by the mid-1990s, were threatened with extinction by Supreme Court decisions and Congressional action.

1990, black families with annual incomes of $50,000 and above more than doubled, from 7 percent to 15 percent.

But the statistics also tell another story.[7] During these same two decades, the number of black families earning $10,000 or less in constant dollars increased from 23 percent to 26 percent. The earlier Kerner Commission warning that America was becoming divided into two unequal societies, one black and the other white, by the 1990s could be applied to the black community, too. One reason was that the job-training programs, which offered administrative middle-class jobs for many African-Americans, did a mediocre to poor job in making the students employable. For example, a study of youths taught under the Job Training Partnership Act (JTPA) found that on the average they earned $200 a quarter less or about 10 percent below the wages earned by a non–JTPA control group. The problem did not appear to be with the quality of the teaching but rather that the training itself was for work in low demand by business.[7] Here we see the paradox of government as the engine for employment training: The beneficiaries are principally those who do the training, not those who are trained. The problems of the job seekers are further compounded by their culture of multi-generational underemployment, which means they usually lack networks of friends and relatives who know where jobs of any kind are likely to be found.

The welfare system on which so many of the inner-city poor subsist is itself loaded with economic disincentives. Individuals on Aid to Families with Dependent Children (AFDC) lose their benefits as soon as they have assets in excess of $1,000, so that they have no motive to save money to further their education and hence improve their employment possibilities. Moreover, in twenty-six states, AFDC parents—almost all of them women—who take a full-time job even at minimum wages lose their welfare checks, which discourages them from seeking work. Public housing tenants, most of whom are on welfare, are also discouraged from improving themselves economically since, under a federal rule, their rents are pegged at 30 percent of their income; as a result, even a modest increase in their earnings will be largely consumed by the rent increase that follows.

The Family Support Act of 1988 allows states to drop AFDC mothers (and others) from the welfare rolls if they don't participate in education and training programs. (Apparently it is more important to teach welfare mothers how to get jobs than it is to teach them how to raise their babies, a view that society does not hold when it comes to middle-class mothers.) To the extent the Family Support Act and subsequent legislation succeeds in putting welfare recipients to work at minimum wage* jobs—they aren't likely to do better than that, considering their skill level—several goals presumably will be met: The welfare budget will be reduced; the very poor will be motivated to break their dependence on welfare by learning what it is to be wage earners; and teenage girls, knowing they are going to have to get jobs, won't get pregnant in order to get AFDC allotments. This odd view of human psychology ignores what might happen if these girls had greater access to birth control methods and had many choices available to them in life, so that having babies would not be the only means by which they could have a sense of accomplishment and worthwhileness as human beings.**

Assuming it is feasible to replace the present low-cost*** welfare system with low-income jobs, the result will be to resubstitute wage poverty for conditional poverty. Even if that is thought to be a step in the right direction, upper-end economic dislocations would be substantial: A significant portion of the very large welfare man-

* Some critics of welfare have proposed that recipients be required to take jobs paying less than minimum wage. Should that be allowed to happen, the welfare population will become favored over the non-welfare jobless, who won't be hired because, under the law, they would have to be paid at least the minimum scale. Many of these jobless, as a consequence, would be forced onto welfare, where they will get jobs below the minimum; savings to employers would be as considerable as would the growth in poverty.

** Not that teenage mothers make up a considerable portion of welfare recipients on AFDC allotments; they constitute just 5 percent, according to 1993 figures released by the Center for Law and Public Policy.

*** About 1 percent of the 1994 federal budget.

agerial class will not be able to find new jobs in the private sector at their present salaries because they will not have the qualifications that employers need. This is not to say that the welfare system shouldn't be changed to encourage able-bodied recipients to find work. And despite myths to the contrary, even as matters presently stand, they try; the average welfare recipient remains on the dole less than two years. Disincentives should be removed; incentives added. However, when employment is primarily seen as a means of dismantling welfare, attention becomes focused on jobs for the sake of jobs and not upon meaningful employment, which can be defined as work that gives the wage-earner a sense of self-worth and security, and that creates increased disposable income that can be used to purchase more of the goods that capital produces.

Whatever else might be said about the jobs-instead-of-welfare approach, it neglects to deal with the roadblocks to success caused by the demoralizing effect of life in the slums. Needed is a program that will teach useful job skills and at the same time lead to physical improvements of the inner cities, thereby benefiting both the workers who are trained and the people for whom the work is done. Housing rehabilitation can be a significant work provider, and particularly so for young people, who desperately need job qualifications. There is nothing new about this thinking. House rehabbing using indigenous labor has been tried sporadically and usually as a matter of individual initiative, but rarely, if ever, in a purposeful way and on a long-term basis under the guidance of a committed government.*

* In the discussion that follows, the focus is on the nexus between jobs and housing. However, the theory that is described can also be applied to other community needs, including rehabilitation of schools, recreation centers, churches, sidewalks, the planting of parks and trees, the renewal and maintenance of the entire inner-city infrastructure. The Citizens Corps legislation passed on a modest scale by Congress in 1990 and marked for expansion by the Clinton administration would incorporate infrastructure renewal by enlisting youths for one or two years of public service at minimum wages, in return for which they would receive vouchers, beginning at $10,000, for college tuition, for other job-training courses, or for a down payment on a first home.[8]

Edmund Bacon's continuum provides our model for how to proceed. It teaches us that the place to begin, as Bacon did for Penn Center, is with a focal point of stability from which the vectoring can flow. In the case of Penn Center, that was City Hall; in an inner-city neighborhood, it might be a church, a community center, or the block on which a strong community leader resides so that she becomes the energizing force. Whichever, the idea is to establish the continuum at the focal point, leading simultaneously toward it and outward from it, creating sequences, so that the vectors that have been established gain strength as they enter adjacent streets and adjacent neighborhoods, promoting cellular growth along their paths.

Beyond question, it will be more difficult to achieve a Baconian continuum for the inner city than for the downtown. Imaginative ideas for the central city have the capacity to generate business support when they seem potentially profitable. To the contrary, housing rehabilitation in the inner city by the people who live there serves no outsider's immediate pecuniary purposes, save that it will be attractive to artisans, like carpenters and plumbers, who win city contracts to teach the local employees the renovating skills they require.*

Despite the lack of enthusiasm, if not outright opposition, that the inner-city housing renewal continuum will encounter in some quarters, and the problems that will have to be solved in carrying it out, the alternatives have shown themselves to be disastrous. The

---

* A work/school program might be the best approach. Beginning at the tenth grade, or age sixteen, youths who aren't on the college track would have the opportunity to be apprenticed to the artisans on a part-time basis while continuing their education. On-the-job training would make their classroom learning more meaningful to them as they become better able to understand its relationship to earning a living. Our subject here is housing rehabilitation, but apprenticeships would not have to be limited to that field. (The time spent on on-site job training would mean that most apprentices would need a thirteenth year of schooling to complete their credits for a diploma, but at the end of that time, they would be much more employable than they otherwise would have been.)[9]

macro-surgical approach of tearing down whole neighborhoods, either because of their condition or to make way for middle-class housing or industrial ventures, succeeded only in spreading the slums, leading (among other evils) to the population pop-outs described in Chapter Nine. Today, macro-surgery has largely been replaced by micro-surgery in which a single house, a portion of a block, or more rarely an entire block, is razed and replaced. In an immediate-expenditure sense, micro-surgery is economically attractive, since replacement is usually cheaper than renovation; it particularly becomes so when the replacement mode is pre-fabricated houses, which are much less costly than masonry construction.[10]

But the long-range results have to be considered, too, and from that perspective micro-surgery can have no less devastating consequences than macro. A case in point is offered by the pre-fabs. They are entirely foreign to the environment in which they are introduced and have a disassociative visual effect that is not conducive to encouraging a sense of community in neighborhoods where such a spirit is likely to be fragile at best. Were that their only drawback, an argument could be made to accept them. But they have other ill effects. Because they are manufactured elsewhere, they don't help the neighborhood economy. At the same time, as replacement housing, they replace only what they replace; adjoining buildings remain untreated and will eventually have to be condemned, too. By the time they are replaced with still more pre-fabs, the first ones will themselves have begun to deteriorate, setting into motion the next round of blight.

The psychology of the process tends to speed it. As the people of the neighborhood witness the micro-surgery (pre-fab or not), they recognize that their houses, just as was true in the days of macro-surgery, will likely be next. As a result, they have less reason than ever before to try to maintain them. Neither do they have any pride in the new houses, since they represent something government has dumped in their midst. They don't represent something they have done for themselves.

When the therapy of housing rehabilitation replaces the

surgery of house removal as the dominant inner-city housing program, the structural result is more harmonious, and pride of accomplishment becomes possible. The young workers who had been occupationless, supported by the government or supporting themselves through crime, not only learn a craft that can stand them in good stead later in the private sector, but they may reap a spiritual benefit as well. Restoring a house is a creative act. When the task is completed, the workers have the satisfaction of seeing they have made something good out of something bad. They are likely to become protective of the fruits of their work and the neighborhood generally. The sense of accomplishment, in some instances, can have another meaning for them, too. Bacon recalls that when he was working with juvenile gang members, the ambition they most frequently mentioned to him was to make enough money to buy a decent home for their mothers. Housing rehabilitation is a way to allow them to make that gift out of their own hands.

Not all of them will. We must expect failures. Some of those to whom the renovating skills are taught will not profit from them in any manner. They will continue to vandalize, continue to commit crimes. Still others will start out with enthusiasm and quickly discover that hard physical work is not to their taste. Selling drugs is easier and more profitable, and all the other negative factors of poverty will also continue to impinge upon their lives. We may, therefore, be looking for a hundred to benefit and find only ten, look for a thousand and find only a hundred, but if that is all we can find, then we start with the ten or the hundred. The merit of an idea is always more important than any immediate quantification of it, because (as this book has attempted to show), if it is a valid idea, it will have persistence when we have the patience to allow it to, and eventually we will get the hundred or the thousand.

As restoration proceeds, the continuum may take on a whole new direction. An example is provided by the low-income, nearly all-black Point Breeze neighborhood in Philadelphia. The Point

Breeze renewal, prodded into existence by a resident named Mamie Nichols, began with housing rehabilitation. The next step was the painting of wall murals throughout the community. One mural faces a garden that contains a wedding kiosk and that also serves as a center for selling baked good and other wares. Another mural, which shows two little girls holding a gigantic fish on their laps, has a plot of land in front of it on which neighbors grow flowers and vegetables. Elsewhere, abandoned tires have been put to use by filling them with soil and planting them with flowers. A Point Breeze arts festival is held each year.

In Point Breeze and neighborhoods like it in other cities—efforts in Chicago have been particularly impressive as a citizens' counter-offensive against the Daley-era high-rises—we see the continuum displaying its energy, one sequence leading to the next. In Point Breeze, the harmony is by no means completed and may never be. At places, the area remains dotted with government-seized abandoned housing, which could be turned over for rehabilitation but has not been. The government, in this way, seems intent upon enforcing the blight that the residents have been fighting against. Nevertheless, the movement in Point Breeze has been a hardy one that has persisted for many years; the people seem to like what they have done for themselves, and that's why they will probably be able to keep it.

As the Point Breeze story suggests, efforts to save a neighborhood have their greatest chance for success when they are locally generated and then remain under local auspices. Very often, however, a nurturing process is called for, in the manner outlined by Bacon in his 1949 article quoted in Chapter Nine. Under his rubric, the city's agents, be they planners or housing officials, take the time to identify natural communities. This means talking to people to get to understand their idea of the neighborhood, finding out whom they consider to be their leaders, walking their streets, and perhaps above all, as Bacon has written, recognizing "existing community institutions and . . . [using] them [as] a point of departure in its design. These institutions can be given a new dignity and significance . . . through providing them with new settings, and through the opening up of spaces between them to give them a new relationship with each other and with the community."[11] Only when this sense of the total neighborhood has been absorbed will the city's planners and other agents have the right to communicate with the leaders, describe ideas, suggest new rhythms of placement and space; only then are they likely not to be resisted as outsiders but to be seen, instead, as participants in a common purpose.

The agents have other duties, too. They should be able to impart details of financing mechanisms that are available, including those of the private sector. Helping activists locate a bank willing to invest in their community's recovery will be of inestimable value to them, as in Chicago, where the South Side Bank has been an active investor. Often horticulture societies are willing to provide trees, flowers, and shrubbery; the city's agents can put the locals in touch with these sources. However, the choices to be made in house decor, how to improve the appearance of vacant lots and the like, and all the other important decisions are to be made by the people. It's their ideas, not the city's ideas of what they should want, that finally count.

Housing rehabilitation and its ancillary benefits will not work everywhere, at least not at first. Every city has sectors of highly transient populations, of rampant crime. For many years, no doubt, the only feasible policy toward these zones will be containment through a strong police presence. The holistic program we have been outlining, therefore, is one for the long term, and we must recognize that it will have its setbacks and that at places the successes will probably never be more than partial. However, to the extent a city locates and encourages people who seek a better community and makes available training in job skills for those willing to learn them, it is no longer in the business of trying to control chaos, but in the much better business of allowing people the opportunity to define their hopes and of offering the means of carrying them out.

Ultimately we have only two ways of thinking about what is going to happen to our cities, and their welfare depends on which we take. One is to see the urban future proceeding from realities of which we are aware at the moment, which means that our ideas are guided by the constrictions of the moment, too. For instance, we may recognize that the politics of the day are bad, which suggests they will remain bad; that not enough money is available to bring about needed changes, which suggests never will there be enough money; that the city is shabby and crime-ridden, with people fleeing from it, which suggests that it will always be shabby and crime-ridden, with people fleeing from it. Because only the present is considered real, its problems and handicaps force entropic drift, and we and our cities are captured by restrictions we have placed on our own expectations.

The second perspective is the one Bacon described when he said, "My whole life has been in seeing the future as something real." And in preparing for the urban future—whether that be of five or a hundred years from now—we have before us, if we care to heed it, the lesson to be found in the continuum. In New York City, it will be recalled, William Cullen Bryant was one of those who triggered the idea of green space in the city for the enjoyment of its people, and from that initiation Frederick Law Olmsted created a continuum of such elegance and breathtaking beauty in Central Park that it became the inspiration for the greening of cities (and suburbs, too) around the nation by those who lacked his imagination but who learned from it. Similarly, Bacon, inspired by the powerful movement axis installed by his city's founder, conceived Penn Center as a totality of pedestrian movement and organization of space in relationship to the habitat and to the sun above it. From that vision flowed congruent extensions that offer deep and vitalizing directions for the restoration of central business districts and inner cities alike. Bacon's continuum finds its political manifestation and necessary ally in Dilworth's philosophy of the good government that constantly facilitates people's aspirations. Each of these visions of the city have qualities in common. They are humanistic, they are pragmatic, they educate us about potentiality, and so they are and will remain enspiriting.

When we understand only what is, we don't understand what can be.

Notes

Chapter One

1. Led by reformers like Jane Addams in Chicago and Lillian Wald in New York, the settlement house movement had its origins in the late Victorian era. Largely located in working-class neighborhoods of the big cities, the settlement houses acted as a means for people to organize politically around local issues and sometimes petition the government for redress of their grievances. Unifying cultural and social activities were also a part, and sometimes the most important part, of a settlement house agenda. Primarily viewed as a means of assimilating first-generation Americans, the settlement house movement lost steam in the 1920s, following the enactment of the restrictive immigration laws of that period. The settlement houses themselves often continued to be used, but usually under the auspices of a city's recreation department and primarily serving children rather than adults. The early settlement house political thrust can be seen as a progenitor for later community activist groups, as exemplified by Saul Alinsky's pioneering populist programs in Chicago. For a description of suburban settlement houses, see Lewis Mumford, *The City in History* (Harcourt, Brace & World, 1961), pp. 500–501. An excellent biography of Alinsky is Stanford D. Horwitt's *Let Them Call Me Rebel* (Knopf, 1989); see also Nicholas Lemann, *The Promised Land* (Knopf, 1991), pp. 98–102.

2. Edmund Bacon, lecture, University of Illinois, 1991.

Chapter Two

1. Edmund Bacon, "New World Cities," in *American Civilization*, ed. by Daniel Boorstin (Thames & Hudson, 1972), pp. 206–207; *The Park Avenue Railroad Tunnel* (Metro-North Commuter Railroad, 1987); "The Greatest Railroad Terminal in the World" (*Munsey's Magazine*, April 1916), pp. 27–38.

2. John W. Reps, *The Making of Urban America* (Princeton University Press, 1965), pp. 297–299.

3. Jeanne R. Lowe, *Cities in a*

Race with Time (Random House, 1967), p. 9.

4. Reps, pp. 216–217.

5. Mumford, pp. 243 ff.

6. Reps, pp. 163–164.

7. Edmund Bacon, *Design of Cities* (Penguin Books, 1967), pp. 219–221; Reps, pp. 185–192. Oglethorpe's description of the Savannah site is from a letter he wrote to the Trustees, Feb. 20, 1733; "Some of the People ...," from *South Carolina Gazette*, August 25, 1733, both quoted by Reps.

8. Bacon, *Design of Cities*, pp. 131–157.

9. See, generally, Reps, pp. 242–256; Bacon, *Design of Cities*, pp. 48, 222.

10. Proceedings to be had under the Residence Act, November 29, 1790, Reps, pp. 245–246.

11. Undated letter from L'Enfant to Washington, Reps, p. 248.

12. April 10, 1791, Reps, *ibid.*

13. Mumford, p. 407.

14. Undated report from L'Enfant to Washington, Reps, p. 250.

15. Reps, p. 263. A more negative view of L'Enfant's role as a planner is to be found in Mumford, pp. 403–409.

Chapter Three

1. Bacon, *American Civilization*, p. 204.

2. Mumford, p. 7.

3. Cornelia W. Walker, *Mount Auburn* (New York, 1847), quoted by Reps, p. 326.

4. James Silk Buckingham, *The Eastern and Western States of America* (London, 1842), quoted by Reps, p. 206.

5. Andrew Jackson Downing, *Rural Essays*, quoted by Reps, p. 330.

6. Bacon, *American Civilization*, p. 208; David Clow, *Understanding Cities* (Urban Land Institute, 1982), pp. 41–42; Reps, pp. 331–336.

7. Olmsted, Vaux & Co., *Preliminary Report upon the Proposed Suburban Village at Riverside, Near Chicago*, 1868, quoted by Reps, p. 344.

8. Reps, p. 300. Walter D. Moody, *Wacker's Manual of the Plan for Chicago* (Chicago Plan Commission, 1912), pp. 111–113.

9. Reps., pp. 300, 302.

10. Bacon, *American Civilization*, pp. 209, 226; Reps, pp. 497–502, for events leading to, and construction of, White City.

11. Richard Slotkin, *Gunfighter Nation* (Atheneum, 1992), pp. 63–65, 97–98.

12. Candace Wheeler, "A Dream City" (*Harper's New Monthly Magazine*, LXXVI, 1893), quoted by Reps, pp. 501–502.

13. Louis Sullivan, *The Autobiography of an Idea* (Dover Publications, 1956, reprint of 1924 edition), pp. 324–325.

14. Reps, pp. 514–517.

15. Daniel H. Burnham and Edward H. Bennett, *Plan of Chicago* (Commercial Club of Chicago, 1909).

16. *Wacker's Manual*, p. 45.

17. *Wacker's Manual*, pp. 86–92. On Burnham's plan generally, see also Reps, pp. 517–519.

18. Reps, pp. 502–514; Bacon,

American Civilization, pp. 226–228; Bacon, *Design of Cities*, p. 222.

19. Lawrence M. Friedman, *History of American Law* (Touchstone, 1973), p. 262.

20. Bacon, *Design of Cities*, pp. 228–229.

21. Bacon, *City as Sequence* (*Dichotomy*, University of Detroit School of Architecture, 1990), p. 19.

22. Edmund Bacon, "Bringing Us Back to Our Senses" (*Ekistics*, Jan.–June 1988), p. 112.

23. Bacon, "Bringing Us Back to Our Senses," p. 110.

24. Bacon, "Bringing Us Back to Our Senses," *ibid.*

Chapter Four

1. Charles Abrams, *Future of Housing* (Harper & Bros., 1946), p. 212.

2. *Urban Renewal: People, Politics & Planning*, ed. by Jewel Bellush and Murray Hausknecht (Doubleday Anchor, 1967), pp. 4–5 (hereafter referred to as "Bellush").

3. Lowe, p. 23.

4. Bellush, p. 5.

5. Bellush, p. 6.

6. The language is quoted by Walter F. Mondale in a 1971 speech entitled "Toward Domestic Justice," delivered to the American Society of Planning Officials, published in *Planning 1971*, p. 8.

7. Ickes had been a political reformer in Chicago in the late nineteenth century and subsequently became an adherent of Theodore Roosevelt's Progressive platform. See

Roy Lubove, *The Progressives and the Slums* (University of Pittsburgh, 1962), quoted in Bellush, pp. 20 ff. See also, generally, Jacob Riis, *How the Other Half Lives* (Charles Scribner's Sons, 1890).

8. Patrick Geddes, *Cities in Evolution* (Williams & Norgate, Ltd., 1949, reprint of 1915 edition), pp. 69 ff., 190–191.

9. Bellush, p. 7.

10. Bellush, *ibid.*

11. Bellush, p. 9.

12. Eliel Saarinen, *The City* (Massachusetts Institute of Technology Press, 1966, reprint of 1943 Reinhold Publishing Co. edition), p. 231.

13. Bellush, pp. 8–9.

14. Abrams, pp. 210 ff.; Robert Weaver, "The Urban Complex," in Bellush, p. 94.

15. Abrams, p. 219.

16. Abrams, *ibid.*

17. Lowe, p. 28.

18. Abrams, *ibid.*

19. Lemann, pp. 239–240.

20. Bellush, p. 9.

21. George Reedy, *From the Ward to the White House* (Charles Scribner's Sons, 1991), pp. 157 ff.

22. Robert Caro, *The Power Broker* (Knopf, 1974), p. 516.

23. Caro, p. 511.

24. Caro, p. 487.

25. Caro, pp. 453, 487.

26. Caro, p. 453.

27. Daniel H. Burnham, "A City of the Future Under a Democratic Government," *Transactions of the Town Planning Conference*, London, October 10–15, 1910 (Royal Institute of Architects, 1911), pp. 372–373.

Chapter Five

1. Reps, p. 525.
2. Lowe, pp. 60–62, for discussion of New York Planning Commission.
3. The history of the Philadelphia Planning Commission is based primarily on Bacon's recollections; see also "Philadelphia Plans Again," *Architectural Forum*, Dec. 1947, pp. 66–67.
4. Herbert W. Starick, "Putting Planning in the Decision-Making Process," *Planning 1964* (American Society of Planning Officials), p. 29.
5. *Architectural Forum, ibid.*
6. *Architectural Forum*, p. 84.

Chapter Six

1. Arthur Mann, in Introduction to William L. Riordon, *Plunkitt of Tammany Hall* (E. P. Dutton & Co., 1963 edition of book first published in 1905), p. xiv.
2. Mann, *ibid.*
3. Reedy, p. 26. The 200,000 figure for 1851 contrasts with 5,000 in 1835. Irish emigration to the United States did not begin with the potato famine. A fairly steady stream of Irish arrived in the New World during the colonial period and in the years immediately following the Revolution. While economic motivations, then and later, were always significant, a sizable number of the immigrants were rebels fleeing for their lives from British rule, including the anti-Federalist polemicist Matthew Carey, who became one of America's leading publishers. (See also John

Guinther, *Philadelphia* [Continental Heritage Press, 1983], pp. 68, 72, 97–98.)
4. Reedy, pp. 35 ff.
5. Reedy, p. 47.
6. Reedy, p. 59, 65; Mann, *op. cit.*
7. Riordon, p. 3.
8. Riordon, pp. 91–93.
9. Jane Addams, "Why the Ward Boss Rules" (*International Journal of Ethics*, 1898), quoted by Reedy, pp. 192–198.
10. John Guinther, *Moralists & Managers: Public Interest Movements in America* (Doubleday Anchor, 1976), p. 101.
11. But see also Reedy (pp. 51–55), who points out that the Irish Catholics weren't welcome in the big-city Republican parties during the late nineteenth century, whereas the Democratic parties were in disarray following the Civil War and readily susceptible to takeover by the Irish politicians.
12. David Kairys, "Freedom of Speech," in *The Politics of Law*, ed. by David Kairys (Pantheon Books, 1982), pp. 142–144.
13. Reedy, pp. 161–162.
14. Mike Royko, *Boss* (E. P. Dutton, 1971), pp. 67–68.
15. Bureau of Labor Statistics estimate, 1992.
16. Taylor Branch, *Parting the Waters* (Simon & Schuster, 1988), pp. 359–76.

Chapter Seven

1. Lincoln Steffens, *The Shame of the Cities* (McClure, Phillips & Co.,

1904, from Hill & Wang reprint, 1957), p. 137.

2. Penn made this comment in connection with his Frame of Government for his new colony.

3. The history of the political reform movement in Philadelphia is based on contemporary newspaper accounts and interviews with participants; on Edmund Bacon's recollections; and on Harold Libros, *Hard-Core Liberals* (Schenkman Publ. Co., 1975).

4. *Philadelphia Home Rule Charter* (*Legal Intelligencer*, 1959 edition).

5. See esp. Joel Garreau, *Edge City* (Doubleday, 1992).

Chapter Eight

1. Lowe, p. 107.

2. Lemann, p. 6.

3. Olmsted, Vaux & Co., quoted by Reps, pp. 16–17.

4. Mumford, p. 492.

5. Mumford, p. 504.

6. Caro, p. 911.

7. Caro, p. 930.

8. Caro, pp. 890–891.

9. Zachary Weiss, "Mechanisms for Citizen Participation in the Planning Process," *Planning 1971* (American Society of Planning Officials), p. 142.

10. Caro, p. 930.

11. Lowe, p. 39.

12. Guinther, *Moralists & Managers*, p. 178.

13. Caro, pp. 947, 949.

14. Reps, p. 93.

Chapter Nine

1. Quoted by Bacon in "Urban Redevelopment," *Planning 1949* (American Society of Planning Officials), p. 19.

2. Charles R. Cherington, "Metropolitan Special Districts," in *Metropolitan Analysis*, ed. by Stephen B. Sweeney (University of Pennsylvania Press, 1953), p. 133.

3. *Housing: A Quality Survey* (City of Philadelphia, 1951), p. 3.

4. *Housing Quality Survey, ibid.*

5. *Housing Quality Survey, ibid.*

6. Bacon, *Planning 1949*, p. 20.

7. Lowe, p. 35.

8. Lowe, p. 81.

9. Lowe, pp. 87–89.

10. Caro, p. 777.

11. Bellush, p. 12.

12. Bacon, *American Civilization*, p. 233.

13. Lowe, pp. 69–70.

14. Caro, p. 962; Lowe, p. 74.

15. Caro, pp. 962–963; Lowe, *ibid.*

16. Caro, pp. 962–963.

17. Lowe, pp. 52–53.

18. Caro, p. 492.

19. Caro, pp. 492–494.

20. Caro, pp. 963–965.

21. Caro, p. 980; Lowe, pp. 75–83.

22. Lowe, p. 192.

23. Caro, pp. 714–729, 982–983.

24. Caro, p. 970.

25. Lowe, p. 83.

26. Caro, p. 981.

27. Lowe, p. 75.

28. Caro, p. 1012.

29. Caro, pp. 980–981.

30. Bellush, p. 13.

31. Lowe, p. 85.

32. Bellush, p. 15.

33. Martin Anderson, *The Federal Bulldozer* (MIT Press, 1965), quoted in Bellush, pp. 392–393.

34. Herbert J. Gans (*Commentary*, April 1965), quoted in Bellush, p. 467.

35. Gans, p. 468; Bacon, *American Civilization*, p. 234.

36. Gans, pp. 467–468.

37. Gans, p. 468.

38. Bacon, *American Civilization*, p. 234.

39. Robert Weaver, *The Urban Complex* (Doubleday, 1964), in Bellush, p. 94.

40. Frank Friel and John Guinther, *Breaking the Mob* (McGraw-Hill, 1990), pp. 28–29.

41. Lemann, p. 92.

42. Lemann, *ibid.*

43. Harrison Salisbury, *The Shook-Up Generation* (Harper & Bros., 1958), in Bellush, pp. 426–427.

44. Lee Rainwater, *Behind Ghetto Walls* (Penguin, 1973).

45. Bacon, *American Civilization*, p. 233.

46. Salisbury, p. 430.

47. See Lemann, generally, esp. Parts One and Two.

48. Richard Wright, *12 Million Black Voices* (Viking, 1941), p. 93.

49. Lemann, esp. pp. 59–107.

50. Bacon, *American Civilization*, p. 234.

51. Lemann, pp. 133, 145, 149.

52. Lemann, pp. 197–199.

53. Guinther interview, 1973. See also Lemann, p. 199, for a very similar story involving an Atlanta woman.

54. "Model Cities—flush it," was a note taken by John Ehrlichman following a meeting with Nixon a few days after Nixon's inauguration as President. Lemann, p. 218.

55. Lemann, pp. 207–208.

56. Lemann, p. 201.

57. *Philadelphia Inquirer*, May 6, 1992.

58. Interview, Maureen Kennedy, HUD, 1995.

59. Garreau develops this thesis throughout *Edge City*.

Chapter Ten

(The information in this chapter is principally based on interviews with Bacon and with officials in Pittsburgh, Baltimore, Minneapolis, St. Paul, Milwaukee, and San Antonio. See also acknowledgments.)

1. Saarinen, p. 55.

2. Stefan Lorant, *Pittsburgh* (Author's Edition, 1988), p. 675.

3. Thomas Hine, *Philadelphia Inquirer*, August 11, 1991.

4. Interview with author, 1991.

5. David Osborne, "Government That Means Business," *New York Times Magazine*, March 8, 1992, pp. 24, 26, from Osborne and Ted Gaebler, *Reinventing Government* (Addison-Wesley, 1992).

6. Bacon, *Design of Cities*, p. 291.

7. Friel, pp. 288–289.

Chapter Eleven

1. For Chicago convention discussion, see Royko, pp. 183–185.

2. Lemann, p. 242.

3. Royko, p. 165.

4. Royko, pp. 32–58, for biological sketch

5. Royko, pp. 5–6.

6. Royko, p. 158.

7. Royko, p. 16.

8. Lemann, pp. 301–302; *Statistical Abstract of the United States* (U.S. Department of Commerce, 1985), p. 23.

9. Royko, p. 133.

10. Royko, *ibid.*

11. Royko, p. 134.

12. Lemann, p. 272.

13. Lemann, p. 234.

14. Lemann, pp. 234–240; David J. Garrow, *Bearing the Cross* (Morrow, 1986), pp. 431–525.

15. Unless otherwise attributed below, the biographical information in this section was first published in a different form in "Requiem," by John Guinther (*Philadelphia Magazine*, April 1974).

16. Peter Binzen, "Prince of the City" (*Inquirer Magazine*, December 17, 1989), p. 12.

17. Binzen, p. 13.

18. Binzen, p. 13; interview with Henry Sawyer (1992).

19. Binzen, *ibid.*

20. Binzen, *ibid.*

21. The reporter was Bernard McCormick, then of *Philadelphia Magazine*.

22. Interview with Marilyn Gelb (1991).

23. Evelyn Trommer and Marilyn Gelb were the first two; Lisa Richette was the third.

24. Binzen, p. 18.

25. Sawyer interview.

26. Binzen, p. 34.

Chapter Twelve

1. Bureau of Census, 1990.

2. *New York Times*, June 14, 1992.

3. Bureau of Census, 1993. The gap between black and white high school graduation rates had narrowed by 12 percentage points between 1973 and 1993. However, during the same period, the gap had widened between blacks and whites attending college: White enrollment went up from 30 percent to 43 percent, black only from 24 percent to 30 percent; the differential thus more than doubled.

4. Ralph Estes, *Analysis of Enterprise Zones* (Institute for Policy Studies and Center for Advancement of Public Policy, 1992).

5. See also *Hobbling a Generation*, report of the National Center on Institutions and Alternatives, September 1992.

6. *Philadelphia Inquirer*, Nov. 1, 1992.

7. *Mandate for Change*, Progressive Policy Institute (Berkeley Books, 1993), p. 138.

8. *Mandate for Change*, pp. 144–145.

9. *Mandate for Change*, pp. 141–143.

10. Thomas Hine, "Housing That Looks Out of Place" (*Philadelphia Inquirer*, September 8, 1991).

11. Bacon, *Planning 1949*, p. 23.

Acknowledgments

During the course of the writing of this book, in addition to Edmund Bacon, many people offered their help. I particularly want to acknowledge the contributions of Gerald Maier, who served as Project Manager of Market East in Philadelphia, and R. Damon Childs, Bacon's successor as Executive Director of the Planning Commission; Sue Hurley and Ken Ford as sources for the Latimer Administration and development in St. Paul; Jon Wellhoefer of the Milwaukee Redevelopment Corp.; Dawn Hagen of Minneapolis; Jenny Stacy of Savannah; Mary Poppenberg of Pittsburgh; Suzanne Satagaj of San Antonio for the history of the Riverwalk, and the Conservation Society of San Antonio for additional information; Eileen Drelick of Penn Central Corporation; Henry Sawyer and Marilyn Gelb for their reminiscences of Richardson Dilworth. Thanks also for their help to Otto Reichert-Facilides, Susan McAninley, Sharon J. Wholmuth, Elizabeth Finkler, Leonard Fruchter, and as always to my daughter, Carol, and my agent, Elizabeth Frost Knappman of New England Publishing Associates.

Work on this book was generously supported by a grant from the Graham Foundation for Advanced Studies in the Fine Arts.

Illustration Credits

Title page and p. 102, photograph by Ezra Stoller, © Esto; p. 2, photograph of model by Courtlandt V. D. Hubbard, inset photograph by Sharon J. Wohlmuth; p. 22, drawing courtesy of Edmund N. Bacon and the Archives of the Penn Central Corporation; p. 45, illustration courtesy of The New-York Historical Society, New York, NY; p. 53, painting by Lewis Edward Hickmott, courtesy of the Chicago Historical Society; p. 56, illustration courtesy of the Library of Congress; p. 209, photograph by Andrew A. Wagner; p. 210, photograph by Edmund N. Bacon; p. 211, photograph courtesy of the Rouse Company; p. 214, photograph © Thorney Lieberman; p. 220, photograph courtesy of the City of St. Paul; p. 221, photograph courtesy of the San Antonio Convention and Visitors Bureau; p. 227, drawing by Edmund N. Bacon; p. 232, photograph © 1992 H. Durston Saylor, Inc., courtesy of H. Durston Saylor.

Diagrams 1-9, 20-21 by Susan McAninley.
Diagram 10 by John W. Reps, from his *The Making of Urban America*. Copyright © 1965 by Princeton University Press, renewed 1993. Reproduced by permission of Princeton University Press.
Diagram 11 by Elliot Arthur Pavlos. Courtesy of Edmund N. Bacon.
Diagrams 12-19 by Edmund N. Bacon.

Index

Page numbers in *italics* refer to illustrations.

Daley, Richard J. (*cont.*)
  as Cook County Democratic
    Committee chairman, 240–41,
    243
  Democratic National
    Convention and, 237–38,
    247
  elected mayor, 240
  in Hamburg Social and Athletic
    Club, 239
  King and, 245–47
  police violence and, 237–39,
    258
  voters and, 244, 245
Daley, Richard M., 238
Dash, Samuel, 251, 256
Daus, Melvin, 79
Denver, Colo., 177
Depression, Great, 62–63, 65, 67,
    72–73, 74, 77, 78, 113, 162,
    260
Detroit, Mich., 40, 47, 48
  downtown, 209, *210*
  Renaissance Center, 208–9, *210*,
    216, 228, 231–32, 261
Dilworth, Richardson, 133, 139,
    157, 225, 247–57, 260, 261
  background of, 248
  blacks and, 250, 251
  charter ripper amendments and,
    252, 253
  city council and, 254–55
  as district attorney, 139, 250–51,
    257
  elected mayor, 247, 251–52
  government and politics as
    viewed by, 253, 256–58, 281
  McCarthy and, 248–49
  1947 mayoral campaign of, 134,
    135, 136, 250, 252
  patronage and, 252, 253, 254
  reelected mayor, 255
  schools and, 255, 256
  war service of, 248

Dowling, Robert, 153, 208
Downing, Andrew Jackson, 44, 46,
    78
Dragos, Stephen F., 215
drugs, 66, 266, 267–68, 278
Dubinsky, David, 116

Edwards, Emily, 220
Eisenhower, Dwight, 183*n*
Elliott, George, 94–95
employment:
  blue-collar, decline in, 269–70
  fair practices in, 272
  highway building as source of,
    162
  housing rehabilitation as source
    of, 275, 276, 277–78
  poverty and, 66–67, 269–72
  suburban, transportation to,
    166–67
  training in, 273, 276*n*
  welfare and, 273–75
  work/school programs, 276*n*
English colonies, 168
enterprise zones, 266*n*
entropy, 17–18, 19, 20, 130, 155,
    203, 206, 259–60
Equitable Life Insurance, 151, 153,
    208
Erieview Plaza, 61
Europe, medieval, 23, 26
expressways, *see* highways
extra-territoriality, 167–68, 171

Family Support Act (1988), 274
Federal Housing Administration
    (FHA), 64–65, 70, 77–78, 162
First Class Cities Act, 139
Flint, Mich., 72–76, 79, 82, 83, 88,
    89–90, 92, 114, 146
Ford, Henry, II, 208, 209
Ford, James, 69
Forten, James, 128
France, 39, 40